Solutions to Social Problems

Lessons from Other Societies

SECOND EDITION

D. STANLEY EITZEN
Colorado State University

CRAIG S. LEEDHAM
Arizona State University

ALLYN AND BACON
Boston   London   Toronto   Sydney   Tokyo   Singapore

Series Editor: Sarah L. Kelbaugh
Editor in Chief, Social Sciences: Karen Hanson
Series Editoral Assistant: Lori Flickinger
Production Editor: Christopher H. Rawlings
Editorial-Production Service: Omegatype Typography, Inc.
Composition and Prepress Buyer: Linda Cox
Manufacturing Buyer: Julie McNeill
Cover Administrator: Jenny Hart
Electronic Composition: Omegatype Typography, Inc.

Library of Congress Cataloging-in-Publication Data

Solutions to social problems : lessons from other societies / [edited by] D. Stanley
Eitzen, Craig S. Leedham.—2nd ed.
  p.   cm.
  Includes bibliographical references.
  ISBN 0-205-32107-0
  1. Social problems. 2. Social problems—United States. 3. Social policy. 4. United
States—Social policy. I. Eitzen, D. Stanley. II. Leedham, Craig S.

HN17.5 .S653 2001
361.1'0973—dc21

00-024892

Printed in the United States of America

10 9 8 7 6 5 4 3 2 1   05 04 03 02 01 00

Text credits appear on pages 265–266, which constitute an extension of the copyright page.

CONTENTS

Preface

This collection of readings is intended to supplement traditional textbooks for courses dealing with U.S. social problems. It fills a void because social problems textbooks, generally, have two fundamental shortcomings: (1) they focus too much on U.S. society, and (2) they are long on the descriptions of social problems and short on the policies to alleviate them. The readings included in this text are from other societies and demonstrate successful alternatives for overcoming the social problems that plague the United States.

This unique approach is timely and important for at least four reasons. First, social problems in the United States are worsening. To illustrate: the number of the poor and the near poor is increasing; the income inequality gap is widening; incidents of racial discord are increasing; health care is rationed according to one's ability to pay; the inner cities continue to crumble from an inadequate tax base and a shortage of jobs; and the degradation of the environment continues. These social problems require solutions or the United States will continue in a downward spiral.

Second, contemporary students must be prepared to live in a global environment. As workers and consumers they are vitally affected by the global economy. In our interdependent world the political events from around the globe impinge on the United States, affecting expenditures, taxes, public policies, and military strategies. Expanding our knowledge and our appreciation of other societies is important as we adjust to being responsible citizens of the world, as well as those of the United States.

Third, the current political climate comprised of both Republican and Democrat voters and elected officials is inclined toward the dismantling of the more than sixty-year-old welfare state, which began under President Franklin Roosevelt. The emerging ideological consensus has three related propositions: (1) government subsidies exacerbate social problems rather than solve them; (2) individuals must rely on their own resources and motivations if they are to succeed; and (3) individuals who fail are to blame and must suffer the consequences for their failure. The key questions: Is this trashing of the welfare state a good idea? What will be the likely consequences? Will it solve or intensify social problems? Comparing the United States with more generous welfare states will help to answer these important questions.

Finally, a comparative examination of public policies regarding social problems will demonstrate what works and under what social conditions. This is an important precondition for the formation of creative and workable social policies that will reduce or eliminate social problems in the United States.

The book is divided into five parts. Part One focuses on two important foundational issues: first, a comparison of the United States with other advanced industrial societies on a number of dimensions, and second, a consideration of why the United States fails to adopt social policies that appear to solve social problems in other industrial societies. Each remaining part centers on specific social problems. Part Two examines problems of inequality (poverty, income inequality, gender inequality); Part Three looks at institutional problems (families, schools, labor, and health care delivery); Part Four concentrates on environmental and urban problems; and Part Five addresses the attempts by societies to control individual deviance (crime and drugs).

For each of the social problems considered, one or more articles has been selected. These articles either describe the situation in a single country or in multiple countries, or expressly contrast the situation in a country or countries with that of the United States. We have limited the sample of countries to the major industrial nations (Canada, the countries of Scandinavia and Western Europe, Australia and New Zealand, and Japan). In each instance, we invite the reader to assess *critically* the situation in the United States and in the country or countries under examination, considering questions such as, Will the successful public policies used elsewhere work in the United States? If not, why not? If possible here, how might they be implemented?

While engaged in this comparative exercise, we must guard against the tendency to be either overly defensive about the United States or, at the other extreme, too accepting of the social policies of other societies. Regarding the first instance, we must acknowledge the magnitude of our social problems as a precursor to finding appropriate solutions. Regarding the second possibility, we must recognize that we cannot simply import the social policies of other societies without some modification. As William Julius Wilson has said,

> The approaches [used in Japan, Germany, and the Western European nations] are embedded in their own cultures and have their own flaws and deficiences as well as strengths. We should . . . learn from the approaches used in other countries and adapt the best aspects into our own homegrown solutions.[1]

We would like to thank the following reviewers for their suggestions in putting together the second edition—George Dolph, LaSalle University; Sharon Methvin, Cameron University; Kenneth Rothrock, Bowling Green State University; and Lee Garth Vigilant, Framingham State College. We appreciate their thoughtful comments.

D.S.E.
C.S.L.

---

1. William Julius Wilson, *When Work Disappears: The World of the New Urban Poor* (New York: Alfred A. Knopf, 1996), p. 220.

PART ONE

Introduction

Section 1:   The Comparative Approach to Social Problems

1

U.S. Social Problems
in Comparative Perspective

D. STANLEY EITZEN AND CRAIG S. LEEDHAM

Social problems in the United States are worsening. Since 1970 Marc Miringoff of Fordham University has been compiling an "Index of Social Health" for U.S. society (Miringoff and Miringoff, 1999). This index, which is like a Dow Jones (stock market) average for social problems, has declined from a composite score of 76.9 (out of 100) in 1973 to 43 in 1996. Among the indicators improving in those twenty-three years were infant mortality, high school dropout rates, poverty among those over age sixty-five, and life expectancy. Among the declining indicators were child abuse, children in poverty, youth suicide, average weekly earnings, health insurance coverage, and the gap between the rich and the poor.

Not only are social problems in this country worsening but also, for the most part, the United States does not compare favorably with other modern, advanced nations. This introductory essay addresses three fundamental questions. First, how does the United States compare to the other advanced industrial countries on a number of social problems? Second, what are the consequences of U.S. social policies regarding social problems? And, third, why doesn't this nation adopt public policies that other countries have found to be successful in reducing or eliminating certain social problems?

WE'RE NUMBER ONE: THE UNITED STATES COMPARED TO ITS PEERS

Americans are extremely competitive. We want to be the best in all things: Olympic victories, world records, getting to the moon first, harnessing the atom, finding a cure for AIDS, or whatever. So far, we have done remarkably well in these and other competitions. But one area in which we outrank the other modern nations is not a source of pride—*we are number one, or nearly number one, in the magnitude of our social problems.*

3

Andrew Shapiro has compiled data on the nineteen major industrial nations—Australia, Austria, Belgium, Canada, Denmark, Finland, France, Germany, Ireland, Italy, Japan, the Netherlands, New Zealand, Norway, Spain, Sweden, Switzerland, the United Kingdom, and the United States (Shapiro, 1992). Of these nations, the United States ranks number one in real wealth, number of billionaires, executive salaries, physician salaries, amount of space in homes, defense spending and military capability, ethnic diversity, percentage of population with access to safe drinking water, and percentage of residents enrolled in higher education.

Unfortunately, however, the United States also ranks first in murder rate, reported rapes, robbery rate, incarceration rate, number of drunk driving fatalities, cocaine use, greenhouse gas emissions, acid rain, forest depletion, hazardous waste per capita, garbage per capita, number of cars per capita (and use of cars rather than public transportation), inequality of wealth distribution, bank failures, divorce, single-parent families, number of children and elderly in poverty, homelessness, reported cases of AIDS, infant mortality, death of children younger than five years, and teenage pregnancy.

Also, among these nations, the United States ranks *last* in spending on the poor; fully immunizing preschoolers against polio, DTP (dipphtheria-tetanus-pertussis), and measles; giving humanitarian aid to developing countries; in the percentage of people with health insurance; and providing paid maternity leave. In addition, although the United States was not last, it ranked fifteenth in women's wages as a percentage of men's; fifteenth in life expectancy; and ninth in early childhood education.

Some additional facts underscore the depth of social problems in the United States relative to its peers:

• Compared to its industrialized counterparts, the United States (1) has the highest incidence of poverty; (2) experiences the longest periods of people being in poverty; and (3) provides the least amount of income security to the poor (Danzier and Gottschalk, 1995; *Children's Defense Fund,* 1998). Moreover, the United States ranks first in the percentage of its children under age six in poverty (at 21.6 percent in 1997), a rate three to five times that of Western European nations (*The Nation,* 1996:7). In a study of eighteen industrialized nations, poor children in the United States ranked sixteenth in living standards (Rainwater and Smeeding, 1995).

• The United States is the only industrialized nation without some form of universal health care. It does, however, have the most advanced health care system in the world, and it spends 35 to 40 percent more for health care than the other industrialized countries. But because health care in the United States depends on a person's ability to pay, the overall indicators of good health are low: (1) Data from 1992 showed that the United States ranked twenty-second worldwide in overall infant mortality (and the worst among the industrialized nations). The infant mortality for U.S. blacks was more than twice the national average. (2) The United States ranks first among the industrialized nations in the percentage of infants born with low birth weight, in the proportion of children dying before age five, and in the percentage of preschoolers *not* immunized. (3) The country ranks fifteenth in life expectancy.

- The United States has the most unfair distribution of wealth and income in the industrialized world (Smeeding and Gottschalk, 1998).

- "None of the other industrialized democracies has allowed its city centers to deteriorate as has the United States" (Wilson, 1996:218). "No European city has experienced the level of concentrated poverty and racial and ethnic segregation that is typical of American metropolises. Nor does any European city include areas that are as physically isolated, deteriorated, and prone to violence as the inner-city ghettos of urban America" (Wilson, 1996:149). Many U.S. cities have child poverty rates higher than 35 percent and black child poverty rates of more than 50 percent (*The Nation,* 1996).

- Compared to its peers, the United States ranks first on a number of crime and criminal justice dimensions: (1) The country ranks first in percentage of population who have been victims of a crime. (2) It is number one in murder rate. (3) Similarly, the United States is preeminent in the murder rate of children. (4) It is also first in reported rapes, with the U.S. rate nearly three times higher than that of Sweden, the industrialized country with the second highest rate. (5) The United States imprisons a greater percentage of its population than any other industrialized nation (in 1995 the U.S. incarceration rate was 600 per 100,000 compared to 55 to 120 per 100,000 in the other industrialized societies) (Currie, 1998:15).

- Overall, the United States spends more than most developed nations for education (as measured by percentage of its gross domestic product). However, when the amount spent is divided into private and public spending, most of the spending is for private education (for the education of the well-to-do); in this category the country is ranked first among the nineteen major industrial nations, but it ranks only seventeenth in public spending for education as a percentage of gross domestic product (GDP) (Shapiro, 1992:55).

- A comparative study of child supports (e.g., housing, health, education, welfare allowances, and tax benefits) for families in fifteen nations ranked Luxembourg, Norway, France, and Belgium among the most generous countries; Denmark, Germany, the United Kingdom, Australia, and the Netherlands were among those providing middle-range provisions; and Portugal, Italy, Ireland, Spain, Greece, and the United States were the least generous with child benefit packages (Bradshaw et al., 1993).

The litany of U.S. social problems could go on, but the point has been made: *the United States has more serious social problems than are found in the countries most similar to it.* These other societies, like the United States, are modern, affluent, industrialized, democratic, and capitalist. Why, then, are the social problems in the United States of such greater magnitude? That is the question answered in the next section.

THE CONSEQUENCES OF U.S. SOCIAL POLICIES

Let's begin by describing the differences between the United States and the other developed nations on the dimensions that might affect the severity of social problems within societies. Most significant, the nations comparable to the United States devote a greater percentage of their gross domestic product to social expenditures. The United States chooses to spend a smaller proportion of its budget on social security and welfare programs (housing, food, health, and family allowance to single parents) than do other advanced industrialized nations.

In contrast to the United States, the advanced industrial societies provide excellent, publicly funded health care for all their citizens. In the United States, workers who do not have health insurance (about one-fourth) are not eligible for Medicaid, which is reserved for the poor. Those who do receive Medicaid often find the health services are insufficient for their needs. Moreover, because Medicaid does not compensate doctors as well as private health insurance does, many doctors refuse to take Medicaid patients.

The other industrialized countries also provide much more support for parents than the United States does in such areas as family allowances, housing subsidies, publicly subsidized child care, and paid family leaves from work. In this country, child care for working parents is tax deductible, a provision that expands the benefits as the parents' income increases, thus offering the working poor little benefit. The other developed countries have programs that provide maternity (and sometimes paternity) leaves with pay, whereas United States law requires only that companies employing more than fifty workers must allow *unpaid* maternity leave. Workers in smaller enterprises may or may not receive family leaves depending on the whim of their employers.

The United States differs from the other developed countries in the way public education is organized. Education in this country is decentralized, with each of the 15,000 school districts responsible for much of the financing and curriculum decisions for the local schools. This is in sharp contrast to the other countries in which national standards are set and schools are financed much more equally.

Prekindergarten programs are universal in the other developed countries; access to such programs is dependent on parents' resources in the United States. Compensatory preschool programs for the disadvantaged are underfunded in the United States, with only about one-fourth of those eligible actually receiving programs such as Head Start. Contrast this with the 100 percent of four-year-old French children and 98 percent of Belgian and Dutch children enrolled in preprimary programs. As a result of these differences, U.S. students graduating from high school are more varied in their skills and aptitudes (and this is correlated with parents' income and with the wealth of school districts) than are their counterparts in other industrialized countries.

Public education is taken more seriously elsewhere. In contrast to the United States, teacher salaries are higher, more resources are spent on public education, the school year is longer. And, for those eligible, higher education through graduate school is subsidized.

The differences in worker benefits are considerable when the United States is compared to its more generous peers. Take wages, for example:

> *Total compensation—wages, health benefits, vacations—for the typical U.S. worker in manufacturing has either remained flat or declined since the mid-1970s while it has increased by 40 percent for a European worker in a comparable job. Average compensation for a manufacturing worker in the United States is $16 an hour; in Germany it is $26. During the 1980s, the wages for low-income U.S. workers who lacked any college education dropped 15 percent when adjusted for inflation, whereas those for comparable workers in Europe increased 15 to 20 percent. (Wilson, 1996:154)*

In most of these comparable societies, national law requires that workers receive benefits such as strong job security; four-week, paid vacations; an ample minimum wage; and generous unemployment benefits (in some of these societies this is $1,000 per month indefinitely). In the United States, in contrast, job security is weak; paid vacations are not universal but depend instead on seniority and job status; and unemployment benefits are meager and short in duration. Moreover, more than twelve million workers labor for poverty wages, usually without health coverage or pension plans, and about one-fourth of the entire workforce are temporary workers, part-timers, and "independent contractors" working for low wages, no health and pension benefits, and few, if any, basic legal protections for their health and safety on the job (Sweeney, 1996:34–36).

Most significant, the gap between the chief executive officers and the average blue-collar workers who make the products is enormous—419 times as much in 1998. This measure of income inequality is much greater in the United States than in the other industrialized nations and is getting wider—up from 120-to-1 in 1990. Actually the gap is even greater because the executives in the other countries pay higher taxes on their relatively lower incomes than do U.S. executives. Moreover, the workers in the other countries receive much more in nonmonetary compensation (e. g., universal medical care, subsidized child care) than do U.S. workers (Fischer et al., 1996:102, 122).

Wealth inequality is also much more skewed in the United States than among its peers. In 1990, for example, the richest 1 percent of U.S. families owned about 40 percent of household wealth (more, by the way, than the bottom 90 percent), more than in any other advanced nation. In Canada the richest 1 percent owned 25 percent while in the United Kingdom it owned only 18 percent (Fischer et al., 1996:124–125). This is a reversal from the situation in the early twentieth century.

> *The evidence seems to suggest that in the early part of this century (the 1920s are the earliest period for which data are available), wealth inequality was much lower in the United States than in the United Kingdom, while U.S. figures were comparable to Sweden. America appeared to be the land of opportunity, whereas Europe was a place where an entrenched upper class controlled the bulk of wealth. By the late 1980s, the situation appears to have completely reversed, with much higher concentration of wealth in the United States than in Europe. Europe now appears the land of equality. (Wolff, 1995:21)*

As we have seen, U.S. policies concerning citizens are much different than are the policies of the other developed nations. The other societies are much more generous to their citizens, providing social supports that encourage equal opportunity and provide for the basic needs of income maintenance, housing, job security, and health care. To reiterate, the other developed societies have much more comprehensive programs that minimize economic deprivation and insecurity. The few supports found in the United States are now under severe attack. The irony, as James Carville has said, is that "we have the thinnest, most pathetic social safety net of any industrialized country" (Carville, 1996:26). Yet, the Republican-controlled Congress with the aid of the New Democrats (including President Clinton) have eliminated the Aid to Families with Dependent Children and reduced welfare benefits, allowing the states to devise and administer the program. Food stamps, legal services to the poor, housing subsidies, school lunch programs, and the like have been reduced and are always under the threat of further reductions or elimination.

The prevailing ideology has two postulates. First, the unequal distribution of economic rewards is none of the government's business. Americans value individualism and the market economy. The obvious result is inequality and that is good because it motivates people to compete and it weeds out the weak. Whatever suffering occurs is not the fault of society but lies, rather, in the actions of society's losers.

The second postulate of the current conservative creed is that government efforts to reduce poverty and class inequality actually cause those very problems. Welfare dependency, in this view, is the source of poverty, illegitimacy, laziness, crime, unemployment, and other social pathologies. Proponents of this opinion agree with Charles Murray that only when poor people are confronted with a "sink or swim" world will they ever develop the will and the skill to stay afloat (Murray, 1984).

Acceptance of these two postulates leads to the obvious solution: do away with the welfare state and the quicker the better. This view leads to the following related questions: Will dismantling the welfare state be beneficial or will it create chaos? Will society be safer or more dangerous? Will crime rates increase or decrease? Will more or fewer people be on the economic margins?

We believe that the answers to these questions are self-evident. Society will be worse off rather than better off. The number of people on the economic margins will rise. Homelessness will increase. Crime rates will swell. Public safety will become much more problematic.

One result will be the exacerbation of income and wealth inequality. This phenomenon has serious implications for society. As one sociologist has concluded, "growing inequality erodes social solidarity" (Gitlin, 1995:225).

Criminologists have shown that poverty, unemployment, and economic inequality are powerful determinants of street crime (DeKeseredy and Schwartz, 1996). Crime rates (e.g., homicide, robbery, and rape) are much higher in the United States than in the more generous welfare states. As a consequence, not only is society more dangerous, but also it must bear the economic cost of imprisoning so many.

The generous benefits in the social democracies are costly, with income, inheritance, and sales taxes considerably higher than in the United States. In 1991, for example, the total tax burden (as a percentage of that country's GDP) was 29.8 percent in the United States (virtually tied with Australia for having the lowest taxes), compared to 37.3 percent in Canada, 39.2 percent in Germany, 44.2 percent in France, and 56 percent in Sweden (Steinmo, 1993). The trade-off is that these other countries have comprehensive, universal health care systems. Pensions and nursing home care are provided for the elderly. Families are supported with paid parental leaves. Jobs are well paid and relatively secure. Most important, poverty is rare, street crime is relatively insignificant, and the people feel relatively safe from crime and the insecurities over income, illness, and old age.

The United States, in sharp contrast, has the highest poverty rate by far among the industrialized societies, a withering bond among those of different social classes, a growing racial divide, and an alarming move toward a two-tiered society. The consequences of an extreme bipolar society are seen in the following description by James Fallows:

> *If you had a million dollars, where would you want to live, Switzerland or the Philippines? Think about all the extra costs, monetary and otherwise, if you chose a vastly unequal country like the Philippines. Maybe you'd pay less in taxes, but you'd wind up shuttling between little fenced-in enclaves. You'd have private security guards. You'd socialize only in private clubs. You'd visit only private parks and beaches. Your kids would go to private schools. They'd study in private libraries. (quoted in Carville, 1996:87)*

The United States is not the Philippines, but we are experiencing a dramatic rise in private schooling, home schooling, private recreational clubs, and the number of walled and gated affluent neighborhood enclaves on the one hand and ever greater segregation of the poor, and especially poor racial minorities, in already segregated and deteriorating neighborhoods and inferior schools on the other. Personal safety is more and more problematic as violent crime rates increase among the young. Finally, democracy is on the wane as more and more people opt out of the electoral process (only about 40 percent vote in presidential elections and many fewer in off-year and local elections), presumably because, among other things, they are alienated and believe their votes do not count (consistently, the United States has the lowest voter turnout among the industrialized nations).

In sum, the comparison of U.S. policies with those of the generous welfare states leads to the following conclusion: we ignore the problems of poverty, wealth inequality, and a rationed health care system at our own peril. If the country continues on the present path of ignoring these and other social problems or reducing or eliminating programs to deal with them, Americans will be less secure, more people will be defined as problems that require greater control, and at an ever greater social and economic cost.

BARRIERS TO THE ADOPTION OF MORE GENEROUS WELFARE STATE POLICIES

If the social policies of the other developed societies minimize social problems, why doesn't the United States adopt them or at least try to modify them to fit our situation? There are significant barriers that make such social changes very difficult.

First, there is the fundamental American belief in competitive individualism. Americans celebrate and support individual rights. Seymour Martin Lipset puts it this way:

> *Citizens have been expected to demand and protect their rights on a personal basis. The exceptional focus on law here as compared to Europe, derived from the Constitution and the Bill of Rights, has stressed rights against the state and other powers. America began and continues as the most anti-statist, legalistic, and rights-oriented nation. (Lipset, 1996:20)*

The high value Americans place on individualism has several implications, all of which work against efforts for the collective good. First, the individual is exalted, which makes working for group goals difficult. Americans typically do not want to pay taxes for the good of others. Opinion surveys taken in various developed countries, for example, reveal that Americans are much less prone than Europeans and Canadians to favor measures to help the underprivileged (Lipset, 1996:145). Second, government intrusions into personal lives or into local schools or communities are opposed. Third, there is a resistance against efforts to establish preferential rights for disadvantaged groups (e.g., affirmative action based on race or gender). Fourth, Americans combat government handouts to the undeserving. Finally, the strong emphasis on competitive meritocracy means that individuals are believed to be advantaged or disadvantaged because of their skills, effort, and motivation or the lack thereof. Thus, the affluent are venerated and the poor vilified.

A second barrier to the adoption of welfare state policies is political. To begin, the majorities in the federal and state legislatures are political conservatives, which means they will opt for reducing or eliminating the welfare state rather than expanding these government programs. The political debate in these assemblies is from the right to the political center, with little, if any, voice from the political left. As the U.S. population ages (the baby boomers are now reaching fifty), and the sunbelt states continue to attract population disproportionately, this tendency to elect centrist and right-of-center politicians will increase. Another political barrier is the two-party system, where both parties market their appeals to the center. Moreover, the major parties are financed by big business and wealthy individuals, both of which favor low taxes and reduced social programs. Also, the two-party system that has evolved in the United States creates structural difficulties for third parties attempting to emerge as viable alternatives.

One of the necessary ingredients for a generous welfare state is the existence of a heavily unionized workforce. Strong unions use their collective clout to support issues favorable to the working class, as evidenced in Canada and the welfare states of Europe. The labor movement in the United States has fought for Social Security, Medicare, Medicaid, FHA mortgages, the GI Bill, civil rights legislation, voting rights legislation, student loans, and an increased minimum wage. In the past, U.S. unions were a powerful force for economic security and social justice. But that was forty years ago when unions were strong. In the mid-1950s, 35 percent of all U.S. workers belonged to unions, 80 to 90 percent in major industries such as auto and steel manufacturing, and coal mining. This percentage slipped to 28 percent in the mid-1970s and now it is only 13.8 percent in 1998. Weak unions do not present a countervailing force against powerful business interests. The result is that efforts to expand the welfare state in the United States have no powerful ally. And, with labor's loss of power, we are experiencing a growing meanness in public policy (Sweeney, 1996:7).

CONCLUSION

The political-social-economic system of a society does not just evolve from random events and aimless choices. The powerful in societies craft policies to accomplish certain ends within the context of historical events, budgetary constraints, and the like. Addressing the issue of inequality, Fischer and his colleagues say:

> The answer to the question of why societies vary in their structure of rewards is more political. In significant measure, societies choose the height and breadth of their "ladders." By loosening markets or regulating them, by providing services to all citizens or rationing them according to income, by subsidizing some groups more than others, societies, through their politics,

build their ladders. To be sure, historical and external constraints deny full freedom of action, but a substantial freedom of action remains. . . . In a democracy, this means that the inequality Americans have is, in significant measure, the historical result of policy choices Americans— or, at least, Americans' representatives—have made. In the United States, the result is a society that is distinctly unequal. Our ladder is, by the standards of affluent democracies and even by the standards of recent American history, unusually extended and narrow—and becoming more so. (Fischer et al., 1996:8)

In other words, the level of inequality in the United States is by design (Fischer et al., 1996:125).

Social policy is about design, about setting goals and determining the means to achieve them. Do we want to regulate and protect more as the well-developed welfare states do or should we do less? Should we create and invest in policies and programs that protect citizens from poverty, unemployment, the high cost of health care, or should the market economy sort people into winners, players, and losers based on their abilities and efforts? Decision makers in the United States have opted to reduce the welfare state. Are they on the right track, or can the policies of the generous welfare states, with modification, reduce the social problems in the United States? If societies are designed, should the United States change its design?

REFERENCES

Bradshaw, J., J. Ditch, H. Holmes, and P. Whiteford. 1993. "A Comparative Study of Child Support in Fifteen Countries." *Journal of European Social Policy 3*(4): 255–271.

Carville, James. 1996. *We're Right, They're Wrong: A Handbook for Spirited Progressives.* New York: Random House.

Children's Defense Fund. 1998. *The State of America's Children Yearbook 1998.* Washington, DC: Children's Defense Fund.

Currie, Elliott. 1998. *Crime and Punishment in America.* New York: Metropolitan Books.

Danziger, Sheldon, and Peter Gottschalk. 1995. *America Unequal.* New York: Russell Sage Foundation.

DeKeseredy, Walter S., and Martin D. Schwartz. 1996. *Contemporary Criminology.* Belmont, CA: Wadsworth.

Fischer, Claude S., Michael Hout, Martin Sanchez Jankowski, Samuel R. Lucas, Ann Swidler, and Kim Voss. 1996. *Inequality by Design: Cracking the Bell Curve Myth.* Princeton, NJ: Princeton University Press.

Gitlin, Todd. 1995. *The Twilight of Common Dreams.* New York: Henry Holt.

Lipset, Seymour Martin. 1996. *American Exceptionalism: A Double-Edged Sword.* New York: W. W. Norton.

Miringoff, Marc, and Marque-Luisa Miringoff. 1999. *The Social Health of the Nation: How America Is Really Doing.* New York: Oxford University Press.

Murray, Charles. 1984. *Losing Ground: American Social Policy 1950–1980.* New York: Basic Books.

The Nation. 1996. "State of the Children." *The Nation* (June 17):7.

Rainwater, Lee, and Timothy Smeeding. 1995. *Doing Poorly: The Real Income of American Children in Comparative Perspective.* Luxembourg Income Study Working Paper Number 127 (August).

Shapiro, Andrew L. 1992. *We're Number One! Where America Stands—and Falls—in the New World Order.* New York: Random House Vintage Books.

Smeeding, Timothy M., and Peter Gottschalk. 1998. "Cross-National Income Inequality: How Great Is It and What Can We Learn From It?" *Focus* (University of Wisconsin-Madison Institute for Research on Poverty) *19* (Summer/Fall):15–19.

Steinmo, Sven. 1993. "So, How High Are Taxes?" *Denver Post* (March 13):Dl.

Sweeney, John J., with David Kusnet. 1996. *America Needs a Raise.* Boston: Houghton Mifflin.

Wilson, William Julius. 1996. *When Work Disappears: The World of the New Urban Poor.* New York: Alfred A. Knopf.

Wolff, Edward N. 1995. *Top Heavy: A Study of the Increasing Inequality of Wealth in America.* New York: The Twentieth Century Fund Press.

2

Canada: A Kinder, Gentler Nation

PETER DREIER AND ELAINE BERNARD

This article analyzes in what ways Canada is different from the United States. Although there are important similarities between these two neighbors, Canada's approach to solving social problems is quite different and much more successful. The key appears to be Canada's multiparty political system, which is more efficient than the U.S. system in translating public opinion into public policy and a strong labor union movement.

IS CANADA A MORE HUMANE, LIVEABLE SOCIETY THAN THE UNITED STATES?

On issue after issue, the answer is yes. A quick glance at the statistics on page 14 reveals that Canada has less poverty, better unemployment insurance, less crime, fewer infant deaths, and less hazardous waste than the United States. On most indicators of social well-being, Canada outperforms the US, typically by a wide margin.

Canada's experience suggests that activist government does not inevitably lead to bureaucratic red tape, erosion of the work ethic, a decline in personal freedom, or a weaker economy. Indeed, on many economic indicators—productivity gains, budget deficits, export growth—Canada surpasses the United States.

The current debates about national health insurance have brought Canada to the attention of many Americans. But there clearly is much more that Americans can learn from their neighbors to the north.

Some pundits argue that the differences in public policy between Canada and the US are rooted in different social values and views about government. Americans, they say, prize individualism and the private market, while Canadians put a higher premium on government activism to solve common problems. But public-opinion surveys reveal that the views of ordinary citizens in Canada and the US on social values and the role of government are more alike than different. The key distinction—for reasons discussed below—is that in Canada, public opinion is more easily translated into public policy.

Source: Peter Dreier and Elaine Bernard, 1992. "Canada: A Kinder, Gentler Nation," *Social Policy 23* (Summer), pp. 6–19.

Social Policy Index

On most indicators of national well-being, the social democracies of Western Europe outperform both the United States and Canada. But in most cases, Canada outperforms the US, typically by a wide margin. For example:

- 20.4% of American children live in poverty, compared with 9.3% of Canadian children.
- 10.9% of elderly Americans live in poverty, compared with 2.2% in Canada.
- The US spends more on health care—12.4% of its GNP ($2,566 per capita)—than any country in the world, while still not providing coverage for all of its citizens; Canada spends 9% of GNP ($1,795 per capita) and provides universal coverage for all residents.
- The US infant mortality rate of 10 deaths per 1,000 live births is the highest of the 19 major industrial countries; Canada's rate is 7 deaths per 1,000 live births.
- Canada ranks 7th in life expectancy (77 years); the US ranks 15th (75.9 years).
- The US does not have a national maternity leave policy; Canadian women receive 17–18 weeks of paid maternity leave.
- The US ranks first in the world with 9.4 murders per 100,000 population; Canada ranks third with 5.5 murders per 100,000 population.
- During the late 1980s, the US was the world's most prolific producer of hazardous waste—110,000 tons of hazardous waste per 100,000 people; Canada ranked second with less than one eighth that rate: 12,500 tons per 100,000 people.
- The US spends 4.77% of its GDP in public dollars on education, compared with 6.53% in Canada.
- When 14-year-olds in 17 countries were given a science test, the US ranked 15th, above only the Philippines and Hong Kong; Canada ranked fourth.
- The US has won the most Nobel prizes in science, but 28 nations have more scientists and technicians per capita than the US. Canada ranks fourth, with 257 scientists and technicians per capita; the US has 55 per capita.
- In 1991, corporate CEOs in the US (in firms with sales over $250 million) received an average remuneration of $747,500, 25 times the average pay of manufacturing employees. Their Canadian counterparts received $407,600, 12 times the average pay of manufacturing workers.
- American workers get 10.8 paid vacation days per year—last among 19 major industrial nations; Canadians are next to last, with 14.7 paid vacation days per year.
- The US has one of the lowest voter turnout rates of any industrialized democracy—53 percent on average in the 1980s for presidential elections. In Canada, the rate of turnout among eligible voters is generally some 20 points higher—the '80s average was 72 percent in national elections.

These facts are drawn from Andrew L. Shapiro, *We're Number One: Where America Stands—and Falls—in the New World Order* (New York: Vintage, 1992); *The World Almanac 1992* (New York: Pharos Books, 1991); and Ruy A. Teixeira, *The Disappearing American Voter* (Washington, DC: Brookings Institution, 1992).

Canada certainly is not an ideal society. On many social issues it lags far behind the social democracies of Western Europe. But because Canada is similar to the US in so many ways, it offers an important model. With some modifications, what works in Canada is likely to work in the United States.

One-Way Mirror

The United States and Canada share over 3,000 miles of border, and each is the other's largest trading partner. In many respects, the two countries are as close as any in the world. Yet in spite of extensive cultural and economic integration, the relationship between the United States and Canada can perhaps best be described as something like a one-way mirror. In general, Canadians know a great deal about their neighbor to the south, but people in the US tend to know very little about Canada. Most Americans know that Canada is big, sparse and cold; that the best professional hockey players hail from Canada; that the French-speaking residents of Quebec are unhappy about their relationship with the rest of Canada; that Canada welcomed American draft resisters during the Vietnam War; and that, at least in the movies, "the Royal Canadian Mounties" always get their man.

Most American visitors to Canada find themselves very much at ease in a setting where, aside from the novelty of seeing labels written in English and French, most consumer products and brand names are the same as in the United States. The same popular culture—from music to sports to best-selling novels—is available on both sides of the border, and the population has a standard of living virtually identical to that of the US.

But much of this familiarity derives from US dominance of Canadian commerce and culture. While publications like *Time, Newsweek* and the *New York Times* are widely read in Canada, few Americans can find *Maclean's Magazine* or the Toronto *Globe and Mail* at their local newsstand. Canadians watch American-made TV shows and films on a daily basis, but Canadian productions rarely are shown in this country. And although many Canadian journalists, entertainers, and celebrities have "crossed over" into the US market, they have usually done so by "passing" as Americans: Few people in the US are likely to be aware that Peter Jennings, Margaret Atwood, or Michael J. Fox are Canadians. And how many Americans know that the social democratic NDP (New Democratic Party) won election in 1990 to lead the government of Ontario, Canada's largest province? Most Americans cannot name Canada's Prime Minister (Brian Mulroney), its capital city (Ottawa), the political party in power (Progressive Conservative), or more than one or two of the nation's 10 provinces. Canadian politics, economics, history, and distinct popular culture are virtually invisible to most people in the US, even those living near the Canadian border.

In the past few years, however, people on this side of the border have been hearing about one aspect of politics that Canadians have long taken for granted: a universal healthcare system. In light of skyrocketing health costs in the US and 37 million citizens without health insurance, a growing number of experts and politicians have looked admiringly at Canada, which provides decent health for all its citizens while holding down healthcare expenditures and operating at a reasonable cost to government. "It's Not Perfect, But It Sure Works," *Business Week* (March 9, 1992) told its readers. Echoed the *New York Times* (July 23, 1992): "Canada's Medical System Is a Model. That's a Fact.". . . .

A Frontier Society

Despite the obvious existence of huge social and economic inequalities in the US, American politics has rarely developed a coherent progressive political force based on class.

Some scholars have sought to explain this vacuum as a result of the country's frontier culture, ethnic diversity, and ethos of individualism. But, like the United States, Canada is, in essence, a frontier society populated by continuing waves of immigration—requiring it to deal with the continued absorption of new people, languages, religions, and cultures. And, like the US, Canada has confronted the challenge of creating a single sense of nationhood among peoples varied in language and culture, and spread out over a vast territory.

The US and Canada share a link as British colonies, although for Canada that history continued well into the twentieth century. The British and French wrestled for control of what is now central and eastern Canada. British forces defeated the French in 1759, but under the Treaty of Paris, Quebec was permitted to maintain a strong French and Catholic culture—much to the anger of the English colonies to the south. The Quebec Act of 1774 guaranteed the French population in the British colony of Quebec the right to their religion (Catholicism) and French civil law.

It wasn't until 1867, through an act of British parliament called the British North America Act, that the colonies united in confederation to form Canada. Over the next century, the confederation assumed increasing powers, admitting the western territories as new provinces, while gradually the territories moved from colony to nation.

With a population of 26.5 million, Canada is approximately one-tenth the size of the US. The geographical territory of Canada is immense—the break up of the Soviet Union has made it the largest country in the world. However, since much of the territory is cold and barren, the majority of Canada's population lives in a long band in the south of the country within 200 miles of the US border. One-half of Canada's population lives in the three metropolitan areas around Toronto, Montreal, and Vancouver; all three cities are within an easy car drive of the US. And while Canada has ten provinces and two northern territories, the two large central Canadian provinces—Ontario and Quebec—account for over 60 percent of the population.

Regionalism, Race, and Culture

Like the US, Canada has been torn by regional differences throughout its history. In the United States, the South has long played a key role in limiting national policies on race, labor, industrial development, and increased wages. Race has been a major factor, but so has the region's low-wage agricultural and industrial economy, leading southern politicians in Congress to resist pro-union legislation and federal standards for social programs. The politics of "states' rights," and the resistance to a strong national government, has meant that Washington has played a minimal role in equalizing regional disparities.

Canada's regional economic differences are played out around competing interests in fishing, lumber, farming, resource extraction, manufacturing, and finance. No less than in the US, this requires a careful balancing act in Parliament and within the major parties. Provinces not only fight for their political autonomy, but also for getting their "fair share" of federal resources for social and economic development. But . . . the wealthier provinces have not resisted "equalization" policies to assist the poorer regions. In fact, they have typically viewed it as in their self-interest to promote national economic development that requires improving the social and economic conditions in Canada's poorer areas.

Like the US, Canada is torn by ethnic conflict. In particular, there are the long-standing grievances of Canada's French-speaking population centered in Quebec and Canada's indigenous peoples (the Cree, Inuits, and other Indian nations within Canada). Dissatisfaction among both groups has led to an intense constitutional crisis that has threatened the very unity of Canada.

Quebec has long viewed itself as a "nation" within Canada, and has periodically spawned nationalist parties and movements seeking separation and the creation of an independent French-speaking state in North America. Indeed, the most recent constitutional crisis in Canada—which revolves around the failed Meech Lake Accord—has its roots in the unfinished business of Canadian nation-building.

In the early 1980s, Liberal Prime Minister Pierre Trudeau sought unanimous agreement from the provinces in order to adopt a written constitution for the country through patriating (placing under Canadian jurisdiction) the act of British parliament—the British North America Act—that outlined the basis of confederation and the division of powers between the federal and provincial governments, which was Canada's founding document. Along with the proposed constitution, Trudeau also negotiated the adoption of a Charter of Rights and Freedoms, essentially a Canadian Bill of Rights. Quebec objected to some provisions of the constitution and to the Charter of Rights and Freedoms as an encroachment on its longstanding rights, and refused to sign the final agreement. In response, Trudeau adopted the legislation without Quebec's support, leaving Canada in the dubious position of having a constitution that one province, with one quarter of the population of the country, has never ratified.

The Meech Lake Accord of 1988 was an effort by Progressive Conservative Prime Minister Mulroney to bring Quebec into the Canadian constitutional fold by recognizing it as "a distinct society." The Accord proposed enshrining in the constitution the concept that Canada was the product of two founding nations—one English and one French. Such a formulation was objected to as an insult to the large number of Canadians with neither English nor French roots—more than 50 percent of the country's population. In addition, Canada's indigenous population objected to once again being excluded from constitutional talks. The Accord proposed giving additional powers to all provinces, something it was widely felt would undermine the power of the federal government and might serve as a barrier to current and future universal social programs. In the end, the Meech Lake Accord was defeated by the clock; it failed to receive approval by all provinces before its three-year time limit ran out.

Today, Canadians are again negotiating a constitutional accord—only this time wider consultation has taken place, and the indigenous people have received assurance that their demand for self-government will be recognized. It is hoped that an accord can be concluded that will redefine Canadian federalism so as to satisfy the national aspirations of Quebec, while at the same time preserving a significant role for the federal government in assuring equality of treatment for Canadians regardless of which province they live in.

Canada is hardly lacking in regional, ethnic, cultural, and national divisions. But whereas in the US racial and regional divisions have long dominated discussions of social-welfare policy—undermining support for assistance to the poor and to cities—in Canada there is generally not the same inflammatory conflation of race/region/poverty. Despite the ongoing conflict between French- and English-speaking Canadians, poverty is not significantly higher in Quebec than elsewhere in Canada; in fact poverty rates are much lower than in the English-speaking maritime provinces. There is little discussion of an "underclass" in Canada, and the question of "welfare chiselers" or the social pathologies of the poor is much less a part of mainstream political debate.

The exception to this rule is Canada's indigenous people, long denied basic rights and subject to racist and paternalistic rule by successive Canadian governments.

Economic Factors

Canada's more "collectivist" tradition is rooted in the need to promote national unity across a wide geographic area and between economically distinct regions. Government's strong role in these areas carried over into social policy and labor relations. In the post–World War II period, the major sectors of the business community (represented by the "Progressive Conservative" and "Liberal" parties) have been less resistant to an expanded social contract than their counterparts in the United States.

In economic production, Canada is the smallest of the top seven OECD countries. Its GNP is $500 billion, compared to $5,200 billion for the United States. Yet its GNP per capita ($19,030 in 1989) is similar to the United States ($20,910). Canada has been an active player in the global economy, and is heavily dependent on trade. In the same year, imported and exported goods accounted for 46.1 percent of its gross domestic product—this makes Canada less open than Germany, about the same as Italy and Britain, and more open than France, Japan or the United States.

The major fact of Canadian economic life—much resented by Canadians—is its historic role as a "junior partner" to the United States. As Richard Lipsey and Murray Smith put it in *Taking the Initiative,* "Like it or not, Canada is a small country living next door to a giant." Canadians often want to keep their distance from the US for fear of "being swallowed up culturally, economically and politically by the US colossus." Indeed, much of their fierce nationalism is rooted in resistance to economic and cultural control by the United States.

It is nevertheless undeniable that Canada's economy is very much dependent on its southern neighbor. For Canada, 70 percent of imports and 75 percent of exports are traded with the US; for the US, Canada makes up 17 percent of imports and 22 percent of exports. Direct American ownership of and investment in Canadian business is substantial, although it has declined since the late 1960s as a result of both Canadian policies and market conditions. But since the signing of the Canada–US Free Trade Agreement in 1988, US ownership has again been on the increase.

In 1987, before the passage of the US–Canada Free Trade Agreement, the US controlled 83 percent of transportation equipment, 67 percent of rubber products, 54 percent of chemicals and chemical products, 47 percent of petroleum and coal products, 46 percent of electrical products, 45 percent of mining and mineral fuels, and 42 percent of machinery industries in Canada. Needless to say, at these levels of ownership, American business has a high profile. This has led to an ongoing debate in Canada over "free trade" with the US. Canadians were profoundly ambivalent about the US–Canada Free Trade Agreement. With the combined effects of a recession and dislocation related to the Free Trade Agreement, today a majority of Canadians in every region in the country are opposed to it.

One final note on economic factors: during the 20th century, a tremendous amount of the United States's political, economic and cultural life has been devoted to staking out its position as a global superpower. Since the end of World War II, at least a third— and often considerably more—of the United States's annual federal budget has been devoted to military and related matters. In Canada, only a tiny part of the federal budget (8.7 percent in 1990) is related to military costs, and correspondingly little political energy has been devoted to fighting the Cold War.

Political Structures

From its very beginnings, Canada's federal government was viewed as an instrument of national unity, forging a collective community out of disparate regions and cultures. As Andrew Jackson observes, the federal government played a strong role in creating a transcontinental economy, overcoming the geographic isolation of the Western, Central, and Atlantic parts of Canada, and resisting US economic and cultural domination. This was accomplished by government-initiated tariffs, regulations, and, in the 20th century, publicly-owned enterprises in transportation, broadcasting, natural resources and other sectors. Even Canada's Conservative Party and much of the business community recognized the importance of creating a national railway system, and later a national airline, to help bind the country together economically. Similarly, support has been widespread for a national broadcasting system (the Canadian Broadcasting Corporation) to promote Canadian culture and identity in the flood of American and British cultural imports.

This helps explain the origins of Canadians' support for activist government. The US Constitution focuses on "life, liberty and the pursuit of happiness"—a creed that emphasizes the rights of individuals and is silent on the role of the community. Its Canadian counterpart focuses on "peace, order, and good government"—with an emphasis on collective goals and relations. This difference may be key to the separate evolution of the two systems.

Federalism and the Role of Provincial Government

Canadian federalism features a division of powers between the federal and provincial levels of government. In comparison to US states, the Canadian constitution allocates significant powers to the provinces, including health care, education, social programs, labor law covering almost 90 percent of the workforce, resources, and business within their own province. With recent constitutional negotiations, it also is likely that provinces will expand their powers to include at least some powers regarding immigration. With only 10 provinces (as opposed to 50 states in the US), sheer size paired with shared constitutional responsibility has forced new forms of consultation—such as First Minister Conferences between the federal and provincial ministers.

The division of powers within Canadian federalism has led to considerable experimentation at the provincial level, which in turn has often been transferred to the national level or disseminated throughout the country. For example, Canada's universal, single-payer health care program was first developed by the NDP provincial government of Saskatchewan. The federal government promoted its transfer throughout the country by offering matching funding to provinces that adopted a program following the guidelines first developed in Saskatchewan. The federal government, in this and other instances, has been innovative in seeking ways to promote a national program in areas where constitutionally it clearly does not have the power to act.

The nature of Canadian federalism has also been a boost to minority parties in Canada, especially in Western Canada, historic home of the social democratic NDP, and in Quebec, where various nationalist parties have appeared throughout this century. In the Canadian political system, a party that wins power at the provincial level can bring about significant change—change that has the potential of being adopted nationally. The NDP, which has never garnered more than 20 percent of the popular vote in a federal election, exerts considerable influence in Canadian politics, especially now that it forms the provincial government in Canada's largest province, Ontario, and also governs in British Columbia (the third largest province), Saskatchewan and the far northern Yukon. As a result, 52 percent of Canadians are now governed by NDP provincial governments.

The Parliamentary System

Canada operates under a variant of the British system of parliamentary government. In the US, voters elect a chief executive (president, governor) separately from the legislative branch, making it possible for different political parties to control each branch. In Canada, the government is formed by the party (or the several parties in coalition) representing the majority in the House of Commons. The Prime Minister selects the Cabinet from among the elected members of Parliament. The Prime Minister and Cabinet face daily questioning from opposition members while Parliament is in session. Strong party discipline usually guarantees that the government speaks with one voice. This system makes it less likely that the government will be stalemated by policy differences, which is so common in the United States, leading many observers to view Washington as dominated by gridlock and inertia.

Though not without patronage, by comparison to the US, the party (or parties) in power at both the federal and provincial levels in Canada get to appoint relatively few people to run the government. Most positions are secured through a career civil service, which is expected to carry out the policies and serve the elected government. Perhaps as a result, Canadians are less likely than Americans to view their governments as havens for political patronage and favoritism. The Canadian upper chamber, the Senate, may be one obvious exception. Members of the Senate are directly appointed by the Prime Minister. This body has little power, but it has long been viewed as a patronage plum. (Recent constitutional discussions have moved toward making Canada's Senate equal and elected—with six members from each province—and to charging it with the responsibility of safeguarding regional interests at the federal level.)

Voting, Elections, and the Party System

Both the US and Canada have almost universal adult suffrage. But while citizens in both countries must be registered in order to vote, the responsibility of the government in assuring registration marks a major difference between Canada and the US. In Canada, when an election is called, a complete national registration is carried out in a matter of weeks by a federal government agency (called Elections Canada) charged with the responsibility of overseeing elections. In national elections, over 70 percent of eligible voters normally go to the polls. In the US, where the onus is on the individual citizen to register and the process is frequently complicated, barely above 50 percent of the eligible electorate regularly vote in a presidential election year, and even less in off-year elections.

Unlike many European democracies, Canada does not have proportional representation to assure some measure of representation for minority parties based on the percentage of popular vote they achieve. Rather, as in the US, members of the respective legislatures are chosen in winner-take-all elections, in which the candidate with a plurality of votes wins. However, because there are usually more than two candidates vying in each electoral district, candidates frequently win with less than 50 percent of the vote in their district. This leads to greater political turnover. It also increases the chances for minority party candidates, as they do not need a clear majority to win.

In the United States, parties select candidates through a combination of primaries, conventions and conferences. With the exception of Michigan and Minnesota, neither major political party even has a formal membership. Rather, voters simply choose to indicate their preference—Republican or Democrat—as part of the registration process. As a result, US political parties are very loose organizations, subject to extensive state regulation of their primary processes. Party politics is dominated by candidate-centered campaigns vying to be the party standard-bearer. Each individual seeking to win a party nomination must pull together a campaign apparatus, raise money, fashion positions on issues, and garner endorsements.

In Canada, political parties are membership bodies that are self-governed, with individuals deciding to join a political party and agreeing to abide by the policies and constitution of the organization. Political parties hold nominating conventions in each district, and party members living in that district vote at a specially convened nominating meeting to select who will represent their party in the election. The parties play a major role in assisting candidates with their campaign, fundraising, and organizing. In return, candidates and elected officials running on the party banner are charged with carrying out the program of their respective parties. It is a rare event when an elected official votes against the party caucus in the federal or provincial parliaments. On those occasions when it does happen, the individual is often disciplined by being tossed out of the caucus or expelled from the party altogether.

Political parties in Canada are much more coherent and ideological than their American counterparts. In contrast to the US, there are few topics in Canadian politics left out of political debate because of bipartisan agreement. From the separatist *Parti Québecois* to the social democratic NDP in Central and Western Canada to the more recent right-wing populist party—the Reform Party—there is a considerably livelier political debate and broader mainstream political spectrum in Canada than in the US.

Business interests tend not to dominate Canadian politics to the same extent as they do in the United States, although this is starting to change. In the last federal election (1988), business interests weighed in heavily with support for the Free Trade Agreement and the Tories during the last weeks of the campaign. There also has been an ongoing business-sponsored campaign against the Ontario NDP government since its election in 1990. Electoral finance laws are much stricter in Canada. There are tight limits on how much individual candidates' campaigns and political parties are permitted to spend in an election. Election campaigns are generally less expensive, and there is some federal financing for candidates. through tax credits for individual political contributions and for candidates garnering more than 15 percent of the vote.

Election campaigns are less predictable than in the US. There is no set election date—though federal elections must occur at least every five years. Elections are intense, but last only a few months. Both the public and private broadcast media are *required* to provide each party with free air time. And there are limits on what each party can spend on paid advertising.

The Role of Labor

In both the US and Canada, labor unions tend to support one party—the Democrats and the NDP—but the similarities end there. From the 1930s through the 1960s, the US labor movement translated its influence in the Democratic Party into progressive social and economic legislation, but since then its influence has waned and labor has become isolated from other social movements. Even during the Carter Administration, when Democrats also controlled both houses of Congress, the unions could not win any significant reform of the nation's labor laws. . . . Labor union membership in the US has been declining since the mid 1950s, while in Canada it has continued to increase. Today, unions represent approximately 37 percent of the Canadian workforce, compared with 16 percent in the US.

In Canada, the labor movement cofounded the NDP in 1961, along with the Cooperative Commonwealth Federation (a farm, labor, socialist party formed in 1932). The largest labor federation in the country, the Canadian Labour Congress (CLC) is formally affiliated with the party. Unions always have played a major role in the NDP, assisting in the formulation of party policy and accounting for close to one-fourth of the delegates at party conventions. Senior labor leaders sit on the leadership bodies of the party in most jurisdictions. Today, Nancy Riche, one of two vice-presidents of the Canadian Labour Congress, is president of the federal NDP. Many labor activists have been elected to party offices and have run as NDP candidates in provincial and federal elections. In Ontario, for example, 27 out of 55 NDP members of the provincial parliament are trade unionists.

Because most labor legislation and much social legislation is a provincial responsibility, labor has been able to play a major role in shaping social and economic conditions in provinces where the NDP has held power. The social democratic Saskatchewan government, for example, was the first North American jurisdiction to give public employees collective bargaining rights. The NDP has also promoted a higher minimum wage, labor-law reform, and pay-equity legislation.

Labor in Canada also tends to have a broader political vision than its counterpart in the United States. . . . A "social unionism" perspective—incorporating the concerns of working people on the job and as citizens of the larger society—frequently brings labor into alliances with other progressive movements, including the women's movement, environmentalists, the peace movement, and housing activists, among others. The NDP serves as a vehicle through which all of these groups can work together politically and gives labor a voice in politics not easily relegated to the charge of representing a "special interest group." The NDP is more than a political party for labor. It is a political coalition that provides a permanent structure for labor and other progressive groups to work together.

Canada in Transition

Canada today is a country in crisis. The neo-conservative policies of Prime Minister Mulroney and the federal Progressive Conservative Party are forcing a significant social and economic restructuring. Free Trade, first with the United States and eventually to include Mexico, is a cornerstone in this restructuring, along with privatization and deregulation. Under the guise of a desirable democratic goal—reducing government influence in people's lives—the Canadian federal government is signing away its power to act for the society as a whole. It is subordinating government and democratic decision-making to the market place and corporate power.

Domestically, in response to the demands of indigenous people, Québecois, women, trade unionists and other activists for social justice, the federal government has initiated a new round of constitutional reforms that threatens permanently to enshrine this business-driven restructuring of the Canadian political system. Prime Minister Mulroney once boasted, "Give me 10 years and you won't recognize this country." Yet, until recently, few believed he could unravel so much of the country's social fabric in such a short period of time.

In spite of the crisis that the business/Tory offensive has provoked, Canada's right-wing forces have had a hard time selling their agenda. There are a number of reasons for this. Canadians view their society as a compassionate society, especially when compared to their closest neighbor, the United States. Because Canadians traditionally have seen the role of government as more than simply an instrument of big business, the right's efforts to discredit government's economic role and its attack on public enterprise have met much resistance. There is still a general acceptance in Canada of an activist government providing universal social programs, equalization programs between provinces and regions, and agricultural supply marketing boards to preserve the family and small farm.

In opposing Free Trade and the demands of business, a growing number of Canadians have demonstrated new support for the idea that government's role should be to assure the welfare of the citizens, not simply to create an environment within which business can prosper. This is the essence of the New Democratic Party's social democratic approach, and it appears to have found fertile ground in recent provincial elections.

In an unprecedented show of unity, in recent years labor, farmers', women's, anti-poverty, aboriginal, environmental, peace, church, cultural and senior citizens' groups have joined together to form a national organization—the Action Canada Network (ACN)—to oppose free trade and to struggle against the restructuring of Canada along continentalist and market-oriented lines. Moving beyond the narrow single-issue focus of most coalitions, the ACN has been successful in showing Canadians that the trade debate is really about many of the fundamental assumptions of Canadian society that are now undergoing significant change and challenge.

Most of the groups opposed to the neo-conservative program in Canada, including the ACN, recognize that while opposition is important, it is not enough. What is needed is an alternative program for a new Canada, which rejects the narrow nationalism of protectionism, but also seeks to assure that the government of Canada has sufficient powers to pursue the goal of social justice. However, in this age of multinational corporations and globalization, social justice can no longer be confined to the borders of the nation state. Much of the pressure on Canadian social programs is the pressure to harmonize downward with US programs.

Lessons for the United States

While mainstream America is debating the pros and cons of Canada's health-care system, American progressives have an opportunity to broaden the focus to include other aspects of Canadian social and economic policy.

On the policy level, Canada's success offers Americans a nearby example of what is possible in a society much like their own. It provides a national "laboratory" to explore the potential for activist government.

On the political level, American progressives can take heart from the long-term efforts, and the recent victories, of the NDP. Despite differences in social, economic and political structures between the two countries, the key lesson from the NDP's success is the importance of building a broad coalition that unites progressive forces and of developing a coherent political vehicle to vie for power.

In terms of both policy and politics, American progressives can begin by helping to expand Americans' awareness of the Canadian experience and its success stories. We must begin to turn the one-way mirror into a two-way mirror. We must work to improve coverage of Canada in the American media. We need to expand the interchange between American and Canadian policy makers, journalists, unionists, and other activists. Labor organizations, popular movements, foundations and universities can host forums and exchange visits.

The left in the United States is currently in disarray. Progressive forces are constantly regrouping into new organizations and coalitions out of exasperation with the existing two parties and their frustrations with previous progressive efforts. American progressives always seem to have one foot inside and one foot outside the electoral system. They have learned how to build single-issue social movements and, in many cases, to inject these issues into the mainstream political debate.

They have had less success in translating single-issue movements into forces that can contend for political power at the local, state or national levels. There are always efforts by progressives to gain a stronger foothold inside the Democratic Party, but rarely does a particular strategy last more than one or two electoral cycles. Occasional efforts have been made to create a third party out of the fragments of the left, but although the notion seems to be gaining ground this time around, the past two decades are strewn with the short-lived efforts of the Progressive Alliance, the Citizens Party, the Rainbow Coalition, the Coalition for Democratic Values and dozens of other national attempts to build political bridges on the left. Even within the movements for labor, women's rights, peace, environmentalism, racial justice, community renewal, recent history has been characterized more by fragmentation than common agendas and strategies.

As John Judis perceptively argues in *The American Prospect* the failure of the labor movement to serve as the political "glue" binding together a social democratic movement (as it does in so many other countries) is both a cause and a consequence of the left's failure. In the absence of a strong and progressive labor movement, other elements—single-issue groups, charismatic candidates, temporary coalitions and alliances, backed by foundations and direct mail fundraising—fill the political void. So perhaps the most crucial lesson from the NDP's experience and success is the importance of taking the "long view" of politics. The NDP has not been an "overnight success," but a party that gradually has evolved by focusing on nuts-and-bolts and building a political constituency base over time—in essence, by engaging in a long-term political battle of position.

Since 1984, there has been a conservative national government in Ottawa that has tried to roll back social and economic programs along the same lines as the Reagan/Bush and Thatcher Administrations sought. The fact that Prime Minister Brian Mulroney has been considerably less successful than his role models in Washington and London is largely due to the political strength of Canada's progressive social movements.

The "free trade" agreements being negotiated between Canada and the US have been another major source of pressure for Canada and the US to become homogenized. Yet as the two countries are drawn closer together, it is important that they seek equilibrium at the higher level, not the lower. On many fronts, that means making sure the US becomes more like Canada, and not the other way around.

3

Remedying Social Problems

JOE R. FEAGIN AND CLAIRECE BOOHER FEAGIN

This excerpt describes the Swedish welfare state and how it differs from the United States. It addresses criticisms leveled at the Swedish system, arguing that the system actually surpasses the United States in personal freedom, freedom of the press, and civic participation. Most importantly, Sweden compared to the United States has a higher standard of living, better health care for all citizens, and less poverty. Sweden, faced with the same economic problems of the other industrialized nations, has somewhat reduced the magnitude of the welfare state, despite the opposition of the large working class.

Since 1900 all capitalistic societies, including the United States, have seen considerable government intervention on behalf of working people. But some capitalistic societies have experienced considerably more government intervention than others. Indeed, nations such as Germany, Finland, and Sweden are often mistakenly seen by many Americans as "socialist" because of the extent of this government social intervention. But these are not socialist countries; they are countries with capitalistic economies and a fully developed social welfare state.

For example, in the 1930s Sweden began moving in the direction of large-scale social service reforms, including modest nationalization of industry, public ownership of enterprises, and expanded social services that greatly benefitted rank-and-file citizens. Most production of goods and services in the Swedish economy has remained in the hands of capitalist-controlled private enterprises, with government ownership confined primarily to railroads, mineral resources, a public bank, and liquor and tobacco operations. Sweden's blue-collar and white-collar workers organized strong unions and were able to force considerable concessions from the capitalist class. The social democratic government, in power for most of the past 60 years, developed one of the world's best social welfare systems. It implemented a broad range of people-oriented social service programs, supported by taxes on larger incomes, landed estates, and the profits of cor-

Source: Excerpt from Joe R. Feagin and Clairece Booher Feagin. 1994. *Social Problems: A Critical-Conflict Perspective,* 4th ed. (pp. 444–447). Englewood Cliffs, NJ: Prentice-Hall.

porations, to protect all Swedish citizens from poor housing, poor health care, poverty incomes, and lack of jobs. Labor and capital worked out a cooperative agreement whereby labor got a welfare state and capitalists got labor peace.[1]

In Sweden a laid-off worker has access to a state-run employment agency with which employers must by law list their job openings. Once a job is found, the worker receives government assistance for relocation. If no job is available, job-retraining programs and unemployment insurance benefits are provided. Swedish law also requires substantial advance notification of layoffs to give workers time to find new jobs. When necessary, the government has expanded public employment programs to reduce unemployment levels. As a result, unemployment rates since World War II have been relatively low. Sweden's well-developed welfare state has resulted in a wealthy and productive country; its per capita gross national product has been among the highest in the world.

In the mid-1950s Sweden became one of the first nations to implement a national health insurance program, which covers hospital and doctor costs. Patients choose their own physicians. Prenatal care, delivery, and postnatal care are free, and new mothers receive a lengthy paid leave from work. All schoolchildren receive free medical and dental care. A special program provides most of a worker's income for time lost because of sickness. Sweden's excellent health statistics include one of the lowest infant and maternal mortality rates in the world. In the late 1950s a government-supported pension plan was initiated, and since then a broad variety of other programs has been implemented. Working fathers, as well as working mothers, may take leave from work to help care for an infant, and if they are insured they receive an income supplement for time missed from work. Parents receive a cash bonus for each child and tax-free child care allowances. A large proportion of Swedish children of working parents are provided with safe government child care facilities. The Swedish government has also provided subsidies to help low-income families obtain adequate housing. Involuntary homelessness is not a serious problem in Sweden.[2]

Conservative criticism of the Swedish welfare state claims that taxes are twice as high in Sweden as in the United States. It has been estimated that for the late 1980s all direct and indirect taxes on individuals and corporations amounted to about 30–35 percent of the gross national product in the United States and 50–60 percent in Sweden. The Swedes do pay more taxes, particularly those who are better off, but not as much more as many critics claim. But in opinion surveys, the majority of Swedes have said they are willing to pay higher taxes in order not to have such problems as chronic unemployment, homelessness, and health care rationed by income. For their taxes all Swedes receive an array of benefits and services that help to prevent major social problems such as the inadequate health care received by many moderate-income Americans, homelessness, and widespread unemployment with no hope of employment. In addition, if we were to add the cost of the private medical insurance carried by many Americans (estimated at 5–20 percent of a typical household's income), as well as the cost of medical care not covered by insurance and the cost of private social services such as day care centers to the taxes Americans pay, Swedish and U.S. "taxes" are much more nearly equal. What the Swedes pay for through the tax system, we in the United States buy, if at all, from private enterprise— and we often get less-adequate (or no) health care, child care, and other services as a result.

Indeed, Americans may pay more, everything considered, for all services than do the Swedes—and receive less.

Conservative criticism of Sweden's welfare state also targets its alleged lack of personal freedom, the laziness it creates, the problem of suicides, alcoholism, and inefficiency. Yet on closer inspection, not one of these criticisms holds up very well. Sweden has greater political and press freedoms than the United States. The Swedish national media present a wider array of political and economic opinions on a regular basis than the U.S. media. By providing lower-income people with the means to think beyond struggling for food and shelter to higher needs such as active political participation, Sweden's welfare state has expanded freedom. Moreover, the welfare state has certainly not made Swedes lazy; Sweden has had one of the world's highest postwar growth rates, high earned per capita incomes, and advanced educational programs. And accusations that suicide and alcoholism are closely correlated with the growth of the Swedish welfare state are not supported by the data. Suicide and alcoholism are problems in Sweden, but they have been problems since *before* the welfare state developed, and Sweden's national health care system has provided major remedial responses to both problems.[3]

The only criticism that seems to have some truth in it is inefficiency. Hospital beds are adequate in number, but there are sometimes not enough doctors. Health services are specialized and heavily used; and there are sometimes long waits for elective health care. But this problem exists because all Swedes, not just the rich and affluent, can avail themselves fully of the medical facilities. Indeed, some argue that the U.S. system is more wasteful and inefficient, since it probably costs hundreds if not thousands of lives yearly, such as those of poor mothers and infants who could be saved if a Swedish-type infant and maternal care system were widely available.[4]

The progressive critique of the Swedish welfare state seems more serious. This critique points out that for all its advances in human services, Sweden still has a sharply unequal income distribution, a small capitalist class that owns and controls most of the production facilities, and a large group of modest-wage workers. Organizations of capitalists have a greatly disproportionate influence on day-to-day societal and government operations. Labor unions are much more influential in Sweden than in the United States, because a very large proportion of workers belong to them, but capitalists are more powerful than labor. In addition, Swedish capitalists, like U.S. capitalists, often press for lower wages for Swedish workers, arguing that workers elsewhere will work for much less.[5]

Since 1989 Sweden has experienced increasingly serious economic problems, caused to a substantial degree by some 20 powerful multinational corporations taking capital out of the country. In 1991 the Swedish Social Democratic Party was replaced by a coalition of four conservative parties. Responding to the needs of large corporations for higher profits, the new government dealt with the economic crisis by cutting some government social programs and humanitarian aid and by supporting policies that will lead to the transfer of income from working people to corporations. Workers were forced to take some cuts in sick pay, workers' compensation, and pension benefits; income support to students was cut; and a planned increase in benefit payments to families with children was cancelled. The anger of working people was reflected in the resolution adopted by one union: "We tolerate no proposals that undermine child benefits . . . work accident insurance, social assistance, pensions and other social safety nets for the most vulnerable groups. Let the swindlers and the speculators pay for the banks' losses."[6]

The new Swedish government's plan to allow employee benefit levels to be determined through collective bargaining is a major departure from Sweden's long-standing policy of providing public social benefits to all people, regardless of their degree of need or their position in the labor market. Walter Korpi, a professor of social policy at Stockholm University, has suggested that this new policy will increase inequalities between the less powerful blue-collar union workers and the more powerful white-collar union workers. "The risk for benefit inequalities . . . will become more pronounced the farther down minimum benefit levels are set by the state."[7] In Sweden, just as in the United States, the class struggle between workers and employers can be seen in the struggle over state-provided social services.

NOTES

1. The Swedish Institute's "Fact Sheets on Sweden" series, 1979–1990. See also Norman Furniss and Timothy Tilton. *The Case for the Welfare State* (Bloomington: Indiana University Press, 1977), pp. 134–36.
2. "Fact Sheets on Sweden"; Furniss and Tilton, *The Case for the Welfare State,* pp. 131–43.
3. Furniss and Tilton, *The Case for the Welfare State,* pp. 144–47.
4. Ibid., pp. 144–45.
5. Ibid., pp. 147–49.
6. Eero Carroll, "Swedish Austerity: Benefits at Risk," *Multinational Monitor,* January–February 1993, p. 35.
7. Quoted in ibid., p. 35.

PART TWO

Problems of Inequality

Poverty

THE UNITED STATES CONTEXT

Using the official statistics on poverty (which understate the magnitude of this social problem), 13.3 percent of the United States population in 1997 (35.6 million people) were poor. According to the U.S. Bureau of the Census (1998), the likelihood of being poor in the United States is increased for (1) *racial minorities* (27.1 percent of all Latinos, 26.5 percent of all African Americans, and 14.0 percent of all Asian Americans were poor in 1997, compared to 11.0 percent of all whites), (2) *women* (two-thirds of impoverished adults are women), (3) *children* (19.9 percent of all those under age eighteen and 21.6 percent of those under age 6), (4) *elderly women* (one in five women age seventy-five and over is poor compared to only one in ten men), and (5) *those living in certain places* (in central cities compared to the suburbs, and in four rural regions—the Mississippi Delta, which is primarily African American; the Rio Grande/U.S.–Mexico border, which is largely Latino; the Native American reservations of the Southwest and Plains; and Appalachia, which is predominantly white).

The U.S. poverty rate is the highest in the industrialized world. Child poverty has worsened over time. Among those under eighteen, poverty has increased from 14.9 percent in 1970 to 19.9 percent in 1997, a 33 percent increase. Addressing child poverty, and true of the overall poverty rate as well, Marc Miringoff and Marque-Luisa Miringoff state: "The United States has the worst record among the industrialized nations in reducing the poverty of children. Government programs reduce the poverty rates of children far more effectively in other countries than in the United States" (Miringoff and Miringoff, 1999:80).

In 1996, Congress and President Clinton addressed the poverty problem with a massive overhaul of the U.S. welfare system—the Personal Responsibility and Work Opportunity Act of 1996. This legislation, contrary to the welfare systems in other industrialized nations, eliminated aid to single mothers (Aid to Families with Dependent Children); left welfare programs up to the individual states but financed by the federal government; required the states to demand that parents work within two years of receiving cash assistance; mandated a five-year lifetime limit on assistance, which states can reduce if they wish; cut $54.5 billion from various federal assistance programs targeted for the poor; denied a broad range of public benefits to legal immigrants; and capped the federal money given to the states at $16.4 billion annually, which means no adjustment for inflation or population growth (Eitzen and Baca Zinn, forthcoming).

Is this shrinkage of an already weak safety net for the poor the solution for solving the poverty problem? The early results are not encouraging. On the positive side, 2.4 million people left welfare for work, although this may have been largely the result of a prolonged economic boom in which jobs were relatively plentiful. Negatively, welfare reform has made the poorest (i.e., those below half of the poverty rate) even poorer. A study by the Center on Budget and Policy Priorities found that the average income for the most destitute single-mother households fell from $8,624 in 1995 to $8,047 in 1997 (cited in Sawyer, 1999:34). Research by the Children's Defense Fund shows that the number of children in the extreme poverty category grew by 426,000 from 1996 to 1997 (cited in Freedman, 1999:57A). A fundamental problem for those leaving welfare is that they typically work at low-wage jobs with few if any benefits. Their minimal income must now cover food, housing, child care, and health care costs, and this makes their existence all the more tenuous.

REFERENCES_____

Eitzen, D. Stanley, and Maxine Baca Zinn. (Forthcoming.). "The Missing Safety Net and Families: A Progressive Critique of the New Welfare Legislation," *Sociology and Social Welfare.*

Freedman, Dan. 1999. "Welfare Reform Critics Cite Growth of Poverty," *Rocky Mountain News* (August 22):57A.

Miringoff, Marc, and Marque-Luisa Miringoff. 1999. *The Social Health of the Nation: How America Is Really Doing.* New York: Oxford University Press.

Sawyer, Kathy. 1999. "The Poorest Get Poorer," *The Washington Post National Weekly Edition* (August 30):34.

U.S. Bureau of the Census. 1998. "Poverty in the United States: 1997," *Current Population Reports,* P60-201 (September).

4

Why the U.S. Antipoverty System Doesn't Work Very Well

TIMOTHY M. SMEEDING

This author argues that public policies in the United States, compared to other industrialized countries, have kept the poverty rate higher than those found elsewhere. The other nations outspend the United States to alleviate poverty. Moreover, the tax and transfer systems of the other nations are better suited to fighting poverty and to promoting economic independence. The article ends with six lessons from these nations that the author feels would improve the United States' antipoverty system.

It is most illuminating to compare the effect of the United States' income security policy on poverty with the policies of other similarly modern nations during the 1980s to address the question of how antipoverty programs affect the poor. This allows us to evaluate the impacts of our own policies in relation to those of our allies, friends, and neighbors who, it turns out, have very different and much more effective means of fighting poverty through public programs.

POVERTY ACROSS NATIONS AND OVER TIME

Thanks to the Luxembourg Income Study (LIS) database, we are able to directly compare income and poverty status across a wide range of nations. Essentially LIS is a large microdatabase that contains the same household income survey database that is used to measure poverty in the United States (Current Population Survey), and also similar surveys from eighteen other nations. From LIS, we have selected a set of seven other nations that are very close to the United States in terms of economic status and data set structure for this comparison. These nations are: Canada and Australia (two similarly large, predominantly English-speaking and geographically diverse nations); and five European nations: Sweden, plus four European Community countries: Germany, the Netherlands,

Source: Timothy M. Smeeding. 1992. "Why the U.S. Antipoverty System Doesn't Work Very Well," *Challenge* 35 (January/February), pp. 30–35.

France, and the United Kingdom. For all of these but the United Kingdom, we have comparable data at two points in time: one around 1979–1981 and one around 1985–1987. The years are given by the availability of the other nations' datasets. The U.S. data are for 1979 and for 1986.

Every comparison of poverty involves two elements: income, or some other measure of economic well-being, and a poverty line to which income is compared. Our income definition is the same as that used by the U.S. Census Bureau, except that we add Food Stamps to money income and also take account of federal income and payroll taxes, including the effect of the Earned Income Tax Credit (EITC) on poverty status. The "official" poverty rates produced by the Bureau of the Census do not take account of Food Stamps or the EITC, thus neglecting the impact of two prime instruments in our national war against poverty. Our estimates take these program effects into account.

Our poverty definition uses the same differences for family size as those built into the U.S. poverty line, but sets the poverty line at 40 percent of median income in each country in each period. We chose the 40 percent line because of its closeness to the U.S. poverty line. In fact, the U.S. poverty line was 40.7 percent of median LIS income in 1986 and 42.1 percent in 1979. The result was a set of LIS-based poverty rates that were very close to the official U.S. poverty rates [see Table 4.1].

In fact, the LIS numbers yielded poverty rates that are a bit below the official figures, rates that include the effects of two of the programs that the U.S. government excludes from its figures. The estimates below come as close as possible then, to measuring the comparable level of poverty that one would find if we used the U.S. poverty line definition in each country.

We begin by comparing poverty rates using the 40 percent figures across nations (Table 4.2) and over time (Table 4.3). In the mid to late 1980s the level of poverty in the United States was a clear outlier, compared with any other similar nation, including Canada—our closest neighbor. With the exception of childless adults, U.S. poverty rates were at least twice as high as those in all other nations studied. Particularly noticeable are the poverty rates for elderly and children, the two most vulnerable groups of citizens in all nations. Here we find U.S. poverty rates that are 3.8 to 2.8 times as high as those in other nations when measured by the same poverty definition. U.S. children have by

TABLE 4.1   U.S. Poverty Rates from Two Sources (in percent)

CATEGORY	1979		1986	
	LIS	OFFICIAL U.S.	LIS	OFFICIAL U.S.
All Persons	10.8	11.7	13.3	13.6
Elderly (65 or over)	12.9	15.2	10.9	12.4
Adult (18–24)	8.3	8.9	10.5	10.8
Children (17 or under)	14.7	16.4	20.4	20.5

Source: For official United States poverty rates: U.S. Department of Commerce, Bureau of the Census, 1991: Tables 1, 2.

TABLE 4.2   Comparable Poverty Rates across Several Nations in the Mid-1980s*
Percent of People below 40 Percent of Adjusted
Median Family Income after Tax and Transfer

	U.S.** 1986	CANADA 1987	AUSTRALIA 1985	SWEDEN 1987	GERMANY 1984
All People	13.3	7.0	6.7	4.3	2.8
All Elderly	10.9	2.2	4.0	0.7	3.8
All Adults	10.5	7.0	6.1	6.6	2.6
With Children	12.7	6.6	6.6	1.5	2.0
No Children	8.4	7.4	5.5	9.7	3.0
All Children	20.4	9.3	9.0	1.6	2.8
	NETHERLANDS 1987	FRANCE 1984	U.K. 1986	AVERAGE	RATIO OF U.S TO AVERAGE
All People	3.4	4.5	5.2	5.9	2.3
All Elderly	0.0	0.7	1.0	2.9	3.8
All Adults	3.9	5.2	5.3	5.9	1.8
With Children	2.8	4.4	6.3	5.4	2.4
No Children	4.9	6.1	4.4	6.2	1.4
All Children	3.8	4.6	7.4	7.4	2.8

Source: Luxembourg Income Study.

*Income includes all forms of cash income plus food stamps and similar benefits in other nations, minus federal income and payroll taxes. Income is adjusted using the U.S. Poverty Line Equivalence Scale.

**The ratio of the U.S. Poverty Line for a three person family to the adjusted median income was 40.7 percent in 1986. Thus, the 40 percent line is close to the official U.S. poverty line. See text for additional comments.

far the highest poverty rate of any group, in any nation, at any time (Table 4.3). Even our elderly—for whom we have made great strides in alleviating poverty in the 1970s and 1980s—had poverty rates far above those in other nations. In fact, the only country with double digit poverty rates for any group in the mid to late 1980s was the United States. All other nations studied did a better job of fighting poverty than we did.

[Table 4.3] looks at changes in poverty in these same nations over time—from a year around 1979–1981 to a year around 1985–87. Despite their high level of poverty, the U.S. elderly did better than average in terms of change in poverty over the 1980s—other nations' old did not improve as much as ours did. But, of course, other nations' elderly all started, and stayed, at a level of poverty less than half of ours. Overall, and particularly for children, the United States had the sharpest increase in poverty among its citizens during the 1980s. This increase was far above the average increase in other nations studied. For instance, the LIS data show a 5.7 percent gain in child poverty over this period (the official U.S. poverty rates recorded a 4.1 percent jump). On average, other nations recorded a less than 1.0 percent gain in child poverty over this period. Canada managed to *reduce* overall poverty by 0.5 percentage points and to *reduce* child poverty by 0.9 percentage points. Clearly the United States had by far the highest poverty rates

TABLE 4.3 Changes in Poverty Rates over Time across Several Nations*
Percent of People below 40 Percent Adjusted Median
Family Income after Tax and Transfers

	ALL PEOPLE	ALL ELDERLY	ALL ADULTS	ALL CHILDREN
United States**				
1979	10.8	12.9	8.3	14.7
1986	13.3	10.9	10.5	20.4
Change	2.5	−2.0	2.2	5.7
Canada				
1981	7.5	4.7	6.6	10.2
1987	7.0	2.2	7.0	9.3
Change	−0.5	−2.5	0.4	−0.9
Australia				
1981	6.2	2.8	5.4	8.6
1985	6.7	4.0	6.1	9.0
Change	0.5	1.2	0.7	0.4
Sweden				
1981	2.9	0.1	4.2	2.1
1987	4.3	0.7	6.6	1.6
Change	1.4	0.6	2.4	−0.5
Germany				
1981	2.7	5.0	2.5	1.3
1984	2.8	3.8	2.6	2.8
Change	0.1	−1.2	0.1	1.5
Netherlands				
1983	5.5	2.3	6.8	4.0
1987	3.4	0.0	3.9	3.8
Change	−2.1	−2.3	−2.9	−0.2
France				
1979	4.6	2.3	5.1	4.7
1984	4.5	0.7	5.2	4.6
Change	−0.1	−1.6	0.1	−0.1
United Kingdom				
1986	5.2	1.0	5.3	7.4
Average				
Wave 1	5.7	4.3	5.6	6.5
Wave 2***	5.9	2.9	5.9	7.4
Change	0.2	−1.4	0.3	0.9

Source: Luxembourg Income Study.

*Income includes all forms of cash income plus food stamps and similar benefits in other nations, minus federal income and payroll taxes. Income is adjusted using the U.S. Poverty Line Equivalence Scale.

**The ratio of the U.S. Poverty Line for a three-person family to the adjusted median income was 40.7 percent in 1986 and 42.1 percent in 1979, thus, the 40 percent line is close to the official U.S. poverty line. See text for additional comments.

***Wave 2 Average includes United Kingdom 1986.

and suffered the sharpest increases in poverty among the nations studied here during the 1980s. But were our poverty rates so high because of poor economic conditions or because of the inadequacy of our income security safety net?

INCOME SECURITY POLICY EFFECT ON POVERTY

What worked in reducing poverty in the United States and other nations in recent years? The majority of the effects of public income security policy—government tax and trans- fer policy—on poverty can be isolated by comparing the poverty rate *before* taxes and transfers with the rate *after* taxes and transfers using the same poverty line. This produces an estimate of the direct antipoverty impact of policies aimed at reducing poverty. The after or "post" tax and transfer poverty rates are the same as those in Tables 4.2 and 4.3. We present figures for all people, for the three major age defined subgroups, and finally for children in single parent families—a group of increasing policy focus in all nations studied.

Poverty prior to taxes and transfers (so-called "pre" tax and transfer poverty) almost entirely depends on the status of the market economy. Only levels of earnings and other market income sources affect poverty *prior* to taxes and transfers. In fact, the U.S. *pre*-tax and transfer poverty rates are much closer to the other nations than one might expect (see top line, Table 4.4). Our pre-tax and transfer rate in 1986 was 19.9 percent, com- pared to a 22.4 percent rate in other nations. In fact, then our government programs take place in an environment that begins with below-average market based poverty rates. The big difference between the United States and other nations is in the *change* in poverty produced by public income security policy in the form of tax and transfer programs (third line, Table 4.4). Here the U.S. system reduces poverty by only 6.6 percentage points as compared with a 16.5 percent average effect in other nations. In fact, the impact of U.S. policy on pre-tax and transfer poverty was the least for *every* subgroup investigated. Among all children, for instance, the U.S. tax and transfer system reduced poverty by only 1.9 percentage points; among single parents the U.S. effect was to reduce child poverty by only 3.9 points. For other nations, these impacts averaged 9.4 and 33.7 points, respectively. Even in Canada, our closest neighbor, the effect of tax and transfer pro- grams on poverty among all children was to produce a 6.4 point decrease and among the children of single parents a 19.5 point decrease.

The 1980s produced higher market income-based poverty rates in all countries (Table 4.5). Apparently the long period of sustained economic growth in the 1980s did not affect the growing inequality in wage income or the concentrated effect of long-term unemployment on low-income households. In the United States, *pre*-tax and transfer poverty rose by 1.4 points for 1979 to 1986. In other nations, the increase averaged 1.1 points; in Australia and Canada, 0.5 points. However, in all nations *but* the United States, the change in *post-tax and transfer poverty was less than the change in pre-tax and trans- fer poverty rates: In other nations, the effect of the tax and transfer system on poverty increased while in the United States the income security system's impact on poverty decreased.* This was true for all subgroups of the U.S. poor. Again, the United States did

TABLE 4.4 Transfer System Effectiveness: The Impact of Taxes and Transfers on Poverty in Several Nations in the Mid-1900s

	US86	CN87	AS85	SW87	GE84	NL87	FR84	UK86	AVERAGE
All People									
Pre (Tax and Transfer Income)*	19.9	17.1	19.1	25.9	21.6	21.5	26.4	27.7	22.4
Post (Tax and Transfer Income)**	13.1	7.0	6.7	4.3	2.8	3.4	4.5	5.2	5.9
Change	−6.6	−10.1	−12.4	−21.6	−18.8	−18.1	−21.9	−22.5	−16.5
Aged 65 or Older									
Pre (Tax and Transfer Income)	46.5	50.2	54.5	83.2	80.1	56.1	76.2	62.1	63.6
Post (Tax and Transfer Income)	10.9	2.2	4.0	0.7	3.8	0.0	0.7	1.0	2.9
Change	−35.6	−48.0	−50.5	−82.5	-76.3	−56.1	−75.5	−61.1	−60.7
Adults (18–64)									
Pre (Tax and Transfer Income)	12.8	11.5	12.9	13.4	9.8	17.4	17.6	18.1	14.2
Post (Tax and Transfer Income)	10.5	7.0	6.1	6.6	2.6	3.9	5.2	5.3	5.9
Change	−2.3	−4.5	−6.8	−6.8	−7.2	−13.5	−12.4	−12.8	−8.3
Children (17 or younger)									
Pre (Tax and Transfer Income)	22.3	15.7	16.4	7.9	8.4	14.1	21.1	27.9	16.7
Post (Tax and Transfer Income)	20.4	9.3	9.0	1.6	2.8	3.8	4.6	7.4	7.4
Change	−1.9	−6.4	−7.4	−6.3	−5.6	−10.3	−16.5	−20.5	−9.4
Children in Single Parent Families									
Pre (Tax and Transfer Income)	58.1	56.6	70.2	23.2	46.0	70.3	43.1	71.2	54.8
Post (Tax and Transfer Income)	54.2	37.1	34.6	2.0	15.9	3.8	13.1	8.5	21.2
Change	−3.9	−19.5	−35.6	−21.2	−30.1	−66.5	−30.0	−62.7	−33.7
Other Children									
Pre (Tax and Transfer Income)	15.7	11.7	11.3	5.2	6.9	9.2	19.4	22.2	12.7
Post (Tax and Transfer Income)	14.1	6.6	6.6	1.5	2.3	3.8	4.0	7.3	5.7
Change	−1.6	−5.1	−4.7	−3.7	−4.6	−5.4	−15.4	−14.9	−6.9

Source: Luxembourg Income Study.

*Pre-tax and transfer poverty compares family income based on earnings, property income, and private transfers (private pensions, alimony, and child support) to the same 40 percent after-tax and transfer income poverty line used in earlier tables.

**Post-tax and transfer poverty includes the effect of direct taxes, including negative taxes such as the U.S. Earned Income Tax Credit, and public transfers on poverty. The "post" tax transfer poverty rates are the same as those in Table 4.1

least well for poor children. Our pre-tax and transfer child poverty rate rose by 3.3 points but our post-tax and transfer rate rose by 5.7 points. In the other countries the poverty increases were much more muted. Canada and Australia managed to decrease child poverty during the 1980s.

These numbers present a very negative picture of the U.S. tax and transfer system compared with that of other nations. The findings here corroborate evidence that we first presented for children in the early 1980s in one of the world's leading scientific journals, *Science.* They reinforce our early-1980s evidence for other population groups as well

TABLE 4.5 Transfer System Effectiveness over Time: Impact of Taxes and Transfers on Property in Several Nations in the Mid-1980s

	United States			Average of All Other Nations***		
	1979	**1986**	**CHANGE**	**WAVE 1**	**WAVE 2**	**CHANGE**
All People						
Pre (Tax and Transfer Income)*	18.5	19.9	1.4	20.6	21.6	1.1
Post (Tax and Transfer Income)**	10.8	3.3	2.5	5.7	6.0	0.3
Change	−7.7	−6.6		−14.8	−15.6	
All People 65 and Older						
Pre (Tax and Transfer Income)	52.0	46.5	−4.5	63.9	63.8	0.0
Post (Tax and Transfer Income)	12.9	10.9	−2.0	4.3	3.2	−1.1
Change	−38.1	−35.6		−59.6	−60.6	
All People 18–64						
Pre (Tax and Transfer Income)	11.2	12.8	1.6	12.6	13.6	1.0
Post (Tax and Transfer Income)	8.3	10.5	2.2	5.6	6.0	0.4
Change	−2.9	−2.3		−7.1	−7.6	
All Children						
Pre (Tax and Transfer Income)	19.0	22.3	3.3	13.7	15.1	1.4
Post (Tax and Transfer Income)	14.7	20.4	5.7	6.5	7.4	0.8
Change	−4.3	−1.9		−7.2	−7.8	

	Average of Australia and Canada		
	WAVE 1	**WAVE 2**	**CHANGE**
All People			
Pre (Tax and Transfer Income)*	17.6	18.1	0.5
Post (Tax and Transfer Income)**	6.9	6.9	0
Change	10.7	11.2	
All People 65 and Older			
Pre (Tax and Transfer Income)	56.4	52.4	−4.0
Post (Tax and Transfer Income)	3.8	3.1	−0.7
Change	−52.6	−49.3	
All People 18–64			
Pre (Tax and Transfer Income)	11.5	12.2	0.7
Post (Tax and Transfer Income)	6.0	6.6	0.6
Change	−5.5	−5.6	
All Children			
Pre (Tax and Transfer Income)	15.7	16.1	0.4
Post (Tax and Transfer Income)	9.4	9.2	0.2
Change	−6.3	−6.9	

Source: Luxembourg Income Study.

*Pre-tax and transfer poverty compares family income based on earnings, property income, and private transfers (private pensions, alimony, and child support) to the same 40 percent after-tax income poverty line used in earlier tables.

**Post-tax and transfer poverty includes the effect of direct taxes, including negative taxes such as the U.S. Earned Income Tax Credit, and public transfers on poverty. The "post" tax transfer poverty rates are the same as those in Table 4.1

***Average of Canada, Australia, Sweden, Germany, Netherlands, and France.

(see Smeeding and Torrey, and Smeeding, Torrey, and Rein for further reading). In fact the most recent estimates are even *less* optimistic than those in our earlier publications. They also corroborate the recent evidence on United States–Canada comparisons during the 1980s.

Simply put, U.S. families with low market incomes seem to work as hard as do the families in other nations, as measured by our close to average pre-tax and transfer poverty rates (see also Smeeding and Rainwater for further reading). Others have shown that the U.S. poor are less likely to be long-term dependent on welfare than are the poor in other nations (see Duncan for further reading). But our antipoverty system doesn't work as well as do the systems in other nations. Moreover our system worked *less* well during the 1980s, while other systems continued to prevent high poverty rates, even in the face of increased pressure from worsening unemployment rates and other market income-related changes that drove up pre-tax and transfer poverty in their countries. The major question is *why* do others do better than we do? What programs do they rely on that are absent in the United States?

COMPARING INCOME SECURITY PROGRAMS

The simple answer to why other nations do better than we do is that they put more effort into it: they expend more than we do, and they target it better than we do. That is, the tax and transfer systems in other modern nations are, in general, better suited to fighting poverty and to promoting economic independence than is the U.S. system.

Elderly

The growth in Old Age and Survivors Insurance (OASI) benefits in the United States during the 1970s and 1980s has surely helped reduce poverty among the U.S. elderly. However, the U.S. old age security system is such that there is no effective public pension floor at 40 percent of median income or higher. The Supplemental Security Income (SSI) program, even including food stamps, has a Federal government floor that is only about 35–38 percent of the U.S. median. In other nations, the minimum standard public pension is 48–50 percent of median income or higher. In most nations, the minimum is set in the national social retirement (OASI) system. In others, there are special income-tested benefits to gross up the standard amount to some minimum level (Office of Economic Cooperation and Development, 1998). For instance, in Canada and Australia, minimum income programs for the elderly are set at 52–56 percent of adjusted median income. Among the elderly then, the solution is either to raise the SSI floor or to have a special minimum benefit build into the Social Security program per se. Because the largest single poverty group are elderly women living alone, a special widows' benefit might do the trick. For instance, Canada has combined special widows' benefits with a reasonable income-tested benefit floor for all aged people. Their income-tested program has no assets or wealth test either. The Canadians allow their elderly to hold onto their assets, but then when the elderly no longer need their assets, they levy a national inheritance tax. Perhaps the United States should consider such an approach.

Children and Their Parents

Most of the adult poverty problem in the United States is related to families with children, including single parents, so we discuss these two together. The United States is unique in that it (and Japan) are the only two modern nations that do not have some form of a universal child allowance. In some nations, Canada for example, these allowances are paid via refundable income tax credits. In other nations they are paid via the transfer system in the form of family allowances. In all nations, except for the United States, they are independent of work effort. They are given to parents on behalf of children as a universal right of citizenship. If we were to convert the U.S. personal tax exemption for children to an equivalent cost refundable tax credit—about $800—we would achieve the same floor under all children's incomes that other nations have.

Over and above child allowances, other nations have a set of interrelated programs to help families with children escape poverty. For two-parent families, other nations have more generous unemployment compensation systems that, after some period of extended benefits, are tied to a job-training program. The objective is to help workers in failing industries renew their skills and replace their earnings losses from plant closures with new jobs at decent wages.

For single parents, two additional policies are worth noting. First, there is a system of guaranteed child support (or advance maintenance payments) wherein the state provides insurance against the failure of child support payments by the absent spouse. This system is available in Netherlands, Germany, Sweden and several other nations. It protects against unemployment and/or low wage absent spouses. The second policy is one of providing extensive low cost child care for single parents who want to work. France and Sweden encourage single mothers to work via free or low cost child care, via job protection in the form of parental leave, and via related policies to provide single parents with job training and part-time jobs that allow them to mix work and parenting (see Garfinkel and McLanahan for further reading). In Sweden and France single mothers are much more likely to work than in the United States, Canada, or the United Kingdom (see Kamerman for further reading).

The lessons to be learned here are that other nations have multifaceted and proactive policies that help reduce poverty among all age groups. They do not rely almost entirely on means-tested benefits, as does the United States via the Food Stamps, AFDC, and SSI programs. Other nations also have universal programs that pay child allowances, allow parental leave with pay, guarantee child support, and provide high minimum benefits for the elderly and the permanently disabled.

It goes without saying, of course, that *all* of these countries also have universal tax financed health insurance systems that cover all citizens—rich or poor. There are no poor children who go without Medicaid; there are no poor parents on welfare who fear that taking a job will mean the loss of Medicaid benefits for their families; and there are no long-term unemployed who face either loss of job-related health insurance benefits or a high cost premium to keep their job-related health benefits.

LESSONS FOR THE UNITED STATES

Other countries do better than the United States, but beyond universal health insurance and universal child allowances, each country has its own unique policy mix which fits its own circumstances and national needs. We must also design our own system of antipoverty support. My guess is that we'd want a system that encourages self-reliance rather than reliance on public income transfer programs alone. We'd like a program, or set of programs, which safeguard incentives to work and to become economically independent. We'd like a system that builds on parental responsibility and not one that ignores it.

Based on my studies of other nations, and on my experiences with the U.S. system, I recommended that the United States seriously consider the following measures:

1. Institute a universal refundable child income tax credit of $800–1,000 per child for every child for whom the custodial parent has produced a child support order. This forces unmarried single mothers to identify the father so that child support enforcement can be pursued. In conjunction with the current EITC, this policy should move most if not all working poor families with children off of the poverty rolls.

2. Begin a system of guaranteed child support for all single mothers with a child support order for their children, thus guaranteeing a minimal level of child support for all children in single-parent families where the father has been identified.

3. Move at least to a year-long "Head Start" style child development/child care system for all low-income families with children. Such a system would guarantee at least a year of developmentally oriented preschool for all poor children. Coupled with the opportunity for providing preventive health care (immunizations, lead-based paint exposure checks, other preventive measures) this program would target all low income four- or five-year olds so that at age five or six, every child would be ready to begin formal schooling in good health and with adequate developmental preparation.

4. Provide extended unemployment benefits but then connect them to targeted reemployment and training efforts for unemployed parents. Clearly a good job is the main road to economic independence and to family stability. Job losers should be retrained for new jobs. Our efforts should be targeted toward those who have the most to lose from economic change and deindustrialization: needy parents with children.

5. Raise the minimum SSI benefit to the poverty line and ease the assets or wealth test for the elderly and disabled. If economic independence cannot be achieved due to personal limitations, compassion should lead us to a minimum decent standard of living for the aged and the disabled.

6. Once these systems are in place, provide a two- or three-year limit to the AFDC program as suggested by Ellwood (see References). Once the youngest child is three, the single parent should, with the other help provided by the system outlined above, be ready, willing and able to move toward self-support. The other building blocks suggested above will then provide the necessary help to achieve self-sufficiency.

In summary, where the fiscal will and leadership exist, nations are able to effectively fight poverty. Every other nation studied outperforms the United States in this arena. We need to begin to make poverty a priority in this country, starting especially with poor children, where we tolerate a level of disadvantage unknown to any other major advanced country on earth.

REFERENCES

Greg Duncan et al. "Poverty and Social Assistance Dynamics in the U.S., Canada, and Europe," presented to the Joint Center for Political Studies (JCPS) Conference on "Poverty, Inequality, and the Crisis of Social Policy," Washington D.C., September 19, 1991.

David T. Ellwood, *Poor Support: Poverty in the American Family,* Basic Books, New York, 1988.

Irwin Garfinkel and Sara McLanahan, "Single Mother Families and Social Policy: Lessons for the United States from France, Canada, and Sweden," presented to the JCPS Conference on "Poverty, Inequality, and the Crisis of Social Policy," Washington D.C., September 19, 1991.

Sheila Kamerman, "Gender Role and Family Structure Changes in the Advanced Industrial West: Implications for Social Policy," presented to the JCPS Conference on "Poverty, Inequality, and the Crisis of Social Policy," Washington D.C., September 19, 1991.

Timothy M. Smeeding and Lee Rainwater, "Cross-National Trends in Income, Poverty, and Dependency: The Evidence for Young Adults in the Eighties," presented to the JCPS Conference on "Poverty, Inequality, and the Crisis of Social Policy," Washington D.C., September 19, 1991.

Timothy M. Smeeding and Barbara B. Torrey, "Poor Children in Rich Countries," *Science,* November 11, 1989.

Timothy M. Smeeding, Barbara B. Torrey, and Martin Rein, "The Well-Being of Elderly and of Children: A Framework for Analysis," *The Vulnerable,* John L. Palmer et al., eds., Urban Institute Press, Washington D.C., 1988.

5

Why Canada Has Less Poverty

MARIA J. HANRATTY

The article addresses the essential question: Why is the Canadian anti-welfare system more effective than the U.S. system? The Canadian system differs from the U.S. system on three dimensions: (1) Canada places much greater emphasis on universal, non-means-tested benefits than the United States (e.g., universal health insurance, universal old age security pension, and universal child payments); (2) Canada's means-tested assistance programs maintain less stringent eligibility requirements than programs found in the United States; and (3) Canada's programs have higher benefit levels than U.S. programs.

In Canada, social welfare programs bring one in two poor families out of poverty. In the US, the rate is one in five. Through the 1980s, both the US and Canada saw increases in unemployment and wage inequality. Yet in the US, poverty increased by three points between 1979 and 1986, while in Canada the poverty rate was driven slightly *down*.

Why does the Canadian social welfare system function better than that of the US? One part of the answer is the US's retreat from its commitments to social welfare. In Canada, the 1980s saw an expansion in transfer payments; in the US, they were substantially cut back. Yet that is only part of the story. Canada has a markedly different approach to dealing with welfare policy—a tradition that may point the way for progressives in the US to improve the effectiveness of, and garner support for, increased support for welfare policy.

There are five major social assistance programs for families and working people in Canada (excluding the elderly).

Unemployment Insurance. The federal government offers assistance to workers who have involuntarily lost their jobs. An in-depth study of benefits in the sample year 1986 reported benefits in that year to replace 60 percent of prior earnings, up to a federally-mandated maximum of $396 (in US dollars); benefits in Canada last up to a maximum of 50 weeks. (In the US, by contrast, unemployment insurance is generally available for only 26 weeks—although this has recently been temporarily raised—and in the same test

Source: Maria J. Hanratty. 1992. "Why Canada Has Less Poverty," *Social Policy 23* (Summer), pp. 32–37.

year replaced on average 64 percent of prior earnings up to an average weekly maximum of $184.)

Family Allowances.   The federal government provides annual cash payments to all Canadian families with children; in 1986, this amounted to $379 per child.

Child Tax Credit.   A refundable tax credit is made available by the federal government for all families with children. In 1986, this program paid $454 per child per year to households with annual incomes below $18,800; benefits declined to zero at $26,064.

Social Assistance.   Direct cash assistance is made available to low-income families and individuals. The program, funded jointly by the federal and provincial governments, had an average maximum payment of $266/month for single individuals in 1986; $627/month for a single parent with two children.

Medical Insurance.   As has been much discussed in the US recently, Canada has a universal health insurance program that offers first dollar coverage for most medical and hospital services. The program is funded jointly at the federal and provincial levels, but runs almost entirely at the provincial level.

Generally, Canadian Social Welfare Programs differ from US programs on three dimensions. First, Canada places much greater emphasis on universal, non-means-tested benefits than does the United States. Canada runs a universal health insurance program, a universal old age security pension, and provides universal per-child payments (family allowances) to all households with children.

By way of contrast, in the US, there are virtually no universal programs—means testing is part of every public program to at least some extent. Most US workers are eligible for Social Security, for example, but the amount received depends on the level of earnings. The tradition of universal programs gives a flavor to Canadian discussions of anti-poverty policy that is not found in the United States. The way US and Canadian Catholic bishops split on proposals for a negative income tax highlights the difference between the countries. In the US, bishops supported the idea—which would offer means-tested assistance to low-income households. In Canada, the bishops rejected the notion, calling instead for full employment coupled with improved social insurance and extended universal services.

Second, Canada's means-tested assistance programs maintain less stringent *categorical eligibility requirements* than do programs in the US. In the US, for instance, eligibility for means-tested cash assistance is limited to single-parent families, or to individuals who are aged, blind, or disabled. In other words, the US makes a sharp division between the so-called "deserving" and "undeserving" poor. In Canada, the social assistance program offers aid to all households, although payments to families with children are typically higher than those to employable individuals without children.

Third, Canada's programs have *higher benefit levels* than programs in the US. The average transfer income available to a single-parent family with one child in Canada was $800 in 1986, as opposed to $380 in the US. In the US, AFDC and food stamp payments were below the poverty line in every state except Alaska; in Canada, total social welfare payments exceeded the poverty line in 7 out of 10 provinces.

WELFARE CAN WORK

Comparing poverty levels in the US and Canada points out that differences in the social welfare systems matter. Figure 5.1 indicates that substantially fewer people live in poverty in Canada—seven percent of all families, as opposed to 12 percent in the US. The difference is even more dramatic for single-parent families with children—while 26 percent are poor in Canada, fully *41 percent* are poor in the US. And since these figures do not take into consideration health insurance coverage, which is far more extensive in Canada than in the US, the real gap for many families is even greater than this comparison reflects.

The reason poverty rates are so much lower in Canada is not that poor people earn more money: pre-transfer poverty rates are similar in the two countries (15 percent for the US, 13 percent for Canada). The primary reason is that Canada's transfer system is more generous and more effective. Compared to the US, Canada's welfare system takes more than double the percentage of people out of poverty: 46 percent of all poor people are raised above the poverty line by transfer payments, as opposed to 21 percent in the US.

It frequently has been argued in the US that the most effective way to reduce poverty is to encourage economic growth—transfer programs, many have said, just don't work.

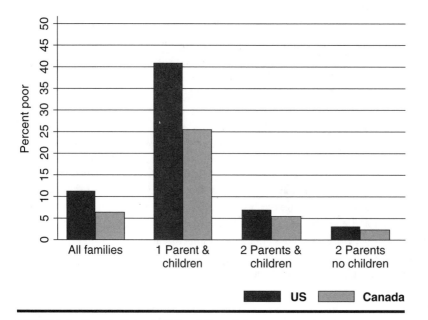

FIGURE 5.1 Poverty Rates in US and Canada*

*For US poverty level, head of family age 18–60.

Throughout this article, the numbers referred to are based on estimates reported for 1986 in two studies by Rebecca Blank and Maria Hanratty: "Responding to Need: Comparative Social Welfare Systems in the US and Canada" (unpublished manuscript, 1991), and "Down and Out in North America: Recent Trends in Poverty Rates in the US and Canada," *Quarterly Journal of Economics,* February, 1992.

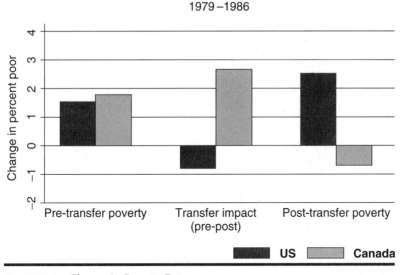

FIGURE 5.2   Change in Poverty Rates

But, while the US economy expanded throughout the 1980s, poverty rates substantially increased. As Figure 5.2 graphically demonstrates, transfer programs *do* seem to work.

Another common concern about transfers, even among those who do believe they effectively reduce poverty, is that they diminish self-sufficiency and decrease the incentive to work. What do the data tell us about this?

One place to look for an answer is in the employment rates of single women with children, since the Canadian and US transfer payments differ most markedly for this group. In particular, if transfers diminished the incentive to work, one would expect to find a large difference in employment rates among single women with children.

Figure 5.3 shows that in Canada, single women with children have *similar or higher* employment rates when compared with those in the US. The employment rate for single women with children under the age of six is 31 percent in the US and 51 percent in Canada; for those with children over six, it is 54 percent in the US and 60 percent in Canada. Transfer payments do not seem to interfere with the incentive to work—or at the least, factors like better job opportunities, child care, and health care seem to be of greater importance to women and children.

WHY IS CANADA DIFFERENT?

What makes it possible for Canada to have a social welfare system that is more effective and more generous than the US? Clearly, it is not that the country is richer—the 1986 per capita income was $15,700, as opposed to $17,500 in the US. Even after controlling for military spending—which is far higher in the US—Canada has fewer resources available to spend on the poor.

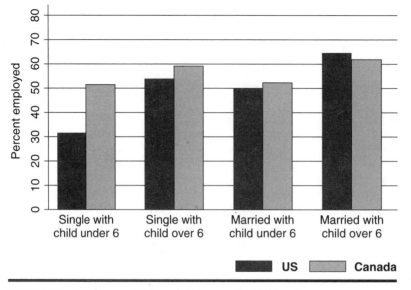

FIGURE 5.3   Employment Rates of Women with Children*
*Figures for 1986.

The reason Canadians have not followed widespread US antipathy to social programs is difficult to isolate. Among the factors that seem to be significant are the following.

• Universality. Because Canada's programs offer more universal coverage than US programs, they attract political support from a broader range of the population.
• Union strength. Unions in both countries have generally pressed for increased social welfare programs, but labor's support carries greater political weight in Canada, which has more than double the unionization rate of the US.
• Minority composition. Canadians generally think of themselves as a more racially homogeneous society than do people in the United States. This may increase the willingness of taxpayers to support social welfare programs, since they perceive the poor to be more like themselves.
• Administrative structure. Canada's social welfare programs offer more discretion to local welfare offices than programs in the US do. This may enable Canadian welfare programs to target and administer aid more effectively, and thus increase the willingness of taxpayers to support the programs.

Reforming social welfare policy in the US will be hotly contested in years to come. What is clear is that social programs can work, and that in a context very similar to the US they have widespread support. Anyone concerned about poverty in the US cannot afford to overlook the experience of Canada.

6

What's Wrong with Current Poverty Policies?

RANDY ALBELDA AND CHRIS TILLY

This excerpt examines the failure of antipoverty policies in the United States. Compared to other industrialized countries, the United States has an ineffective system for fighting poverty. The authors argue that other countries are more successful in lifting families out of poverty because of better tax policies and programs.

The antipoverty policies of the United States do not work very well. The clearest evidence of their ineffectiveness is that poverty has persisted at relatively high levels and has even grown during some periods over the last couple of decades. Does this mean that government action cannot end economic deprivation, or that antipoverty policies have actually contributed to the growth of poverty? Not at all. But our efforts have been incomplete and halfhearted, guided by flawed theories. So it should not surprise us that we have failed to tackle poverty.

A WEAK TRACK RECORD: THE UNITED STATES COMPARED TO OTHER COUNTRIES

Comparison with other industrialized countries helps to place the U.S. anti-poverty track record in perspective. In contrast to these other nations, *the United States has been remarkably unsuccessful in lifting families—especially single-mother families—out of poverty.* Researchers have found that in the late 1980s, not only did the United States have a higher poverty rate for nonelder families (those headed by someone under sixty-five) than six other industrialized countries, *it also had the most ineffective tax and transfer system when it came to pulling those families out of poverty.*[1] To make international comparisons, the researchers defined a family as poor it its size-adjusted income was 50

Source: Excerpt from Randy Albelda and Chris Tilly. 1997. *Glass Ceilings and Bottomless Pits* (pp. 79–81). Boston, MA: South End Press.

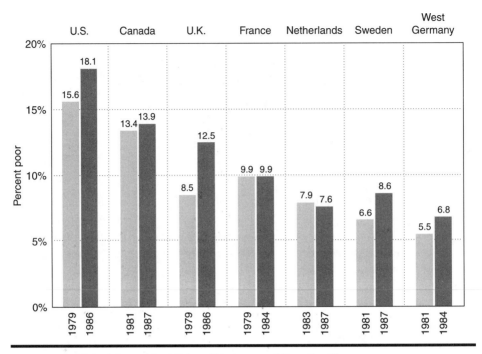

FIGURE 6.1   United States Has Highest Percentage of Poor Families

Percentage of poor among nonelder families in seven industrialized countries, various years

Note: The poverty income threshold is equal to 50 percent of the national median income. Includes only households with heads twenty to fifty-five years old in each country. Data come from the Luxembourg Income Study, and poverty calculations for countries above have not been updated since the mid-1980s.

Source: Joint Center for Political and Economic Studies, *Poverty, Inequality and the Crisis of Social Policy,* September 1991.

percent or less of the national median income among families with heads aged twenty to fifty-five. Figure 6.1 depicts the poverty rates for families with heads in this age range for the United States, Canada, the United Kingdom, the former West Germany, the Netherlands, France, and Sweden in years near 1980 and in the mid-1980s. Figure 6.2 shows the percentage of nonelder families lifted out of poverty by the combination of transfer and tax policies in the same seven nations. It asks the question: Of families who would have been poor *before* receiving government cash aid and paying taxes, what percentage were no longer poor *after* transfers and taxes were applied?

Of the countries studied, the United States had the highest poverty rates—about two to three times those of France, the Netherlands, Sweden, and West Germany. Figure 6.2 helps explain why: U.S. tax and transfer policies had the worst record of lifting families out of poverty. Whereas most countries' policies boosted about half of the at-risk families out of poverty, embarrassingly, U.S. tax and transfer programs actually made families poorer in 1986: taxes pushed more into poverty than transfers pulled out. Since then,

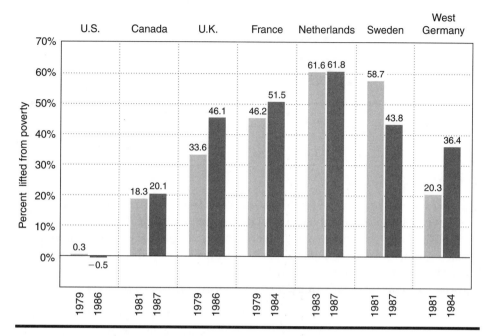

FIGURE 6.2   United States Policies Least Effective in Alleviating Poverty
Percentage of poor, nonelder families that were lifted out of poverty as a result of tax and transfer policies in seven industrialized countries, various years

Note: The poverty income threshold is equal to 50 percent of the national median income. Includes only households with heads twenty to fifty-five years old in each country. Data come from the Luxembourg Income Study, and poverty calculations for countries above have not been updated since the mid-1980s.

Source: Joint Center for Political and Economic Studies, *Poverty, Inequality and the Crisis of Social Policy,* September 1991.

some tax policies have changed—most important, the Earned Income Credit has considerably reduced the taxation of working-poor families. Meanwhile, transfers for poor, nonelder families have actually fallen when adjusted for inflation.

NOTE_____

1. Katherine McFate, *Poverty, Inqulaity, and the Crisis of Social Policy: Summary of Findings* (Washington, DC: Joint Center for Political and Economic Studies, 1991).

SECTION 3

Income Inequality

THE UNITED STATES CONTEXT

Income inequality refers to the gap between the rich and poor. The United States has the most unequal income distribution in the industrialized world (Miringoff and Miringoff, 1999:104). Moreover, this inequality is increasing faster than in any other industrialized country. The disparities in wealth are much larger than income disparities, but we focus on income inequality in this section.

The following facts concern income inequality in the United States.

• The average after-tax income of the richest 1 percent of the population more than doubled between 1977 and 1999, rising 115 percent after adjustment for inflation. The average after-tax income for households in the middle rose only 8 percent over this twenty-two-year period, whereas the average income of the poorest 20 percent actually fell by 9 percent (Shapiro and Greenstein, 1999:1).

• In 1999, 2.7 million Americans with the largest incomes (top 1 percent) were expected to receive as much after-tax income as the 100 million Americans with the lowest incomes (Shapiro and Greenstein, 1999:2). This ratio has more than doubled since 1977, when the top 1 percent had as much as the bottom 49 million.

• In 1998, chief executive officers (CEOs) at the 365 largest corporations were paid 419 times the pay of the average blue-collar workers ($10.6 million compared with about $29,000), compared to a ratio of 120-to-1 in 1990, and 42-to-1 in 1980. If the minimum wage had increased at the same rate as CEO pay between 1990 and 1998, it would now be $22.08 instead of $5.15 an hour. And the average production worker would earn $110,000 a year today, instead of the $29,000 the worker actually makes (United for a Fair Economy data, reported in Ivins, 1999; and Smart, 1999).

This rising inequality gap in the United States has enormous consequences (Eitzen, 1996). If the trend continues, the number of people on the economic margin will rise. Homelessness will increase. Family disruption will escalate. Crime rates will swell. Public safety will become much more problematic. Most generally, this phenomenon of economic inequality has implications for democracy, crime, and civil unrest. Economist Lester Thurow, wondering about this move toward a two-tiered society, asks: "How much inequality can a democracy take? The income gap in America is eroding the social contract. If the promise of a higher standard of living is limited to a few at the top, the rest of the citizenry, as history shows, is likely to grow disaffected, or worse" (Thurow, 1995:78).

54

REFERENCES_____

Eitzen, D. Stanley. 1996. "Dismantling the Welfare State," *Vital Speeches of the Day* (June 15):532–536.

Ivins, Molly. 1999. "Worked Up over Working Class," *Rocky Mountain News* (September 8):37A.

Miringoff, Marc, and Marque-Luisa Miringoff. 1999. *The Social Health of the Nation: How America Is Really Doing.* New York: Oxford University Press.

Shapiro, Isaac, and Robert Greenstein. 1999. "The Widening Income Gulf," *Center on Budget and Policy Priorities* (September 4).

Smart, Tim. 1999. "It Pays Even More to Be the Boss," *Washington Post National Weekly Edition* (September 6):20.

Thurow, Lester. 1995. "Why Their World Might Crumble," *New York Times Magazine* (November 19):78–79.

7

Toward an Apartheid Economy?

RICHARD B. FREEMAN

Freeman argues that the United States is becoming more unequal. The middle class is shrinking, wages are stagnant or declining, and the wealthy are getting an ever bigger proportion of wealth. The result is that the United States is the most unequal of the advanced countries. When comparing inequality across societies, the data actually understate the magnitude of inequality in the United States because the other nations provide more generous universal social programs (e.g., health, pensions, housing). The author points to a number of societal costs that arise with relatively high levels of inequality.

Rising inequality. Stagnant real wages. A declining middle class. High levels of child poverty. Insecure workers. A waning union movement. Homeless people in every city. Bursting jails and prisons. A fraying social safety net.

Does that sound like a third-world economy heading toward disaster? Or perhaps a neo-Marxian vision of the future of capitalism? Or is it a description of the United States moving into the twenty-first century?

Ten to 15 years ago, you or I would have dismissed the preceding inscription of the U.S. economy as soapbox radicalism. Save for the Great Depression, the history of the United States in this century has been one in which economic growth benefits all. From 1910 to 1973, the average employee enjoyed substantial gains in real earnings and increases in leisure time. No honest observer could question the success of American capitalism in delivering middle-class standards of living to workers. But today, despite the nation's great success in creating jobs and maintaining relatively low unemployment, it is not only radical soapbox orators who worry about the ability of our economy to take care of working citizens.

From U.S. secretary of labor Robert Reich on the left to presidential candidate Patrick Buchanan on the right, and from the business press to the mass media, comes the message that something is wrong with the U.S. economy. That something is not the

Source: Richard B. Freeman. 1996. "Toward an Apartheid Economy?" *Harvard Business Review 74* (September/October), pp. 114–121.

country's productivity, technological leadership, or rate of economic growth, though there is room for improvement in all those areas. That something is an issue normally on the back burner in U.S. public discourse: the distribution of the fruits of economic progress. For many, the rise in AT&T's stock after it announced plans to lay off 40,000 employees crystallized the picture of an economy gone haywire, with shareholders gaining and employees losing as a result of innovation and advances in productivity.

Has the distribution of the benefits of economic growth in the United States in fact gone awry? Is the nation heading toward an apartheid economy—one in which the wealthy and powerful prosper while the less well-off struggle? What are the facts? What do they mean? Are there real problems—and can they be solved?

THE SINKING AMERICAN WORKER

The United States has always had a greater degree of inequality than other advanced countries. Inequality, some would say, is the flip side of opportunity and mobility. Some level of inequality is needed to elicit effort, and historically Americans have preferred opportunity and effort to egalitarianism. But in the past two decades, the country's normal high level of inequality, except in the category of gender, has jumped:

- Pay in the upper part of the earnings distribution has risen in comparison with pay in the lower part.
- College graduates have gained in comparison with high school graduates or dropouts.
- Older workers have gained in comparison with younger workers.
- Professionals and executives have gained in comparison with clerical workers, machine operators, and laborers.
- Higher-paid workers within virtually any group—carpenters, lawyers, laborers, clerks, women, men, blacks, whites—have gained in comparison with lower-paid workers.

These changes have occurred despite huge gains in employment—about 17 million new jobs in the Reagan and Bush years and some 8 million in the Clinton years—that in the past would have been associated with rising pay for less-skilled workers and falling inequality.

So what? you may say. Who cares about inequality? As long as living standards are improving for the vast majority, there is no need to ring alarm bells. Put aside envy or jealousy and enjoy the fruits of progress. But the story of recent decades is not one of economic gains for all. On the contrary, the rising tide of inequality has been accompanied by stagnant real wages.

Until the early 1970s, the history of the U.S. job market in this century was one of rising wages—about a 2% increase per year. Compounding that figure leads to a doubling of income every 35 years, virtually guaranteeing higher living standards from one generation to the next.

The rate of growth of real wages from 1973 to the mid-1990s is different. The trend is downward for the most widely used statistical measures of real wages—hourly earnings reported by workers on the U.S. Current Population Survey of households divided by the consumer price index, and earnings reported by employers on the U.S. National Employer Survey, also divided by the CPI. According to the population survey, the median weekly earnings of full-time male workers have dropped by 13% from 1979 through the mid-1990s. According to the employer survey, the average weekly earnings of nonsupervisory private-sector workers (outside of agriculture) have fallen by 12%.

But these measures of real wages are imperfect; for various reasons, they are likely to understate the growth of real earnings. They exclude nonwage compensation—money that goes into health insurance and pensions, for example—which has risen as a share of total wages. And the national employer survey obtains earnings solely for nonsupervisory workers. The most serious problem is that the CPI overstates inflation because it does not fully measure improvements in the quality of goods. And if the rise in inflation is overstated, the growth of real earnings is understated. How much the CPI may be in error is a matter of debate.

Regardless of where one comes out in this debate, there is no gainsaying that the growth rate in real earnings has taken a dive. The growth of fringe benefits has slackened over time, so the bias resulting from their omission has become smaller. And the U.S. Bureau of Labor Statistics has continually improved the CPI. Thus the understatement of growth in real earnings was greater in the past than it is now. In fact, better data may demonstrate an even more severe decline in the rate of growth of real wages in recent decades. Whatever the "true" figures are, the problem of stagnant or falling real wages in combination with rising inequality has created a new group of Americans: economically sinking workers.

In the United States, the big losers in the earnings distribution are men, particularly young or less-educated men. If the fall in earnings greatly increased their employment, the decline in real earnings would have produced at least one benefit: more jobs. But instead, their prospects for work have deteriorated. As inequality in earnings has risen, so too has inequality in the hours people work over the year. The yearly earnings of the low paid and less skilled have fallen by a larger percentage than their hourly pay. In addition, the likelihood that employers will provide low-skilled workers with fringe benefits such as health insurance or pensions has also dropped. The fall in the real earnings of the low paid means that a substantial number of working men earn less than their fathers did two or three decades ago.

Furthermore, low-paid American men are losing ground in comparison with their counterparts in other advanced economies—even as the United States remains the most productive economy in the world. In Western Europe, a male worker in the bottom 10% of the earnings distribution earns 68% of the median worker's income; in Japan, that male worker earns 61% of the median. In the United States, he earns 38% of the median. And a comparison of purchasing power reveals that U.S. workers in the bottom 10% earn less real pay than their counterparts in other advanced countries. Low-paid German workers earn 2.2 times more than low-paid Americans; low-paid Norwegian workers, 1.85 times more. Comparisons of wages based on exchange rates, which are appropriate for business costs, show even greater differences.

It is not just the bottom 10% of U.S. workers that trail the workers in other advanced countries, however. Approximately one-third are paid less, in purchasing-power units, than comparable workers overseas. Not until the third or fourth decile of earnings do Americans do better than Europeans. That so many workers in the United States fare poorly compared with their peers in other countries shows that the problem of low pay is not simply a matter of low-skilled immigrants or poorly educated minority youths. It is a problem of the overall distribution of income.

Because taxes are higher in many countries, comparisons of pay before taxes may seem to exaggerate the disadvantage of low-paid Americans. That would surely be the case if taxes gave nothing back in value, but in most countries they pay for health insurance, pensions, housing subsidies, and other social benefits—the bulk of which Americans purchase from their earnings. Comparisons of wages after taxes are thus likely to *understate* the U.S. disadvantage in pay among low-paid workers.

Nor can U.S. workers depend heavily on the government when they fare poorly in the marketplace. In much of Western Europe, economic assistance programs have created a huge welfare state, which many rely on for years. In the United States, such programs provide an effective safety net provided that workers rebound quickly from their economic problems. But the safety net is weak and has been shrinking in recent years. Declining pay and hours worked translate more commonly into poverty than is the case in other advanced economies. Low-paid Americans who lose their jobs may end up in big trouble: they often lose health insurance, have their cash flow dry up, and have difficulties paying their rent and consumer debt.

The principal way in which poverty is reduced in the United States—except for the elderly who are supported by Social Security—is through higher wages in the job market. As real earnings have stagnated, the downward trend in the poverty rate has slackened, and the rate has increased for families of young workers and for children. Many children are brought up in single-parent families whose welfare benefits have been reduced and whose heads have not had much success obtaining work, though various workfare-style reform proposals may alleviate that problem. But single-parent families on welfare are just one part of the poverty problem. Compared with most other advanced countries, the United States has a higher rate of fully employed working poor. In the 1980s, poverty rates in Canada dropped below those in the United States, not because the Canadian economy boomed relative to the U.S. economy (it didn't) but because Canada has stronger safety-net programs.

The absence of a significant safety net has some advantages. Taxes and fiscal deficits are lower than in most other advanced countries, and citizens have greater incentives to work. But it also means that Americans must rely more heavily on the labor market for their well-being. When the job market turns bad, as it did for the less skilled and the low paid in the 1980s and 1990s, people suffer.

WHO'S RESPONSIBLE?

Nearly everyone has a list of culprits. Pat Buchanan's list focuses on trade and immigration. The AFL-CIO's list includes declining unionization. The Clinton administration stresses technological change. The Republican Congress blames the administration, high taxes, and excessive government spending. If we could identify a single culprit, we'd have a good television drama. But the story of rising income inequality is more complex. Several factors have been at work, and honest analysts weigh their importance differently. Let's examine each factor in turn.

Trade has contributed to the problems of low-wage workers. Losses in pay or employment by those who make products in competition with foreign imports, particularly imported goods from less-developed countries, are the flip side of the much larger benefits that trade brings the nation. U.S. businessman Ross Perot and Anglo-French financier Sir James Goldsmith claim that trade is the main story, but most studies disagree. The estimated effects of trade on the demand for low-skilled labor simply are not big enough for it to dominate the distribution of income in the United States: less-skilled women are most affected by imports from third-world countries, and they have not suffered the economic losses of less-skilled men. Most Americans work in service sector jobs that are not directly affected by trade, and the estimated effects from manufacturing and other traded-goods sectors on the rest of the economy are not large enough to account for the huge rise in inequality.

Immigration has also contributed to the problems of low-wage native-born Americans. Fully one-third of employed high-school dropouts are foreign-born. If they had not immigrated, the wages and employment of their native-born counterparts surely would be higher. But our best estimates suggest that the increased flow of low-skilled immigrants is not the major cause of falling earnings for less-skilled Americans, although it is probably a more important factor than trade. Much of the rise in inequality in the United States has occurred among workers with vocational skills that are unaffected by immigration, such as those of mechanics or lawyers.

The decline of trade unions has contributed to inequality. Unions reduce inequality by standardizing pay among workers, bringing the pay and benefits of their members closer to that of higher-paid executives and professionals, and inducing nonunion companies to raise pay or benefits to avoid unionization. Imagine if 30% of the private sector were unionized, as it was in the 1960s, instead of 11%, as it is today. Would there be less inequality in earnings? Yes. Studies suggest that about one-fifth of the rise in inequality is due to the decline of unions.

The fall in the real value of the minimum wage has also contributed to rising inequality. However, the impact of the minimum wage is felt mostly in the bottom decile, particularly by women and teenagers. Unlike in countries such as France, changes in the minimum wage in the United States do not spill over to many workers.

The Clinton administration has favored technology as the culprit, perhaps because it seems to let policymakers off the hook. No one knows how to predict or control the direction of technological change. There is evidence that computerization has adversely affected low-skilled workers, but the case for technology as the main culprit is underwhelming. Why hasn't the same technology produced massive inequality in other advanced countries? Why, if we have entered a brave new world of accelerating technology, have increases in productivity been moderate? Every generation deals with new technology and often blames it for whatever ills occur: in the 1960s, we had the great automation scare, for example, which blamed rising unemployment on machines and robots.

The influx of women into the job market may also have contributed to the problems of low-wage workers: an increase in the supply of labor drives wages down. But because women's pay has *risen* relative to that of men, and because women and men generally are employed in different industries and occupations, it is difficult to see how women's increased presence in the workforce adversely affects men. Not even the U.S. Senate's Whitewater Committee can blame Hillary Clinton for this one.

Another factor has been the slowdown in the rate of growth of the supply of college graduates. In the 1960s, Jan Tinbergen, the Nobel Prize-winning Dutch economist, wrote that inequality was a race between the increasing demand for highly educated workers due to technology and the increasing supply of such workers due to expanded public education. For most of Western economic history, the increase in the supply of skilled workers has offset the increase in demand for them. In the 1970s, the increase in supply in advanced countries dwarfed the increase in demand, reducing the economic value of education. In the United States, higher education lost some of its attractiveness, and the rate of growth of the college workforce decelerated in the 1980s, contributing to the rise in the earnings advantage of the more educated. In countries where the educated workforce grew more rapidly in the 1980s, differences in pay between more-educated and less-educated workers did not widen much, if at all. In some cases, they even fell. But again, the 1970s slowdown in the flow of young people, particularly men, into college is not sufficient to explain the massive rise of inequality.

The debate over how much weight to give these various factors has enlivened economic conferences and journals. It is an interesting debate, but it is largely irrelevant to the policy question of how, if at all, the nation should respond to the rise in inequality. That is because there is no necessary link between the causes of a problem and potential cures. When someone has myopia, a largely genetic disease, we cure it with glasses or contact lenses. We do not mess with the genes, although they may be the root cause. When you have a headache, you take aspirin rather than go into a long exegesis about where the headache came from.

The same reasoning applies to the problem of rising inequality and stagnant real wages. If a cause of the rise of inequality is trade, should we build a tariff wall around the country? No. Protective tariffs are one of the most inefficient ways to redistribute income that the mind of man has ever conceived. If the United States wanted to help citizens suffering from foreign trade, it could do so with other tools. And if the cause of rising inequality is technological change, should we become Luddites, smash our computers, and march on MIT with pitchforks? Only a devotee of professional wrestling might find that attractive. The heart of the matter is not how we got into the inequality fix but whether we should care about it and what we can do about it.

SHOULD WE CARE?

Rising inequality and falling real earnings reduce the living standards of individuals and families on the lower rungs of the income distribution. Many of those affected will feel alienated from society and behave accordingly.

For people with high incomes, however, inequality has some benefits. If I am rich and you are poor, I can hire you cheaply as my gardener, maid, or nanny. Not surprisingly, the personal services sector has grown with the rise of inequality. Moreover, if the middle class shrinks and buys fewer tickets to basketball games and concerts, there will also be more places for the well-off at those events.

Still, many people in higher income brackets are upset when fellow Americans and their families struggle in a land of plenty. Those distressed by the poverty of others range from bleeding-heart liberals and religious people to the philanthropists and volunteers whose contributions to charities give the United States the largest private charitable sector in the world.

Personal feelings aside, inequality can also impose costs on the entire society, including the rich who don't give a hoot about how their poorer neighbors fare. One such cost is a high rate of crime, which has generated a growing prison population and huge expenses for the criminal justice system. By 1995, more than 2% of the U.S. male workforce was incarcerated, and nearly 7% was under the supervision of the criminal justice system. Mass incarceration may be the reason the crime rate is finally falling, but it is an incredibly expensive way to deal with the problem. Incarcerating a criminal costs about as much per year as sending someone to Harvard. In 1995, the state of California budgeted more for prisons than for higher education. While there is no smoking gun linking the high crime rate to falling real wages or employment opportunities for the less skilled, the economic logic is clear: whatever makes legitimate work less attractive to young men makes crime more attractive. Most studies support that logic.

Another cost of inequality is found in the sense of insecurity at work. When inequality is high, people worry that they may have to work for less pay if they lose their current job. That may underlie the great concern over downsizing among middle-aged men, who are typically unemployed for many months if they are laid off and take a 20% or so wage cut when they finally find a new job. Insecure workers may be less productive, less willing to share their knowledge, and less likely to talk about problems with supervisors than more secure workers. The recent repudiation of the virtues of down-sizing by Stephen Roach, the chief economist at Morgan Stanley, shows that even proponents of lean companies recognize the costs to productivity of a workforce frightened about its future.

Falling real earnings of the low paid may also breed antagonisms between groups as well as general social instability. Animus against CEOs and Wall Street is a logical consequence of rising inequality. When my earnings are falling despite my hardest efforts, whom shall I blame? If year after year, you are getting wealthier and I am getting poorer, who knows what demagoguery might appeal to me?

Inequality has consequences for family structure, as well. There is nothing more antifamily than the falling level of earnings and declining job prospects for less-educated young men. If a young father cannot earn enough to support a family, he is unlikely to try to form one. If he engages in crime and ends up incarcerated, one result is more fatherless children. Hundreds of thousands of children in single-parent homes in the United States have fathers in jail or prison.

Inequality also affects business in various ways. Some businesses—those providing services to the rich—may gain; others—those producing for the great middle class—may lose. Consumer credit defaults may rise. Savings by ordinary citizens, already low, may fall. As the divide between bosses and subordinates grows, many may come to view business unfavorably and support policy interventions harmful to the nation's economy. How much are you making, Mr. CEO?

This list of costs—high crime, insecurity at work, stress on families, skewed business decisions, and political turmoil—is neither exhaustive nor definitive. The magnitude of the costs of rising inequality is not well known, because there is little in our history to provide guidance. But the ultimate cost of increasing inequality lies in the potential for an apartheid economy, one in which the rich live aloof in their exclusive suburbs and expensive apartments with little connection to the working poor in their slums. Just as many South African whites were blind to the plight of nonwhites, so too in an apartheid economy will many of us be blind to citizens of lower economic status—if we are not blind to them already. When was the last time you were shocked by the homeless?

PREVENTING AN APARTHEID ECONOMY

If you are happy about this picture of the emerging U.S. economy—if the benefits of inequality exceed its costs to you—stop reading. The remainder of this article considers ways to reduce inequality and rebuild the middle class. It is a menu of possibilities, not a sales pitch for any specific policy. The economy is a highly complex system that continually surprises us; no one can be sure what will work best to alleviate the trend toward inequality. Still, it is important to put on the table at least some policies that might prevent the development of an apartheid economy.

For starters, many policies on the front burner today won't do much to raise up those at the bottom of the earnings distribution. For instance, some supply-siders believe that faster economic growth by itself will cure the woes of the low paid, and that tax cuts for the wealthy (embodied in a flat tax) or reduced capital-gains taxes are the way to spur that growth. Such views fly in the face of recent experience. The sad lesson of the expansion of the 1980s and 1990s is that even very healthy growth may not improve the pay or income of those in the lower parts of the income distribution. The Reagan-Bush recovery from the 1981–1982 recession was one of the longest and most impressive in U.S. history: employment and income grew significantly. If divided evenly, the $2 trillion increase in the GDP from 1980 to 1994 would have been enough to give roughly $2,000 more to each American family. That's not what happened. Median family income was stagnant. Only the upper 20% had healthy gains in real income, with most of those gains concentrated in the top 5%. The proportion of aggregate income going to the top 5% rose from 15.3% in 1980 to 19.1% in 1993, while the proportion going to 80% fell. Men and especially women had to work more to maintain their standard of living. Nearly a decade of gains in the GDP and in employment were accompanied by falling incomes for the bottom half of American families! Growth alone is no cure for the problems of rising inequality and stagnant real wages.

Some believe that further deregulation of the economy will create more and better jobs. This is the standard solution of the Paris-based Organization for Economic

Cooperation and Development to nearly any economic problem. But the United States has the least-regulated economy among advanced countries. Its problem is not creating jobs but making work pay. There are reasons to cut some regulations, but preventing an apartheid economy is not one of them.

Others believe that cutting the federal deficit will improve the economy so much that real earnings will begin rising rapidly once the markets are assured that deficit reduction is for real. I know of no historical support for that claim, even if cutting the deficit in fact increases investment and growth. There are reasons to cut the deficit, but boosting the earnings of the low paid is not one of them.

Education and job-training programs for the less skilled are popularly suggested solutions to the problem. In the long run, education and training will help reduce inequality by increasing the number of people in higher-paying jobs and by diminishing the number competing for low-wage jobs. But, on their own, such supply-side changes have not yet shown themselves capable of offsetting the market forces that favor the highly paid and skilled.

Many economists expected that the wages of young workers would rise once the baby boomers aged. The logic for this expectation was impeccable—the decline in the number of young people after the baby boom would cause a shortage of young workers in the market—and shortages raise prices. But wages did not rise; instead, the economic position of young job seekers worsened in the 1980s and 1990s. In response, more young people have flocked to colleges and universities than in the past. Eventually, the growing number of college graduates should reduce the difference in pay between graduates of high school and college, but for now the gap remains high. As for government-funded training programs designed to improve the skills of those who do not go to college, even the best such programs increase wages or employment only modestly and cannot conceivably restore losses of earnings of 20% to 30%.

Will higher tariffs, repeal of NAFTA, or other protectionist policies cure the inequality problem? The economic costs of protectionism so dwarf the potential benefits for low-wage workers that they make the cure worse than the disease. What about policies to reduce immigration? They would cut the supply of low-skilled workers, but if the massive decrease in young Americans entering the job market after the baby boom did not improve their economic position, why should modest changes in immigration do the trick?

The problem with many of the policies described above is that they address low wages and rising inequality indirectly rather than tackle it head-on as an issue of income distribution. The topic of distribution has never been popular in the United States. In a society where economic growth benefits everyone, it is sensible to worry about efficiency and growth first and distribution last. In other words, let the Swedes worry about whose slice of the pie is bigger—we'll worry about baking a bigger pie.

But new problems require new solutions, and it behooves us to examine more carefully the redistributive tools at our disposal if we wish to prevent an apartheid economy. The earned income tax credit, which gives cash payments to low-wage workers, tackles the problem of low incomes head-on. At one time, both conservatives and liberals favored it, and the Clinton administration increased the credit in its first year in office. Another redistributive tool is the minimum wage. Like the earned income tax credit, it is not perfect—it is not well targeted at the poor and cannot be raised too high for fear of increasing unemployment—but it does buttress the bottom parts of the earnings distribution.

And we should look at the payroll tax that funds Social Security: the tax is a high, regressive levy on employment that does nothing to increase national capital investment. Perhaps we should combine privatization of Social Security with cuts in the payroll tax for low-paid workers in forming a new national retirement plan. Finally, a more lively and successful trade-union movement—led by a truly new AFL-CIO that succeeded in winning a raise for workers—would help reduce inequality. Perhaps business should rethink what the "union-free" private sector toward which we are headed really means for society.

Having warned you that no one can be sure about the best way to reduce inequality and that some policies won't work much, if at all, I would be insulting your intelligence and mine if I did more than list possibilities. Perhaps a judicious mixture of policies might prove effective. Another mixture might backfire. You may have better policies to suggest. Perhaps, magically, the invisible hand will resolve the problem of its own accord—although if I thought that likely, I would have written a very different article. At this stage, we need to recognize that the country has an inequality problem based on falling real earnings for low-paid workers that is unparalleled at least since the Great Depression. We need to begin debating ways to prevent the United States from developing an apartheid economy. We have a great record of solving problems once we recognize them and put them on the national agenda. Rising inequality and failing earnings for those at the bottom of the income distribution are real problems. Let's start reasoning together about how to solve them.

8

Inequality Here and There

CLAUDE S. FISCHER, MICHAEL HOUT, MARTIN SANCHEZ JANKOWSKI,
SAMUEL R. LUCAS, ANN SWIDLER, AND KIM VOSS

*The authors argue that inequality is not due to the distribution of talent
in society nor to the natural workings of the market. Inequality in the
United States is the result of societal choices based on the cultural support for rewarding difference and the resulting supply-side policies. In
effect, inequality in the United States is by design. As the authors point
out, other nations have designed systems that are less unequal than that
of the United States.*

A glance behind us to American history shows that our pattern of inequality is far from
fixed or naturally determined. A glance sideways to other wealthy nations makes the
same point. The United States has the greatest degree of economic inequality of any
developed country. It is a level of inequality that is not fated by Americans' talents nor
necessitated by economic conditions but is the result of policy choices. The nations with
which we will compare the United States are also modern, affluent, democratic, and capitalist—they are our competitors in the global market—and yet they have ways to reduce
inequality and remain competitive.

The best and latest evidence on how nations compare in levels of inequality comes
from the Luxembourg Income Study (so named because the project is headquartered in
Luxembourg). Social scientists affiliated with the study have collected detailed, comparable data on earnings and income from over a dozen nations. Our first use of their
research appears in Figure 8.1, which speaks to the question of inequality in *earnings,*
specifically earnings of men, aged 25–54, who worked full-time, all year during the mid-
to late 1980s. (Comparable data on earnings were available for only five nations. We are
looking just at men here, because the situation of women in the labor force was in such
flux and varied so much among nations.) The vertical line in the figure serves as an
anchor for looking at inequality in each nation. It represents the earnings of the average

Source: Excerpt from Claude S. Fischer, Michael Hout, Martin Sanchez Jankowski, Samuel R. Lucas, Ann Swidler, and Kim Voss. 1996. *Inequality by Design: Cracking the Bell Curve Myth* (pp. 120-128). Princeton, NJ:
Princeton University Press.

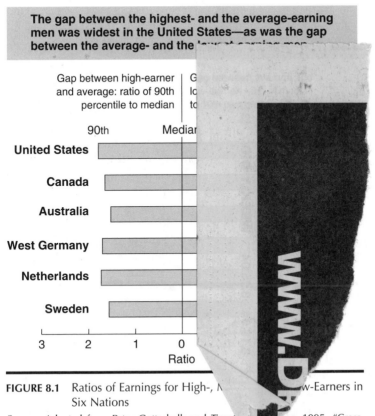

The gap between the highest- and the average-earning men was widest in the United States—as was the gap between the average- and the lowest-earning men

FIGURE 8.1   Ratios of Earnings for High-, M[...]w-Earners in Six Nations

Source: Adapted from Peter Gottschalk and Timot[...]ing, 1995. "Cross-National Comparisons of Levels and Trends in Inequality.[...]orking Paper no.126, Luxembourg Income Study. Syracuse, NY: Maxwell School of Citizenship and Public Affairs, July.

(median) worker. The horizontal bars to the left of the median line display the ratio of the earnings that men near, but not at the top of, the earnings ladder received—those at the 90th percentile in earnings—to the earnings of men at the median. In 1986 the 90th percentile American male worker earned 1.8 times what the median worker earned. The bars stretching to the right represent the same comparison between the median earner and a low-paid worker, one at the 10th percentile of earnings. In the United States, the median worker brought home 2.8 times the amount the 10th percentile worker did. The left-hand bars, therefore, display inequality of earnings between the high-earners and the average; the right-hand bars display inequality between the average and the low-earners. Together, they display total inequality. In the United States, the 90th percentile worker earned five times that of the 10th percentile worker.

These numbers are highest in the United States. That is, the gap in earnings between the rich and the average worker is greater here than elsewhere, as is the gap between the average and the low-paid worker. The contrast between the United States and Europe sharpens further when non-monetary compensation is added to the picture. In most European nations, national law requires that virtually all workers have the kinds of benefits such as strong job security and four-week vacations that in the United States only workers with seniority in major firms have.

These national differences expanded in the 1980s, when inequality increased globally. International economic forces widened the gaps between what the better- and the worse-educated earned in most industrialized nations, but this chasm opened up farthest and fastest in the United States and the United Kingdom. (These were the years of Thatcherite reforms that reduced the role of government in the United Kingdom.) Elsewhere, the gap in earnings between the better- and worse-educated widened less, barely at all, or even narrowed. There seems no clear connection between these differences and other economic trends such as growth rates. The reasons lie in government policies, notably the relative power of unions and the expansions of higher education in the other Western countries.

The biggest contrast in income inequality between the United States and the rest of the developed world, however, appears *after* taking into account how government deals with the results of the market. That means accounting for taxes, tax deductions, transfer payments, housing subsidies, and the like. (Again, we note that this before- and after-government distinction underestimates the role of government. Where, for example, governments require employers to provide certain benefits, there is more market equality.)

To look at international differences in *household income,* we turn again to the Luxembourg Income Study. Peter Gottschalk and Timothy Smeeding compiled comparable data on households' disposable incomes—income after taxes and government support, adjusted for household size—in seventeen nations. In Figure 8.2, we use just the figures for nations with over ten million residents in 1980; our conclusions about the United States would be virtually the same if we showed the smaller nations, too. As in Figure 8.1, the bars to the left of the median display the ratio of a rich household's income (at the 90th percentile) to an average one's income, while the right-hand bars show the ratio of an average household's income to that of a poor one (10th percentile). The rich-to-average ratio is greatest in the United States, 2.1, as is the average-to-poor ratio, 2.9, and so the rich-to-poor ratio, 5.9 (not shown) is much higher than that of the next most unequal nations (4.0 for Italy, Canada, and Australia). In short, the United States has the greatest degree of income inequality in the West whether one focuses on the gap between the poor and the middle or the gap between the middle and the rich. Even these numbers underestimate America's distinctiveness, because they do not count the sorts of "in-kind" help that middle- and lower-income families receive in most other nations, such as free health care, child care, and subsidized housing and transportation. They also underestimate inequality in America by not displaying the concentration of income at the very top of the income ladder.

Western nations generally take two routes to reducing inequality. . . . Some intervene in the market to ensure relatively equal distributions of *earnings* by, for example, brokering nationwide wage agreements, assisting unions, or providing free child care. Others use taxes and government benefits to reduce inequality of *income* after the mar-

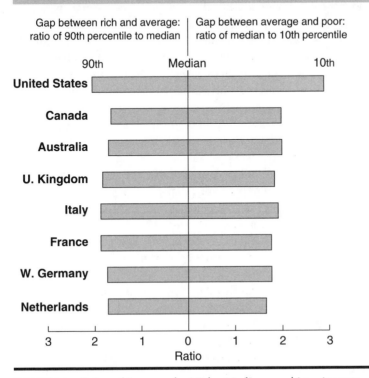

The income gap between the richest and the average household and the gap between the average household and the poorest are both wider in the United States than elsewhere.

| Gap between rich and average: ratio of 90th percentile to median | Gap between average and poor: ratio of median to 10th percentile |

90th   Median   10th

United States
Canada
Australia
U. Kingdom
Italy
France
W. Germany
Netherlands

3   2   1   0   1   2   3
Ratio

FIGURE 8.2   Ratios of Incomes for High-, Median-, and Low-Income Households in Eight Nations

Source: Adapted from Peter Gottschalk and Timothy Smeeding, "Cross-National Comparisons of Levels and Trends in Inequality." Working Paper no. 126, Luxembourg Income Study. Syracuse, NY: Maxwell School of Citizenship and Public Affairs, July.

ket. A few do both seriously, such as the Scandinavian countries. The United States does the least of either. If one sets aside older people, who benefit a great deal from government action in the United States, the net effect of taxes and transfers here is to leave the degree of inequality virtually unchanged from the way it was determined by market earnings.

When everything is accounted for, the Western nation with the most income inequality is the United States. But the United States is also exceptionally unequal in terms of *wealth.* At the end of the 1980s, the richest 1 percent of families owned about 40 percent of household wealth here, more than in any other advanced nation; the richest 1 percent owned only 25 percent of the wealth in Canada and 18 percent of the wealth in Great

Britain, for example. Add the less tangible features of "wealth," such as vacations and security of medical care, and the conclusion is reinforced that Americans are remarkably unequal.

(Some critics of crossnational comparisons contend that one ought not to contrast the United States to other nations, because the United States is distinct in certain ways. We have so many single-parent families, for example. But even looking only at two-parent families, the United States is still unusually unequal. America also seems exceptionally diverse racially and ethnically. But other Western nations also have ethnic diversity, if not the racial caste system we do. And poverty among American whites *only* still exceeds that among white or majority populations elsewhere. Such reservations do not challenge the conclusion that the United States is unusually unequal.)

America's level of inequality is by design. It is not given by nature, nor by the distribution of its people's talents, nor by the demands of a "natural" market. Other Western nations face the same global competition that we do and are about as affluent as we are and yet have managed to develop patterns of inequality less divisive than ours. Ironically, it was not so long ago that Americans were proud of comparing their relatively egalitarian society to the class-riven, hierarchical, decadent societies of Europe. In the last couple of decades, America has become the more class-riven and hierarchical society.

The United States is unusually unequal and Americans are unusually supportive of this inequality. Surveys show that Americans back moves toward expanding *opportunity* but oppose moves toward equalizing *outcomes.* They endorse wage differences among jobs that are pretty similar to the wage differences that they believe exist today (although the real differences are greater than Americans imagine), and they do not approve of government programs to narrow those differences. In a survey of people in six nations, only 28 percent of Americans agreed that government should reduce income differences. The next lowest percentage was 42 percent (Australians), while in the other countries majorities supported reducing income differences. Whether we have as much opportunity as Americans want is debatable but we seem to have a rough match between the desired and the perceived level of outcome inequality. That may be because Americans think that considerable inequality is needed for stimulating productivity and a high standard of living. Is it?

Some commentators straightforwardly defend our current level of inequality. A congressional report in 1995 conceded that the recent trends toward inequality were real but argued, "All societies have unequal wealth and income dispersion, and there is no positive basis for criticizing any degree of market determined [*sic*] inequality." Disparities in income and wealth, some analysts argue, encourage hard work and saving. The rich, in particular, can invest their capital in production and thus create jobs for all. This was the argument of "supply-side" economics in the 1980s, that rewarding the wealthy—for example, by reducing income taxes on returns from their investments—would stimulate growth to the benefit of all. The 1980s did not work out that way, as we have seen, but the theory is still influential. We *could* force more equal outcomes, these analysts say, but doing so would reduce living standards for all Americans.

Must we have so much inequality for overall growth? The latest economic research concludes *not;* it even suggests that inequality may *retard* economic growth. In a detailed statistical analysis, economists Torsten Persson and Guido Tabellini reported finding that, historically, societies that had more inequality of earnings tended to have lower, not higher, subsequent economic growth. Replications by other scholars substantiated the finding: More unequal nations grew less quickly than did more equal societies. . . .

Close examination of detailed policies also suggests that greater equality helps, or at least does not harm, productivity. Researchers affiliated with the National Bureau of Economic Research closely examined the effects on economic flexibility (that is, the ability to shift resources to more productive uses) of several redistributive policies used by Western nations—job security laws, homeowner subsidies, health plans, public child care, and so on. They found that such programs did *not* inhibit the functioning of those economies. Indeed, a study of over one hundred U.S. businesses found that the smaller the wage gap between managers and workers, the higher the business's product quality.

This recent research has not demonstrated precisely how greater equality helps economic growth, but we can consider a few possibilities. Increasing resources for those of lower income might, by raising health, educational attainment, and hope, increase people's abilities to be productive and entrepreneurial. Reducing the income of those at the top might reduce unproductive and speculative spending. Take, as a concrete example, the way American corporations are run compared with German and Japanese ones. The American companies are run by largely autonomous managers whose main responsibility is to return short-term profits and high stock prices to shareholders and—because they are often paid in stock options—to themselves as well. Japanese and German managers are more like top employees whose goals largely focus on keeping the company a thriving enterprise. The latter is more conducive to reinvesting profits and thus to long-term growth. Whatever the mechanisms may be, inequality appears to undermine growth. Americans certainly need not feel that they must accept the high levels of inequality we currently endure in order to have a robust economy.

A related concern for Americans is whether "leveling" stifles the drive to get ahead. Americans prefer to encourage Horatio Alger striving and to provide opportunities for everyone. Lincoln once said "that some would be rich shows that others may become rich." Many, if not most, Americans believe that inequality is needed to encourage people to work hard. But, if so, *how much* inequality is needed?

For decades, sociologists have been comparing the patterns of social mobility across societies, asking: In which countries are people most likely to overcome the disadvantages of birth and move up the ladder? In particular, does more or less equality encourage such an "open" society? The answer is that Western societies vary little in the degree to which children's economic successes are constrained by their parents' class positions. America, the most unequal Western society, has somewhat more fluid, intergenerational mobility than do other nations, but so does Sweden, the most equal Western society. There is no case for encouraging inequality in this evidence, either.

In sum, the assumption that considerable inequality is needed for, or even encourages, economic growth appears to be false. We do not need to make a morally wrenching choice between more affluence and more equality; we can have both. But even if such a choice were necessary, both sides of the debate, the "altruists" who favor intervention for equalizing and the supposed "realists" who resist it, agree that inequality can be shaped by policy decisions: wittingly or unwittingly, we choose our level of inequality.

9

For CEOs, a Minimum Wage in the Millions

HOLLY SKLAR

The gap between what chief executives and workers of U.S. corporations are paid widened dramatically in the last twenty years. While CEO pay rises in the United States, wages and benefits for workers continue to decline. In other industrialized countries, the combination of social values, a strong labor movement, and government regulation keep the wage gap between CEOs and workers smaller.

At the rate executive pay is rising, it won't be long before we start counting yearly compensation in billions. Disney CEO Michael Eisner led the pay parade in 1998 with more than half a billion dollars in salary, bonus, and cashed-in stock options. Eisner's $575.6 million was worth more than half of Disney World's 1998 operating profit. It would take nearly $14 from each of the 41.7 million theme park tickets sold by Disney in Florida last year to cover Eisner's earnings.

Eisner was number one on *Business Week*'s list of executives who gave shareholders the least for their pay for the 1996–1998 period and fourth on the list of executives whose companies did the worst relative to their pay. He still has more than $107 million in stock option gains from previous years yet to be exercised.

The wage gap between CEOs and workers is ten times wider than it was in 1980. Back then, CEOs earned 42 times the pay of average workers. CEOs made 419 times the pay of workers in 1998. That's up from 326 in 1997.

The Boston-based United for a Fair Economy (UFE) dramatizes the CEO-worker wage gap by using the Washington Monument for comparison. If the real 555-foot Washington Monument reflects average 1998 CEO pay, then a scaled-down replica representing average worker pay would be just 16 inches tall—5 inches shorter than in 1997. Back in 1980, the Workers Monument was over 13 feet tall—reflecting a CEO-worker wage gap of 42 to 1.

"In 1980, it would have required a pick-up truck to transport the Workers Washington Monument," says UFE co-director Chuck Collins. "By 1996, you could carry it on an airplane and put it in the overhead luggage bin. The 1998 model fits easily in my briefcase."

Source: Holly Sklar. 1999. *Z-Magazine* (July/August), pp. 63–66.

The CEOs in *Business Week*'s recent survey of executive pay at major companies pocketed $10.6 million on average last year. That's over $29,000 a day, including Saturdays and Sundays. And while fewer workers get health benefits and pensions, CEOs get top-notch health care, subsidized luxury housing and other perks, and truly golden retirements.

CEOs got "a 36% hike over 1997—and an astounding 442% increase over the average paycheck of $2 million pocketed in 1990," says *Business Week.* The five highest-paid executives—Eisner, Mel Karmazin of CBS, Sanford Weill of Citigroup, Steve Case of America Online, and Craig Barrett of Intel—split more than $1.2 billion. How much is $1.2 billion worth? The combined wealth of 24,000 U.S. households at the median net worth (including home equity) of about $50,000.

The CEO's 36 percent average 1998 pay raise beat the S&P 500 stock index, which rose 26.7 percent, and the miserly 2.7 percent raise given blue-collar workers.

According to the AFL-CIO, a worker who earned $25,000 in 1994 would earn $138,350 today if their pay had grown as fast as the average CEO. Too bad workers are still trying to catch up with 1973. A worker earning $25,000 today would have made about $3,400 more in 1973, adjusting for inflation.

In its recent feature on executive pay, the *Wall Street Journal* observes, "Pay for performance? Forget it. These days, CEOs are assured of getting rich—however the company does." CEOs laugh all the way to the bank even when they're fired. Golden parachutes have gone platinum.

A big part of CEO pay comes from stock grants and options to buy company stock that can typically be sold for a large profit. When the stock takes a dive, shareholders can drown, but CEOs with stock options "underwater" are rescued. The options are repriced to assure CEOs the fortunes they expect.

Here's how repricing works: When Cendant stock dropped, a large portion of CEO Henry Silverman's 25.8 million stock options, originally priced between $17 and $31, were repriced at $9.81 so they'd be well under the recent Cendant stock price of $15 a share. He earned $63.9 million in 1998 and has about S400 million in the pipeline.

"Enough is enough," declares the *Wall Street Journal.* "Computer Associates offers a cautionary example of high pay." CEO Charles Wang and other top executives received stock grants for three years beginning in 1995 valued at over $1 billion. Computer Associates had to take a $675 million charge to cover the grant. According to compensation analyst Graef Crystal, the charge "represented 43% of the company's after-tax profit for the whole three years" the plan was in effect.

Computer Associates shareholders will be voting on a resolution in August to establish a maximum ratio between the pay of the CEO and that of the lowest paid worker in the company. Similar shareholder resolutions sponsored by Responsible Wealth, a project of United for a Fair Economy, were introduced at Citigroup, General Electric, AT&T, AlliedSignal, BankAmerica, and BankBoston.

RACE TO THE TOP

While U.S. corporations have promoted a worldwide race to the bottom among workers, they've been leading a race to the top for CEOs. Japanese and European CEOs have typically earned 20 to 30 times the pay of workers, not hundreds of times as much. That's beginning to change. International mergers are one factor. For example, when Daimler-Benz took over Chrysler in 1998, reports *Business Week,* "CEO Jurgen E. Schrempp had to confront the fact that Chrysler CEO Robert Eaton—who earned over $11 million in 1997, including exercised [stock] options—appears to have made more than the rest of Daimler's management board members put together. Worse, Daimler had to pay $395 million—primarily in stock—to Chrysler's top 30 executives to cash out their options. Since cutting the pay of the Chrysler people would be tough, Daimler was forced to boost its own compensation."

In Europe, a combination of social values, union strength, and government regulations [has] kept the CEO–worker wage gap smaller. The United States should be looking more like Europe in that regard, rather than the reverse.

If the CEO–worker wage gap increases this year at the pace it did last year, CEOs will make 538 times as much as workers in 1999. In the year 2000, they'll make 691 times as much. Let's reverse the trend before it gets that bad.

SECTION 4

Gender

THE UNITED STATES CONTEXT

In 1999 women made some significant occupational breakthroughs in the United States: Carly Fiorina became head of Hewlett-Packard, Eileen Collins became the first woman to command a space shuttle flight, and Karen Jurgensen earned the editorship of *USA Today,* the nation's largest newspaper. But despite these highly visible gains, gender inequality in the workforce remains. Women's average earnings—hourly, weekly, or annual—are about 75 percent of men's (the good news is that they are up from 58 percent of men's wages in 1963; the bad news is they are still only three-quarters that of men's wages) (*Focus,* 1998/99:1). There is a long list of occupations in which women make up 5 percent or less of the workforce and where the "glass ceiling" is the thickest (e.g., pilots, navigators, truck drivers, mechanics, carpenters, telephone installers, loggers, material-moving equipment operators, construction workers, and firefighters). Women constitute 90 percent or more of such occupations as secretary, cashier, dental hygienist, child care provider, hairdresser, teacher aide, and receptionist (Sapiro, 1999:469). Generally, the more prestigious the occupation, the lower is the proportion of women. In 1998, for example, only 26 percent of lawyers, 26 percent of physicians, and 33 percent of full-time university or college teachers were women (U.S. Bureau of the Census, 1998:417).

Gender inequality is also manifested in sterotypical media portrayals of women and men; the differences in the socialization of girls and boys at home, school, and church; the unequal financing of women's sports in schools; the greater difficulty that women face from voters when running for electoral office against men; the much greater household demands on wives; and religious traditions that make women subordinate to men.

REFERENCES

Focus. 1998/99. "Women in the Labor Market," *Focus* (Institute for Research on Poverty, University of Wisconsin–Madison) 20 (Winter):1–3.

Sapiro, Virgina. 1999. *Women in American Society,* 4th ed. Mountain View, CA: Mayfield.

U.S. Bureau of the Census. 1998. *Statistical Abstract of the United States: 1998.* Washington, DC: U.S. Government Printing Office.

Comparable Worth
in Industrialized Countries

U.S. DEPARTMENT OF LABOR

This government analysis compares antidiscrimination and equal opportunity measures for women in a number of countries. The countries analyzed are Great Britain, Canada, the United States, Australia, New Zealand, Portugal, Japan, Greece, Belgium, Denmark, Finland, and Turkey.

The significant increase in women's work force participation following World War II, together with the attention directed to the issue by women's groups, has led to considerable international debate on the merits of equal pay. As a result, most industrialized countries have enacted equal employment opportunity and antidiscrimination measures aimed at breaking down the occupational and vertical segregation of women in the labor market. A recent study, sponsored by the Organisation for Economic Co-operation and Development, determined the nature and extent of these initiatives. This report excerpts some findings from that study.

GREAT BRITAIN

Private sector equal pay legislation was first introduced in 1975, when the Equal Pay Act of 1970 (amended by the Sex Discrimination Act of 1975) took effect. This Act provided that all persons doing the same or broadly similar work for the same or an associated employer are entitled to equal pay and equal terms and conditions of employment, unless the employer could show that the difference in pay was genuinely due to a material difference other than the difference of sex.

The Equal Pay Act was amended by the Equal Pay Amendment Regulations of 1983 to extend work value comparisons to include work of "equal value" in terms of effort, skill, and responsibility. Claims under current legislation are brought by individual women, through their unions, to industrial tribunals. Class actions are not possible.

Source: U.S. Department of Labor, Bureau of Labor Statistics. 1992. "Comparable Worth in Industrialized Countries," *Monthly Labor Review 114* (November), pp. 40–42.

The Advisory Conciliation and Arbitration Service has a statutory duty to attempt conciliation cases brought to industrial tribunals under the Act.

CANADA

The Canadian Human Rights Act, which took effect on March 1, 1978, states that it is a discriminatory practice for an employer to establish or maintain differences in compensation between male and female employees in the same establishment who are performing work of equal value based on the standard criteria of skill, effort, responsibility, and working conditions. It covers all federally regulated sectors, including the Federal public service, Crown corporations, and persons employed in banks, airlines, and interprovincial transportation. The Human Rights Commission can initiate complaints and respond to complaints brought by individuals, third parties (such as labor inspectors), or groups.

Provincial equal pay legislation applies to that proportion of the labor force working within a province's boundaries who do not fall within Federal jurisdiction. Federal and provincial equal pay legislation, between them, cover about one-third of the Canadian work force. Every province has legislation mandating equal pay for similar and substantially similar work. However, the scope of provincial legislation varies among jurisdictions.

Labour Canada's Equal Pay Program was established in 1984. Its aim is to eliminate sex-based wage discrimination in the Federal jurisdiction, using a three-step process to determine compliance and to respond to noncompliance. The first step is an educational visit to inform employers of their legal obligations and to provide advice. The second step is a series of monitoring visits to these employers to answer technical questions and to verify progress. The final step is onsite inspection and subsequent referral to the Canadian Human Rights Commission if non-compliance is found.

UNITED STATES

The Equal Pay Act of 1963 provides, in the Federal jurisdiction, for equal pay for jobs requiring equal skill, effort, and responsibility, and performed under similar working conditions. The Act protects most private employees whose employers are covered by the Fair Labor Standards Act, including executive, administrative, professional, and outside sales employees, who are exempt from the minimum wage and overtime provisions. Most Federal, State, and local government workers also are covered under the Act. While this provision is generally held to be applicable only to jobs "substantially equal" in nature, a number of U.S. States have adopted laws that go beyond equal pay for equal work and call for equal pay for work of comparable worth. In any case, most States already have equal pay laws or fair employment laws comparable to the Equal Pay Act or Title VII of the 1964 Civil Rights Act, or both. Title VII makes it unlawful for an employer: 1) "to discriminate against any individual with respect to his compensation terms, conditions, or privileges of employment, because of such individual's sex"; or 2) "to limit, segregate, or classify his employees . . . in any way which would deprive or tend to deprive any individual of employment opportunities or otherwise adversely affect his status as an employee" because, among other things, of such a person's sex. Title VII coverage extends to Federal employees, private employers, State and local governments, educational institutions, and labor organizations having 15 or more employees.

Executive Order 11246 of 1965 requires that every nonexempt contract with the Federal Government contain clauses that impose upon contractors and subcontractors antidiscrimination rules, equal reporting activities, and investigations related to enforcement. The written affirmative action plans required of larger employers with Federal contracts or subcontracts involved a comprehensive requirement for self-analysis of all positions, classifications, compensation, and also recruitment, training, and promotion patterns. When a compliance review identifies problems in the analysis, agreements must be reached to remedy them.

AUSTRALIA

New South Wales was the first Australian jurisdiction to change its Industrial Arbitration Act to entrench the principle of equal pay for equal work in 1958, followed by Queensland in 1964, Tasmania (for public servants only) in 1966, South Australia in 1967, and Western Australia in 1968. Victoria did not specifically introduce any equal pay legislation before 1969.

The establishment of a standard adult minimum wage in 1974 and the extension of equal pay for work of equal value to Australian women workers were industrially determined, and are considered separately.

In 1984, Australia passed its Sex Discrimination Act, administered by the Human Rights and Equal Opportunities Commission. There is no formal definition of equal pay in the Act; instead, it prohibits discriminatory terms and conditions of employment.

NEW ZEALAND

New Zealand has a centralized wage-fixing system, and equal pay legislation applying to both private sector and public sector employees. The Government Service Equal Pay Act, effective April 1, 1961, provided for the elimination of differences based on sex in scales of salary or wages paid to Government employees as soon as practicable after April 1, 1963. The Equal Pay Act of 1972 implemented the principle of equal pay in the private sector. It provided for the removal and prevention of discrimination based on sex in the rates of remuneration of men and women in paid employment in five steps, and full implementation of equal pay by April 1, 1977. It required the parties to adopt a wage-setting instrument, undertake a work classification exercise, and determine rates of remuneration that represent equal pay in accordance with defined criteria rewarding skill, responsibility, and service.

PORTUGAL

According to the Portuguese Constitution of 1976, "all workers without any distinction of sex are entitled to retribution of labour, according to quantity, nature, and quality, thus observing the principle of equal pay for equal work, in order to ensure a decent living." In 1979, Legislative Decree No. 392/79 extended those constitutional principles by requiring that "equal pay for working men and women for equal work or work of equal value done for the same employer, is ensured." The legislation provides that job descriptions and job evaluations shall be based on objective criteria common to the two sexes. It does not cover work at home and domestic service, the state services, and local authorities. However, Legislative Decree No. 426/88 deals with the implementation of equal pay and equal treatment in central, regional, and local administration.

Under the Decree, provisions in individual or collective agreements that are contrary to the principle of equal pay are deemed to be null and void. The legislation further provides that a lower (female) rate of remuneration prescribed in a contract or agreement shall be replaced automatically by the higher (male) rate. Penalties are prescribed for breach of Equal Remuneration Provisions.

JAPAN

The Japanese Constitution of 1946 proclaims the equality of all under the law and condemns any form of discrimination, particularly for reasons of sex, in any field of activity. It provides for the statutory regulation of wages, hours of work, and rest periods. The Labour Standards Act of 1947 repeats the constitutional prohibition of discrimination based on sex with reference to all payments made by an employer to an employee in return for work, and provides for penal measures in cases of noncompliance.

With regard to public services, the National Public Services Act and the Local Public Services Act stipulate that staff salaries must be based on the duties performed and the responsibility carried, and further forbid any discrimination for reasons of sex in the application of their provisions.

The continuance, in spite of the 1947 legislation, of practices such as forced female retirement on marriage and segregation of the work force (enforced by separate recruitment and promotion arrangements) resulted in the Law Concerning the Promotion of Equal Opportunity and Treatment between Men and Women in Employment and Other Welfare Measures for Women Workers, effective April 1, 1986. The law prohibits sex discrimination in education and training, fringe benefits, hiring, placement, promotion, retirement, and dismissal. Like the earlier legislation, it does not make provision for job evaluation methods for segregated occupations. There are no criminal penalties for an employer who does not comply with the law, but an Equal Employment Opportunity Mediation Commission will offer mediation of grievances autonomously.

GREECE

Greece is bound by Article 119 of the Treaty of Rome, which created the European Economic Community, and by the EEC Equal Pay Directive of February 10, 1975. In addition, the Greek Constitution of 1975 specifies that work of equal value should receive equal payment. Law 1414/84 on the Application of the Principle of Equality of the Sexes in Working Relations sets out a requirement that men and women receive equal remuneration for work of equal value, and provides sanctions for violators.

BELGIUM

In Belgium, the EEC Equal Pay Directive was implemented by Convention Collective du Travail No. 25, approved by the Conseil National du Travail (National Labor Board) and enforced by Royal Order in 1975, and hence is binding on all private sector employers in respect of all of their workers. In the public sector, equality of pay between men and women already followed from Article 6 of the Constitution, guaranteeing the equality of all citizens at law, as well as from Article 6bis, proscribing all discrimination.

Subsequently, the Council of the European Communities adopted Directive No. 76/207 in 1976, dealing with equal treatment of men and women, particularly with respect to working conditions. This Directive is directly binding on the Belgian Government. To implement this Directive, Title V of the Economic Reorientation Act of August 4, 1978, was adopted.

DENMARK

The Danish Equal Pay (Consolidation) Act No. 237 of May 5, 1986, gives the following definition of equal pay:

1. (1) No discrimination in terms of pay on the grounds of a person's sex may take place in contravention of the provisions laid down in this Act.

   (2) Any employer who employs men and women shall give them equal pay, including equal pay terms, for the same work or work given the same value.

   (3) This Act shall not be applicable in cases where a similar duty concerning equal pay follows from a collective agreement.

2. An employee whose pay in contravention of Section 1 is lower than the pay of others shall be entitled to claim the difference.

SWEDEN

The principle of equal remuneration, irrespective of sex, for identical appointments, was first introduced in the public sector in Sweden in 1947. In 1960, the Swedish Trade Union Confederation and the Swedish Employers' Confederation agreed on the abolition of specifically women's wages over a 5-year period. It was agreed that women and men should be paid the same for equivalent work, and collective agreements on equality began to extend across the labor market.

In terms of legislation, the question of equal pay is addressed in the Swedish Act on Equality between Men and Women at Work (1980), which prohibits discrimination on the grounds of sex. The Act provides that discrimination on the grounds of sex shall also be considered to exist where an employer applies to an employee less favorable terms of remuneration than those applied by that employer to an employee of the opposite sex where the work they perform is to be regarded as equal on the basis of collective agreement or established practice within the branch of activity, or as equivalent according to an agreed job evaluation, unless the employer can show that the discrepancy in the terms of employment is not due to the employee's sex.

The Act covers both the public and private sectors as regards the prohibition of discrimination. It also has provisions that make it incumbent on an employer to take active steps to promote equality. This part of the law can be set aside by collective agreements to the same effect.

FINLAND

Legislation addressing pay equity came into force in Finland on January 1, 1987, as part of a broader package of equity legislation and covers both the private and public sectors. The Equality Act specifies, in Section 8, that the actions of an employer shall be regarded as discriminatory if (among other things) the employer "applies to an employee conditions of payment or employment less favorable than those he applies to an employee of the opposite sex employed by him in the same work or work of equal value." The concept of work of equal value has not been specified in the Act; nor have "conditions of payment" been further defined. An employer who is found to have violated the prohibition on discrimination is liable to pay compensation.

TURKEY

Equal pay legislation was first introduced in Turkey in 1967 through the Turkish Labour Act No. 931, and covers both public and private sector workers. The State Official's Law of 1965 also includes the principle of equal pay. In addition, the 1982 Turkish Republic Constitution calls for a "guarantee of fair wage" and stipulates that "the State shall take the necessary measures to ensure that workers earn a fair wage suitable for the work they perform and that they enjoy other social benefits."

The Turkish Labour Act No. 1475 specifies that "in an undertaking, no distinction shall be made on grounds of sex between the wages paid to male and female workers performing jobs of the same nature and working with equal efficiency [and that] no provision contrary to this principle may be included in any collective agreement or contract of employment." Formal definitions of equal remuneration and comparable worth are set out in collective labor agreements.

The Complete Report on the comparative experience with pay equity, *Equal Pay for Work of Comparable Worth: The Experience of Industrialised Countries,* Labour Market and Social Policy Occasional Papers No. 6 (Paris, Organisation for Economic Co-operation and Development, 1991), is available from the Directorate for Education, Employment, Labour and Social Affairs, 2 rue Andre-Pascal, 75775 Paris Cedex 16, France.

11

Swedish Sojourn

SUSAN FALUDI

This article begins by comparing the condition of women in the United States with that of women in Sweden. Faludi finds the situation of Swedish women to be superior to that of American women. She focuses on a Swedish feminist organization that was influential in the electoral success of the Social Democratic Party, which stood for, among other things, gender equality.

The myth of the U.S. as the world's best country for women keeps us grateful, and conceals our middle-to-low place on the international totem pole for industrialized democracies, whether the problem is rates of unwanted pregnancies or political participation. It also keeps us from learning what women's movements in other countries have to teach us—not only in Sweden, a nation often ahead of the game in its equality policies, but in many others. For instance: the voter turnout rate in the U.S. is one of the lowest of any democracy. In India, a country with great problems of poverty and illiteracy, nearly 70 percent of eligible women voted in the recent election, compared to the U.S., where only 45 percent of eligible women voted in 1994. In countries as diverse as Canada and Burkina Faso, women's movements have pressured their governments to include questions about women's unpaid work in their countries' census, creating the possibility of attributing value to that work. Without similar measures here, welfare will go on being treated as payment for "nothing," and women who work in the home will continue to be invisible and devalued. That's why having Susan Faludi on a learning sojourn in Sweden is like having your smartest friend come home with exactly the insights you need. She brings us a cautionary tale about modes of including women in government, confirming that fighting for numbers alone may result in nothing more than the appointment of "safe"

Source: Susan Faludi. 1996. "Swedish Sojourn," *Ms. 6* (March/April), pp. 64–71.

*women, and that competent women will be undermined by false
scandals. She gives us an inspiring example of how small support
groups—like the ones we once had but seem to have forgotten—were
effectively used to pressure government. In short, Susan reminds us
that we are not alone. By learning a few tricks from other feminist
movements maybe we can have an impact on our own elections.
Only 40,000 more women voters in the right places could have
prevented the right-wing takeover of Congress in 1994. Only an
increased turnout can take it back in 1996.*

—Gloria Steinem

British feminist Mary Wollstonecraft traveled to Sweden in 1795 during midsummer, that brief Nordic season of warmth and hope, in search of a reason to live. As a practical matter, the author of *A Vindication of the Rights of Woman* came to Scandinavia to clean up the mercantile affairs of her erstwhile lover, a sea captain whose smuggling ship was pirated off by a Norwegian sailor. But she also came to salve a heart broken not only by her paramour but by all the men of politics, in England and in revolutionary France, who had raised and then dashed, again and again, her greatest expectations for women's advancement.

At first, Wollstonecraft's hopes were resurrected in the land of the midnight sun. As she gazed at the untrammeled slopes of wild strawberries and heartsease under a seemingly ever-bright sky, she decided to perceive the luminous landscape as "a good omen." In "the noon of night," as she dubbed the Swedish summer's perpetual half-light, she was renewed in her faith that a passionate "spirit of inquiry" could blaze the way to an enlightened and feminist world. But as three and a half months passed, taking her on a grueling journey across Scandinavia with her year-old baby, the crushing realities of her own betrayed status and that of the women around her sank her spirit once more. "A young woman," she recorded in her travel memoir, *A Short Residence in Sweden, Norway and Denmark,* "who is wet nurse to the mistress of the inn where I lodge, receives only twelve dollars a year, and pays ten for the nursing of her own child; the father had run away to get clear of the expense." It was the same old story, even here, she concluded. She left in despair, a despondency so unrelenting that, shortly after her return to London, she flung herself off Putney Bridge, a thankfully unsuccessful attempt at suicide.

Last spring, the feminist-minded culture editor of *Expressen,* one of Sweden's largest dailies, invited me to come live for two months and to write about what she proudly called "our women's revolution." I decided to read it as a promising augur that the visit would coincide with the 200th anniversary of Wollstonecraft's trip. In part, I wanted to read it that way. If Mary Wollstonecraft had come to Sweden to salve an aching heart, then so had I—albeit the ache of political not romantic disappointment. The brief love affair between American feminists and national politics that culminated in the 1992 presidential campaign was over, the so-called Year of the Woman—in truth only about as long as a Swedish summer—obliterated by the right-wing triumph of the 1994 midterm elections. I was ready for some good feminist political news.

And now it seemed that Wollstonecraft's initial rapture had at last been justified. In 1994, the same year that gave us a Republican-dominated Congress, Swedes elected the most-female government in the world—a parliament that was 41 percent female with a cabinet that was 50 percent female. The speaker of the Parliament was a woman, as was the foreign affairs minister and the deputy prime minister, Mona Sahlin, whose prime mission was to advance women's equality. This new Social Democratic government, Prime Minister Ingvar Carlsson declared in his inaugural address that fall, would stand first and foremost for gender equality. Imagine.

How, I wondered, had Swedish feminists managed such a triumph in the same year that spelled disaster for their American counterparts, and what had they done with this victory? I found a country where women are visible on nearly every level of government; where men are constructively involved in the debate over equality; where women have babies in part because they are assured of state support, not because they have no other choices; and where women enjoy many other advantages only dreamed of in the U.S. And yet, beneath those triumphs, I also found disappointment and restiveness and anxiety among the women who reaped the rewards of political victory. Four months after I left Sweden, the summer over and the leaden skies of the Scandinavian winter prevailing once more, Mona Sahlin would step down in despair. Like Mary Wollstonecraft, she and her sisters in "the women's revolution" had been led "to reflections on the instability of the most flattering plans for happiness," as Wollstonecraft had put it in her Scandinavian memoir. Did the men who made way for women in the Social Democratic party really want gender equality—or were they doling out flattery in exchange for tightening their own grip on the reins?

That men would offer a measure of authority to women and then yank it away is the oldest story in the world. But for the women of Sweden to be hoodwinked, for this to happen in a nation that prides itself on a tradition of women's independence and freedom, is an especially bitter pill. If ever women are to take their rightful place in society, it seems likely that it will happen first in Sweden, where for centuries women have fiercely and successfully guarded their own turf and rights. It is a nation that boasts not only the Viking women (who, with the men off at sea for long stretches, exerted authority in their absence, inheriting land, divorcing when they pleased, and arranging for grave monuments as glorious as the men's) but the fourteenth-century Saint Birgitta and her powerful fiefdom of convents (even the pope feared crossing her) as well as the dairy women who live all summer long in remote mountain communes tending cattle, cowgirls on the range, part of a 500-year-old tradition. But these were all situations where women exercised power in spheres separate from men. What would happen when men were asked to share authority in the same venue? And why would they make room for women—unless they had concluded that the room wasn't all that valuable?

The seeds of the Swedish women's revolution were planted in the days following the election of 1991, when the long-ruling Social Democrats were suddenly elbowed out of power by a conservative coalition that made clear that it intended to cut taxes and rein in social welfare programs—particularly the ones serving women. The coalition was heavily influenced by a right-wing party, the New Democrats, which gave 88 percent of its parliamentary seats to men, and was fond of demonizing day care and discrediting working women's aspirations in general. An antifeminist climate burgeoned. There was talk of reevaluating abortion rights, even accusations that children's allergies were rising because working women were becoming such negligent housekeepers. Anger at women began surfacing elsewhere, in the form of increased domestic violence and rape. And the media fed the fire with hectoring articles on the so-called costs of independence.

By the time the consequences of the conservative government's policies and attitudes became apparent, a resistance group was already mobilized. The Support Stockings got its start as soon as the first sign of a sea change in women's status surfaced: a decline in the number of women in parliament. The proportion of female M.P.s had fallen from 38 percent to 33 percent—the first drop since women's suffrage in 1921. That was enough to set off alarms for Maria-Pia Boëthius, an enormously beloved and respected women's rights advocate and journalist, whose tough-minded investigations of such taboo topics in Sweden as Nazi collaboration, sexual violence, and medical malpractice have won her the admiration of even her most conservative peers. She is also a woman of great enthusiasms and moral intensity—a soul-searcher and seeker on the scale of Mary Wollstonecraft. When I asked her to describe her daily routine, she said to me, "Every morning before I get up, I question everything," then she paused, looked at me intently and added, "including feminism."

The week after the 1991 election, Maria-Pia Boëthius sat at her kitchen table, questioning everything. "I was really worried and felt we have to do something but, Jesus, what do we do?" she said in one of her typical headlong sentences. What she did was invite over nine women she respected, activists from journalism and academe, and they brainstormed over wine and dinner, late into the night. The next week, they each brought five women to another meeting, and all agreed on a simple mission: to support and promote women in politics. They also decided to announce that their membership was secret, except for those who wanted to go public—a strategy that allowed participation by women who wanted to avoid the media's penchant for personal slams against women who stick their necks out for feminist causes. (Only Boëthius and a handful of other Stockings went public and had to weather assaults in the press.) Anonymity piqued the curiosity of the media and the paranoia of the politicians. If the membership were secret, the Stockings figured rightly, the men in power would imagine the group to be a vast web of feminist conspirators. The main inspiration for the Support Stockings is Pippi Longstocking, a national icon, and troublemaking heroine of Astrid Lindgren's children's novels, a girl who can lift horses, hurl cops off roofs, and respects no gender lines.

The Support Stockings, like Pippi, had virtually no money and little in the way of gimmicks besides some stickers warning "Little Sister Is Watching You," which appeared in men's bathrooms in the Parliament building. Yet the Stockings became a nationwide movement in a matter of months. In part, their popularity could be attributed to their Zen-like approach: they led by refusing to lead. When women came wanting to join, they were told to form their own secret societies. Eventually, more than 120 feminist-minded networks sprang up around the country, including a bowling club that doubled as a feminist cell. The flurry of activities culminated in a mobbed women's "tribunal" in Stockholm on International Women's Day in 1993.

The Stockings' popularity among women also came quickly because the founders had been engaged for many years with women who weren't necessarily activists. Women like Ebba Witt-Brattström, a literature professor, or economist Agneta Stark, taught gender issues in the rarefied air of the university; but they also taught shop clerks and bank tellers in free evening lectures in libraries and department stores. This "continuing education" for adults is a long tradition in Sweden, rooted in the social welfare vision of the 1930s, and it is a tradition that has particularly served women.

Women connected across social and economic lines in this movement for another, more basic reason: unlike in the U.S., those lines are increasingly blurry. That sense of commonality is rooted both in the Swedish ideal of redistributed wealth and in the last 25 years of a social system that has genuinely enabled most women to work and have families without major sacrifice. Thanks to a publicly supported bulwark of quality day care, health care, and parental supports, Swedish women have both the highest employment rate and, with the exception of Iceland and Ireland, the highest birthrate of women in any developed European nation. The class divisions are also narrower among women than men, although not necessarily for the right reasons. As in the U.S., women are lumped at the bottom of the job market. "Our success," Ebba Witt-Brattström said to me, "had to do with the fact that never before have Swedish women had so much in common. Now, almost 90 percent of Swedish mothers have had the experience of working outside the home—and working in sectors where women are poorly paid. The wage differences between women are about 4,000 kroner a month at most [about $580] . . . I don't earn much more than the woman at the child care center where my youngest son spends his days." And the result is: "I can feel solidarity with her. She can feel solidarity with me."

The result of all this solidarity was the stunning revelation of a newspaper opinion poll in the spring of 1994 that asked the question, "Would you consider voting for a women's party headed by Maria-Pia Boëthius?" Nearly 40 percent of those polled, women and men, said yes. The politicians went into a panic. Soon after, the Social Democrats announced that they would make every other candidate a woman—and the Support Stockings agreed to hold off on creating a women's party.

The Social Democrats, who had ruled more or less continuously since 1932, were desperate to get back in power. And if positioning themselves as the female-friendly party was the most effective marketing tool, then they were ready to use it. In retrospect, it seems ominous that the party hired a U.S. consulting firm for advice on the campaign—and sought out the youngest and least experienced women they could find to ensure that the party's state would be half female. Older party women who had been fighting for equality for decades were largely ignored. For their deputy prime minister and minister for equality affairs, the Social Democrat party bosses chose Mona Sahlin, who was 37 at the time and made a point of advertising the fact that she had organized the first Barbie doll club in the country—and didn't know nothin' about feminism.

Sahlin's stance on feminism, however, rapidly changed during the campaign, as she experienced waves of personal assaults from the opposing parties and the press, which inspected and denounced everything from her clothes to her maternal instincts. By the time she arrived in office, she was calling herself a feminist, loudly. But whether this would be enough to transform Rosenbad, the central federal government building that stands on the site of a seventeenth-century bathhouse, was another matter. (The name Rosenbad is in homage to the rose petals that once floated in its bathing pool.) By the time I arrived, eight months into the election of the "women's" government, most of the women who were putatively in charge seemed full of doubts about their revolution.

Inside the Parliament building, the convening hall is bright and Scandinavian modern, and on my first day there, the sight of so many women made me rub my eyes with disbelief. There were subtle signs of revolution: a new informality—some of the youngest women legislators wore T-shirts and sneakers—and a new format for the day's question-and-answer session with the cabinet. "This is the first time that the government will be asked questions they don't know ahead of time," Margareta Schwartz, a feminist adviser to Sahlin, and my translator, told me. It was the female speaker who made the change so that M.P.s could get more spontaneous answers from cabinet members.

I sat in the bleachers pondering happily a government where women could change the rules on the boys, and slipped into a reverie of feminist utopia . . . until the women of Parliament began to pose their questions to the cabinet.

"Many of us as women are disappointed," M.P. Rose-Marie Frebran said, addressing Sahlin, and the bitterness in her voice took me aback. "The most important issue this spring is unemployment," she said, and working women were most vulnerable to its ravages. "How is it possible that this passed through your 'eye of equality needle'?"

M.P. Monica Green leaped up. "We were so happy that all issues would be scrutinized from an equality point of view, but has this really happened? We're making *more* women unemployed." The questions kept coming: Why did the budget cuts all seem to come out of women's hides? Why cut family-leave pay? Why were pensions for women shrinking? Why were unemployment benefits down?

Sahlin, the lightning rod for all of this frustration, as the minister for equality affairs, winced and returned the ball to her sister parliamentarians' court: "There are some limits to what a [cabinet] minister can do. She cannot achieve equality here [in Parliament]. You do it, all you women, in the most equal Parliament in the world." In numbers, yes, they were equal, but in the months since the election, women M.P.s and Mona Sahlin herself had begun to wonder if having a lot of women in government was the same thing as having a lot of power—and if government was still a domain that conferred power. Were women's numbers rising on a sinking ship? A ballooning debt, costly financial mistakes made, and the consequences deferred under a predominantly male regime were now to be settled under the regime of the women. Was this a blessing or a curse?

The next morning, Sahlin arrived at the former Långholmen prison to speak before a Young Social Democrats rally. The prison is now a trendy restaurant, with a gift shop hawking T-shirts with pictures of handcuffed inmates—an apt backdrop for a speech full of anxiety about a political system in which its members fear their hands are tied. "If politics loses all possibility for influence, if other powers take over, then we're lost," Sahlin told the young political aspirants. "We're frightened that democracy will lose. People say . . . it's taxes' fault, it's the public sector's fault, it's the European Union's fault. If this goes on . . . where is the vision? To get rid of politics?"

Afterward, sitting at a picnic bench and gazing at an untouched cup of congealing coffee, the 38-year-old Sahlin could speak only of her fears. "I've been in politics 13

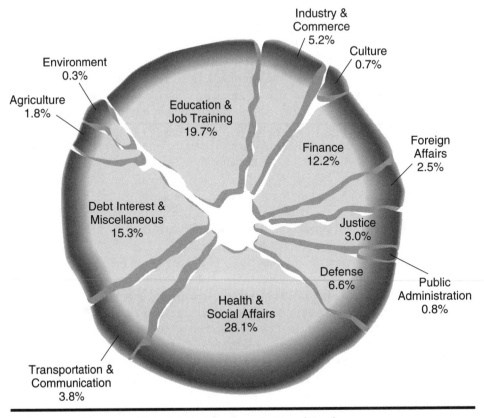

FIGURE 11.1   The Annual Swedish Budget: How the Bread Breaks
Illustrated with *knäckebröd,* a popular Swedish rye crisp bread

years, and the last eight months have been absolutely awful," she said. "No one knows, where is the future? We fail now and all the bad things that have happened to women are nothing compared with what will happen." The euphoria of winning had given way to grave ambivalence and, for some women in politics, utter despair, as they realized that their main assignment—thanks to a prolonged recession and the leviathan deficit that only worsened under the conservatives' tax-cutting reign—was to slash government spending, not to expand women's rights. And worse, those cuts would come, in large measure, out of social programs that represent the biggest chunk of the federal budget— programs that have allowed Swedish women to enjoy that rarest of female experiences: the freedom not to choose between a personal and a public life. Now all that was threatened— and it seemed as if the men in politics were only too happy to let women take the credit for pulling the plug on themselves. Whether they deserved this "credit" is another question: the finance minister, Göran Persson, who has dictated the harshest cuts and wields the most power, is a man.

"It is a terrible time for women to come to power," said Eleanor Wikborg, English professor at the University of Stockholm. "People can only see bad times for a long time ahead and it will hurt women the most." Elizabeth Cederschiöld, who was finishing a biography of Mary Wollstonecraft at the time of my visit, echoed these sentiments. It's a situation that the author of *A Vindication of the Rights of Woman* "would have hated," she said, most especially because of the pairing of the reduction in public support with the rise of a business class that, U.S.-style, allowed for a string of banking collapses in the 1980s and then leaped clear, clutching its golden parachutes. It is a phenomenon whose dangers Wollstonecraft forecast centuries ago, when she warned that a nascent commerce would eventually become an even more brutal "new species of power."

The unprecedented number of women in Parliament "is a fantastic symbol for the world," Maria-Pia Boëthius said to me, "but for women in Parliament it is a shock because they see no power." The power is in the hands of globalized financial institutions, a few hugely profitable Swedish export companies that do much of their hiring offshore, a common market that is compelling Sweden to deemphasize public care, and media monopolies with U.S. roots. Women have been assigned the job of managing the public weal just when the real influence is shifting to the Disneys and the Microsofts. You can walk for blocks past clothing stores and video outlets and movie marquees— and have no clue that you have left the United States. The most prominently featured woman in Stockholm last summer was Pamela Anderson of *Baywatch,* whose bikini-clad likeness was plastered on nearly every bus shelter in town. The advertisement, part of a hugely successful campaign, was for a major Swedish retailer. Feminist graffiti covered many U.S. fashion posters, angry scrawls protesting another import of American vintage—eating disorders.

What the women in politics can and have changed, Boëthius observed, is "the culture of Parliament." This is evident in the creation of a day care center inside the state building, where M.P.s can bring small children. Women like Mona Sahlin have already changed the culture; her style of openness and accessibility, even in the face of criticism, is now called "Sahlinism." When I told her I'd talked to women who said she hadn't taken any concrete steps toward equality, she nodded her head in agreement. "I'm frustrated, too," she said. "I feel I should've done more. . . . But they should come to me with ideas. I need more help." There is a refreshing innocence in such statements—although later I found myself wondering if they didn't suggest naïveté as well.

Ultimately, changing the style of governance is of little import if the substance doesn't change as well—a fact painfully apparent to the women from the Stockings who joined the new government. They may be the most frustrated of all. Ebba Witt-Brattström accepted a post with the ministry of higher education. "I feel like a hostage," she told me as she sat in her government office, mournfully contemplating an old radical feminist poster from the sixties. "Mona will say all the time, 'Be more radical!' . . . We have coffee [in Sahlin's office] every morning where you can be as radical as hell, and then we go to government meetings where all we talk about are cuts we can make in women, children, and family programs." The one "radical" proposal that the ministry was able to put forward— a modest plan to create 30 new professorships for women, a mere 1.5 percent addition to the existing 2,000 posts—generated a firestorm of denunciation from academia and the media. Witt-Brattström was a particular target; the media were full of insinuations about her witchlike brainwashing of students.

If such hostility to professional women's advancement seems out of place in this supposedly progressive nation, that is because Sweden has a well-kept dirty secret: working women's strides have been almost wholly segregated and contained within the public sector. In private businesses, less than 10 percent of all managers are women. In academia, less than 7 percent of professors are women. Even in the Lutheran church, no woman has ever been appointed a bishop. In the prosperous sixties and seventies, women poured into the workplace, but they were diverted to the public sector where the government was looking to staff its rapidly expanding social welfare programs. The result is a his 'n' hers workplace, where 80 percent of men work in the private sector, while 60 percent of women supervise nurseries and change bedpans in the public sector.

With prosperity's end, it is the public sector and *women* that feel the pain. "We have a separated labor market that no other country has," Margareta Eklund, founder of Minerva, a working women's advocacy group, told me, "and so every day that we cut the public sector, hundreds and hundreds of women go out on unemployment." And the losses come at the worst time for pressuring the private sector to hire women, because jobs there are also shrinking, although not as drastically. Eklund had been trying to battle job segregation with a federally funded program she devised to teach men to do women's jobs and vice versa. She started with maids and home repair workers. But with the budget cuts, Eklund's program lost its funding. "It feels like we are being pushed back," she said, just as women were under the conservative government. But at least then it was clear that they were gunning for women. This time it's hard to identify a culprit. As Eklund put it: "I can feel it, but I can't see it."

One such culprit not immediately identifiable may be the Social Democratic party itself. The old working-class party of union men, the Social Democrats have a checkered history with women's rights that stretches back to the enfranchisement of women (they opposed suffrage because they thought, ironically, that women would stymie social change) and forward to the recent remark by one of their trade union leaders that the women in the party were a "shoal of cunts." It was the much smaller Liberal party, from the turn of the century on, that consistently pressed for equality—from property rights to the vote to paternity leave. The last is perhaps most emblematic of the difference in approach between the two parties: the Liberals maintain that women's status won't change until men change, and men won't change until they are just as engaged as women in family life. As Gunilla Thorgren, an adviser on labor issues in the Social Democratic government, keenly observed, "The Liberals are the more radical because they want to *share* sex roles, while the Social Democrats want to *preserve* sex roles."

But the small Liberal party would never be the party in power, capable of creating a government that was half women. And perversely enough, the Social Democrats' triumph in the 1994 elections came at the Liberals' expense, whose constituency shrank from 9 percent to 7 percent. The ironies continue. When asked to show what they've done for women, the Social Democrats point to a number of innovative government policies on equality: an extra month's paid parental leave that families can get only if the father stays home; a toughening of the Equal Opportunities Act and a requirement that private corporations draft plans to eliminate gender pay gaps and promote women; an academy to advance women in corporate management; automatic shared child custody; guaranteed public child care in every county. There's only one catch: all of these policies were designed and pushed through Parliament by the deputy prime minister in the *previous* government, a Liberal politician named Bengt Westerberg. The right-wingers labeled his paternal-leave plank, known as "pappa's month," the "effeminate proposal." But the loudest opponents to the proposal, Westerberg recalled, were the Social Democrats.

"Bengt was more courageous than the women politicians," Maria-Pia Boëthius said. Westerberg has that peculiarly Swedish moral intensity—provoked not by U.S. sentimentality but by an amazing passion for facts and figures, a hyper-rational "spirit of inquiry" that Wollstonecraft would have admired: his feminist awakening came after reading a technical government report on gender power imbalances.

But Westerberg's party is out of favor now, and he is a lecturer on gender equality. (On the upside, he noted to me, he now spends real time with his nine-year-old son, more time than does his working wife.) "Bengt focused on the distribution of power and not the distribution of seats," said Karin Pilsäter, a Liberal M.P., and one of many women's rights advocates who mourn Westerberg's departure from the political arena. "He was very much on the front lines of making it not only a question of women but a question of men." The Social Democrats, by contrast, said Pilsäter, "just woke up one morning and said, 'Oh, we need more women.' But they didn't give their women the power." Pilsäter told me that her greatest fear was that women had been set up for a fall. "I'm very afraid when the next election comes up that they will say: 'See, we put all these women in Parliament and what did they do? Nothing. So we really don't have to do it again.' "

The fall Pilsäter feared came even before the next election. In August, right after I left Sweden, Prime Minister Carlsson announced that he would be retiring, and floated the possibility of Mona Sahlin as his successor. Soon after, a government official "leaked" the news that Sahlin had committed an indiscretion, one so small that had it been committed by a U.S. politician it would barely have merited a news brief (unless the person in question was Hillary Rodham Clinton). Sahlin had used her government credit card to purchase some private items—which is perfectly legal as long as the card user marks the items "private" and reimburses the government, both of which Sahlin did. Her sin: she was a few months late in paying some of these bills. They were not bills for limo rides and nights on the town. They were for diapers and child care. Nonetheless, the opposition parties and the press worked themselves into righteous indignation. The former prime minister under the conservative government huffed: "Mona Sahlin should be placed under financial supervision."

Sixty prominent women signed a public letter of support, in which they declared that "we have sometimes not paid our bills in due time." But it was of no use. By November, Sahlin announced that she was withdrawing her name from consideration as prime minister—and quitting as deputy prime minister for equality affairs "for the sake of the party." The responsibility for equality affairs was promptly bumped down to the ministry of public administration, a lower-profile office that handles such "important" tasks as recreation. At press time, Göran Persson, the finance minister whose promarket policies have caused the most pain to average Swedish women, was expected to be the next prime minister.

It would be difficult to imagine a more bleak ending to such a promising moment in feminist political history. But perhaps it is not an ending, just a false start. As the irrepressible Maria-Pia Boëthius pointed out to me one day as we walked through the summer countryside, the Support Stockings still hold "our trump card." The Stockings had agreed to hold off on forming a women's party—but they never agreed to shelve the idea entirely, she pointed out. Perhaps, I thought, such a party would be more in line with the Swedish tradition of women exerting strength through separatism. But Boëthius has a more radical vision of a women's party. Recently, she told me, she bumped into Bengt Westerberg and she reminded him, "We can still form this women's party." And Westerberg, understanding that the "we" didn't mean women only, nodded and said that this party sounded like the kind he'd like to join.

Boëthius was striding vigorously up a steep stretch of mountain trail as she told this story. She had begun the conversation sounding weary, despairing. But her optimism returned as she wandered across the fields of wildflowers, stopping to exclaim over a fragile tendril she had discovered under a dead mat of leaves or to pluck wild strawberries, which she proffered, like manna, to her hiking companions. There was something in her undaunted nature, and in the fact that it was nature's wilderness that had restored her to hope, that reminded me of the feminist who had exalted over the Nordic landscape all those years ago. Mary Wollstonecraft, I thought, had returned. And in the end, she would prevail.

Age

THE UNITED STATES CONTEXT

Similar to what is occurring worldwide, the population of the United States is aging. In 1900 the percentage of the U.S. population age sixty-five and older was 4 percent. In 1950 it was 8 percent. Now it is 13 percent (35 million), and in 2030 it will likely be about 20 percent, with 70 million retirees, and more grandparents than grandchildren (Treas, 1995).

There are two major problems brought about by an aging society (the following is from Eitzen and Baca Zinn, forthcoming). The first is that the Social Security system will become increasingly inadequate to meet the financial needs of the elderly (Callahan, 1999). The present program, when compared to the federal pensions in other industrialized societies, provides only minimal support. Instead of a universal system that allows the elderly to live comfortably, the Social Security program (1) does not cover all workers; (2) pays benefits according to the length of time workers have paid into the system and the amount of wages on which they paid a Social Security tax (i.e., low-wage workers receive low benefits during retirement); and (3) pays such meager benefits for some that 30 percent of those relying exclusively on Social Security are *below* the poverty line. These problems will escalate in the future as more people become eligible for Social Security, people live longer, and relatively fewer workers (in comparison with the proportion who are old) pay into the Social Security system.

The second problem for the elderly in the United States is paying for health care. Of all age groups, the elderly are most affected by ill health, especially from age seventy-five onward. The U.S. does provide universal health care for those age sixty-five and over through Medicare, but this government program is insufficiently financed. From the perspective of the elderly, only about half of their health care bills are paid through the program, leaving them with substantial costs. The affluent elderly are not hurt because they can afford supplemental health insurance. The poor are not hurt because they are also covered by Medicaid, a separate program that pays for the health care of indigent people. The near-poor, however, do not qualify for Medicaid and they cannot afford additional health insurance.

About 43 percent of today's elderly will use a nursing home in their lifetime (Greenwald, 1999). This is a special concern to the elderly in the United States because nursing home care may cost as much as $3,000 to $5,000 a month. Nursing home patients must pay these costs until their assets reach a low point when Medicaid takes over. The problem, of course, is that this means that few resources remain for the surviving spouse. In other industrialized nations, the government pays for nursing home costs when needed.

REFERENCES

Callahan, David. 1999. "Still with Us," *The American Prospect* 45 (July/August):74–77.
Eitzen, D. Stanley, and Maxine Baca Zinn. (forthcoming). *In Conflict and Order: Understanding Society,* 9th ed. Boston: Allyn and Bacon.
Greenwald, John. 1999. "Elder Care: Making the Right Choice," *Time* (August 30):52–56.
Treas, Judith. 1995. "Older Americans in the 1990s and Beyond," *Population Bulletin* 50 (May), entire issue.

12

The Super-Aged Society

SHIGEAKI BABA

*Of all the advanced industrial societies, Japan has the largest propor-
tion of its population classified as elderly. Thus, Japan is faced with a
number of choices in meeting this age group's needs and in developing
requirements for social services and facilities. Because other industrial
countries will soon face the same problems, Japan's policies will be
watched closely for their successes and failures. Japan's solution
appears to be a combination of proactive government planning and policies (e.g., health, pensions, and services) for the aged, combined with
individual responsibility.*

Aging is fast becoming a major social problem in Japan. In the last four decades, life
expectancy has risen from 63.9 years to 78.7 years (from 65.9 to 81.6 years for women
and from 62.1 to 75.9 years for men). The total population, which was 123.61 million in
1990, is expected to reach 128.64 million in 2007, and by 2025 the numbers aged 65 or
older will exceed 20% of the total population, reaching 27.3% and perhaps a staggering
total of 33.2 million. This means that there will be more than twice as many aged as in
1990, and that Japan will have a vast elderly population on a scale unparalleled by any
other nation in history. Professor Naohiro Ogawa of Nihon University Centre for Population Study reported that, according to his projected estimates, by 2025 the number of
the bedridden old will increase to about 2.8 times that of 1990, and those affected by
senility will be 3.2 times more numerous.

Starting in the 1990s, the Ministry of Health and Welfare has moved into action with
its strategic ten-year Plan for the Aged, focusing on improving and expanding the number of welfare institutions for the elderly as well as providing funding and assistance for
nursing at home. However, the numbers of aged in need of care are increasing rapidly,
and an urgent demand has arisen for establishing community systems and systems for
mutual help among the elderly.

The overwhelming numbers of the elderly are also bound to impose a financial burden on society, with expected increases in national medical expenditure and in individual

Source: Shigeaki Baba. 1993. "The Super-Aged Society," *World Health 46* (May/June), pp. 9–11.

national pension payments. Consequently there are voices in the government urging drastic reforms to the present social security system. Thus, improvements in the life-style of each and every member of Japanese society are now a responsibility of the government, as well as of the people.

QUALITY OF LIFE

Widespread interest in health and well-being characterizes this aging society. Along with activities for fitness and newly developed approaches to the health concept, which are centred more on the role and outlook of the individual, various measures have been taken to encourage improved life-styles for each age group. This approach of examining the quality of life according to people's age groups and their stage in the life-cycle is a recent trend in the area of social philosophy, and is a basic component in establishing healthy, wholesome life-styles as well as the prevention and control of diseases.

However, what is all very well in theory is not so easy to put into practice. For instance, an essential prerequisite to prevent illness and promote well-being is cutting out the smoking habit. Yet Japan's statistics indicate that 74.7% of men and 14.2% of women are smokers. The highest proportion of smokers are among men in their 30s and women in their 20s, while the lowest are among males and females in their 70s or older. The wide difference between the sexes in respect of smoking is a particularly Japanese characteristic.

Furthermore, as many as 2.2 million Japanese are estimated to be dependent on alcohol. According to a 1985 Japan-US joint survey, 76.5% of men and 24.6% of women in Japan were drinkers, the highest figures being 80.1% and 79.2% for men in their 30s and 40s, respectively. There was a similar high ratio among the other age groups for males. Among women, those in their 20s had the highest percentage of drinkers (36.2%). It would seem that steps should be taken to prevent possible risks to the health of newborn babies as a result of high alcohol consumption among these women—who are the ones most likely to become pregnant.

A nationwide survey of views and attitudes to health found that an overwhelming majority of the Japanese spend their leisure hours watching television or listening to the radio. Among the groups studied, 70% or more of men and women with pre-school children and 50% of those with primary school children spend their holidays with their families. The Japanese mostly live in nuclear families, and their family lives are centred around the children.

As for exercise and sports, there are differences between the sexes and between age groups. Women tend to discontinue their sports pursuits at a younger age than their male peers. Participation in sports has been found to correlate directly with interest in health, and the cultivation of sports from an early age is expected to foster awareness about fitness and well-being in the future.

A NEW PROTOTYPE

In contrast to the social concepts of the elderly in the past, a new prototype seems to be emerging—that of the "New Elderly." No other age group is subject to so wide a variation in their individual physical and financial conditions, and accordingly in their needs and requirements for social services and facilities. As the majority of the population become older, in the coming super-aged society, separate consideration will have to be given to those who are fit and able to work, and others requiring nursing and care.

Nutrition and diet in Japan have undergone great changes from the post–1945 era of near-starvation to the rich indolence of present affluence. As life-styles in housing, food and clothing have rapidly become westernized, and as society has progressed due to advances in science, the physical build of the Japanese and also the prevalence of non-communicable diseases have approached those of Western people.

It is customary in Japan for women to be in charge of the kitchen, while men take a more passive role concerning what they eat. This tradition is an important health factor.

Membership in various social and occupational groups also greatly affects eating patterns, while in recent years awareness of the effect of eating on health has been steadily growing. The irregular diet of the increasing numbers of elderly living alone is beginning to emerge as a major social problem.

The social environment is thus undergoing rapid change, with the increase in the numbers of working women, the build-up of population in urban areas, the inner city problems, the rise of the nuclear family, and the aging of society.

CARE FOR THE BEDRIDDEN

The home-nursed or bedridden elderly and those suffering from senility are therefore urgently in need of active government policies and local assistance to ensure their reha-bilitation and care, including the planning and construction of the necessary social infrastructure. Furthermore, preventive measures against such debilitating and chronic noncommunicable diseases as cancer, diabetes, atherosclerosis, cardiovascular diseases, rheumatism and osteoporosis are goals that need to be pursued though interdisciplinary efforts.

Medical surveys conducted on a wide scale will supply vital information on the inci-dence and prevalence of these noncommunicable diseases, suggest countermeasures, and make possible the evaluation of policies and economic support measures already taken. These are the foundation stones of disease prevention in an aging society. In step with these population-based medical surveys and monitoring, various regions have recently intro-duced computerized hospital systems and central databanks to maintain patient records.

Finally, basic community planning that promotes both regional cultural development and the individual's quality of life within the community is a truly vital basis for the strategic promotion of health and well-being. The health of each and every man and woman, at every stage of life, is an essential resource to ensure harmony for all on this planet and for the future of mankind.

13

A Gradual Goodbye

THE ECONOMIST

This article addresses the question of an appropriate retirement age (and government pensions). The situations in Great Britain, France, Italy, Germany, Japan, and the United States are examined. The United States is the only nation with a comprehensive law in recruitment, training, promotion, or dismissal on the basis of age. Despite this seemingly progressive legal stance, age discrimination occurs less frequently in the other countries.

Only a generation ago, retirement in rich countries went by the book. The book generally said that men were entitled to a pension at age 65, women sometimes earlier. Until then, most people diligently worked on. In 1970, in most OECD countries 70–80% of men aged 60–64 were still at work.

Twenty years later that proportion had halved. The other half had quietly taken early retirement, often at their employers' suggestion. The arrangement suited both sides. Employers may have wanted to rejuvenate or reduce their workforce, or perhaps even had to close down. Offering older employees an attractive way out minimised the fuss and upheaval. And employees for the most part accepted eagerly, thinking of their neglected spouses, gardens or golf handicaps. Those who were not so eager did not have much choice. Governments, desperate to keep the unemployment figures down colluded by easing the rules for early retirement and disability pensions. And trade unions often accepted the logic of paying off older workers to make room for younger ones, provided the pill could be suitably sweetened.

Today's workers have got into the way of thinking that it will be their turn next. In France, for example, new rules introduced in the 1970s allowed many people to retire at 60. In 1982 the pension age itself was reduced to 60. "Solidarity contracts" in the 1980s allowed many to go at 55. The railway workers, who recently went on strike against the French government's welfare reform plans, bow out as early as 50. In Europe and America an early-retirement culture has taken root.

Source: "A Gradual Goodbye." 1996. *The Economist 338* (January 27), pp. 5–8.

Yet over the past few years many governments have had to rethink. If people even at the official retirement age can now typically expect to live another 15 or 20 years, an early exit might award them half an adult lifetime of economic inactivity. Since their numbers are growing fast, this will soon become unaffordable. So some countries are now raising their official retirement age, though they are treading softly. America, for example, is increasing the age at which it pays a full social security pension from 65 to 67, but in such tiny steps that it will take until 2022. Britain is bringing women's retirement age up to 65, in line with men's, but will not get there until 2020. Other countries, including Germany, Italy and Japan, are moving the same way.

On the face of it, raising the retirement age seems an ideal way of dealing with a bulge of old people. If people are living longer, they should also be fit for work for longer, and so can contribute to the cost of their own good fortune. However, paying pensions later will not necessarily keep people in work. The old are often the first to be made redundant. Once out of a job, they often find it hard to get another one. One future source of jobs for older people—provided they are fit enough—might be the care of the "oldest old," clearly a growth industry; but the pickings elsewhere will be slim.

Prejudice against older people at work is universal. In an opinion poll taken throughout the European Union, 80% of respondents—of all ages—believed that older workers were discriminated against in job recruitment. "Older" can mean as young as 40. Employers may be behaving quite rationally in discriminating. It often costs more to employ older workers than younger ones. Pay may be linked to seniority rather than to performance, and some occupational pension schemes require larger employers' contributions for older employees. Health insurance can also cost more.

But the main reason that employers steer clear of older workers is that they suspect them of not being up to the job. Again there maybe a grain of truth in this. A World Health Organisation (WHO) study of older people's working capacity recently gathered together the biological facts and concluded that "the definition of an ageing worker could be considered to apply from 45 years." Physical performance, at a peak in the early 20s, declines gradually thereafter. Eyesight deteriorates and hearing gets worse. This may matter less as fewer jobs rely on physical strength, but depressingly the WHO also found that "the speed at which information is processed usually slows down substantially in older individuals." On the other hand, "while older managers take more time to reach decisions, they . . . appear to be as competent as younger managers in overall decision-making."

IN PRAISE OF OLDER WORKERS

According to many employers, older workers—say those over 50—are more reliable, conscientious and loyal than younger ones. They tend to be good at dealing with people and happy to work in teams, though, less likely to turn in a sparkling, rather than merely competent, performance. They are also considered less adaptable than younger workers, slower to grasp new ideas and, most damagingly, less likely to be able to use new technology such as computers. That is not surprising: older employees everywhere are last in the queue for training of any kind. Most employers do not bother to offer it, and employees are afraid to ask.

To some extent, older workers can compensate for their slower actions by experience. In one much-quoted American study of typists aged between 19 and 72, the older women managed to work as fast as the younger ones, despite slower responses, simply by processing longer chunks of text in one go. In any case, differences in performance within each age group are far larger than those between age groups. Since older workers are not a homogeneous group, age is not much use for predicting how someone will perform in a job.

Some employers are taking the hint. In Britain, B&Q, a do-it-yourself chain, has tried staffing some of its stores with over-50s, who are more experienced and better at dealing with customers than younger workers. Sainsbury and Tesco, two large supermarket chains, have recently been recruiting staff up to 69, partly in response to labour shortages. In France, Aérospatiale has introduced incentives for its experienced staff to stay on until 60, and at Société Générale Sucrière employees between 55 and 60 in part-time retirement come to work during the beet harvest. In America, the Travelers Insurance Group offers pensioners the opportunity to come back part-time. There are other examples, but not many: the same names crop up over and over.

Legislation seems unlikely to help spread this good practice. America is the only country with a comprehensive law against discrimination in recruitment, training, promotion or dismissal on the basis of age. Its Age Discrimination in Employment Act, introduced in 1967, originally applied only to people aged between 40 and 65 but was later extended without limit, doing away with mandatory retirement on age grounds altogether. Yet in reviewing the legislation, the American Congress concluded that age discrimination remains an obstacle to employment for older workers, and that "statutory provisions . . . remain incomplete and somewhat ineffective." Opinion surveys show that 80% of Americans—the same proportion as in Europe—believe that most employers discriminate against older workers. Legislation may merely have made employers more careful to hide their prejudices.

Other countries have the odd law here and there, but nothing as comprehensive as America. The only country that has incorporated specific protection against age discrimination is Spain. In France, a legal ban on age limits in job advertisements has been in place for some years, but is widely acknowledged to be ineffective. Something may be done at the European Union level when the Maastricht treaty is revised later this year, perhaps in the form of a general article that would prohibit discrimination on a number of grounds including age. The hope is that this will help to create a climate of opinion against ageism.

GENTLY DOES IT

Changing entrenched attitudes will take time. "The age of retirement will have to go up," says Winfried Schmähl, an expert on work for older people at Bremen University. "People understand what needs to be done—they are just not doing it yet." Another German academic, Gerd Naegele of the Institute of Gerontology at Dortmund University, agrees that the lead time must be long: "It takes 10–15 years for the business culture to adjust." But he also accepts that there are real problems employing older workers: "Many jobs have become psychologically more stressful, even if they are physically easier, and older people often find it difficult to handle that stress."

With retirement ages going up, many more older people are likely to run out of formal, conventional employment some time before they are able to draw their pensions. They will need "bridge" jobs, which are likely to be less prestigious, less well-paid and less skilled than the jobs they had in their main careers. They can also be hard to find. One way out, used widely in Japan and the United States, is for older workers to turn self-employed, usually in the same broad area that they worked in before. This can offer a dignified, flexible way to keep going.

The idea of making retirement less categorical and more gradual is catching on. In Britain, the Carnegie Inquiry into the Third Age, reporting in 1993, recommended flexible arrangements for older workers, including partial retirement, out-placements and secondments. In a recent report Geneviève Reday-Mulvey, of the International Association for the Study of Insurance Economics, and Lei Delsen of Nijmegen University argue strongly against what they call "guillotine retirement." Instead, they advocate a flexible transition period between a full-time career and full retirement, typically lasting about five years, which can both spread the pensions burden and give individuals more choice. The spread of part-time employment in a number of countries may offer opportunities along these lines.

Within Europe, such a policy has been successfully practiced in Sweden for 20 years, and kept more older people at work than elsewhere in Europe, even through a severe recession. Sweden suffers less from age discrimination than other European countries, and is more used to flexible working, to part-time jobs and to state labour-market subsidies. But the scheme proved too good to last: faced with mounting budget deficits, the Swedish government is phasing out the financial incentives by 2000. Perhaps by then the Swedes will take gradual retirement for granted.

Of all the rich countries, Japan keeps its people (or at least its men) at work longest. Although at present the mandatory pension age is only 60, more than a third of Japanese men over 65 are still at work. Since life expectancies in Japan are now the highest in the world—76 at birth for a man, 82 for a woman—that may be a good thing. In a country which by 2030 will have some 32 [million] over-65s, well over a quarter of the population, it would be unwise to encourage expectations of early retirement. To reinforce the message, Japan has reformed its pension system so that by early next century the basic state pension starts at 65, and early retirement will become less attractive. The government also offers various subsidies for firms employing people over 60.

Making this work has required flexibility all round. For example, the regular pay rises that in Japan go with increasing seniority now mostly stop at 50. Workers who retire at the mandatory retirement age of 60 are often re-employed either by their firms or by a subsidiary, but this always involves a big cut in pay and sometimes a move to part-time work. Many retirees become self-employed. In a survey of Japanese employees, some 60% said they wanted to go on working even after 65, possibly part-time—not so much for financial reasons, but because they thought it would help them maintain good health and remain active in society. Perhaps these long-lived people know something the West does not. But perhaps the size of their prospective pension has something to do with it after all.

PART THREE

Institutional Problems

SECTION 6

Families

THE UNITED STATES CONTEXT

The situation of families in the United States is similar to that found in other industrialized nations: a high divorce rate, both spouses in the workforce, and a relatively high number of single parents. Families in the United States, compared to families in similar countries, differ considerably, however, in the relative lack of support they receive from the government and from their employers. Some examples:

• The United States has the highest incidence of unwed teenage births of any of the industrialized countries. Two obvious reasons for this are that it is much more difficult to obtain contraceptives, and sex education is woefully inadequate in the United States. About 60 percent of all pregnancies in the United States are unplanned, occurring because contraceptives are misused or unreliable, or not used at all. One reason is cost: a month's supply of oral contraceptives costs about $13 from a local Planned Parenthood clinic. In sharp contrast, a woman in the Netherlands can purchase *a year's supply* of oral contraceptives for about $8. The free distribution of condoms in schools and health clinics is challenged by many in the United States because they believe that it leads to sexual promiscuity. In keeping with that belief, the 1996 welfare law included $250 million to states for sex education provided that information about contraception not be provided and that it be replaced by an abstinence-only message. In those countries with cheaper contraceptives and a fully informed sex education, teens who are likely to be as sexually active as those in the United States have much lower teen pregnancy rates (e.g., half ours in England and Wales and one-tenth ours in the Netherlands) (Pollitt, 1996).

• The maternity and nursing benefits given to working mothers in the United States are the least generous in the industrialized world (Grimsley, 1998). A United Nations agency found that 80 percent of the 152 countries studied provided *paid* maternity leave to female workers. Working mothers in France and Germany, for example, receive 100 percent of their wages for as much as twenty-six weeks (Jones, 1998). The United States merely "permits" twelve weeks of *unpaid* maternity leave.

• Child care is imperative for families when both parents are in the workforce or for working single parents. Child care in the United States is often expensive and difficult to find. By contrast, in France virtually all three-, four-, and five-year-olds attend preschools at no or minimal charge. For younger children, daycare facilities are heavily subsidized by the government (Folbre, 1995:3.16).

REFERENCES

Folbre, Nancy, and the Center for Popular Economics. 1995. *The New Field Guide to the U.S. Economy.* New York: The New Press.

Grimsley, Kirstin Downey. 1998. "Not Much in the Family Way," *Washington Post National Weekly Edition* (February 23):35.

Jones, Del. 1998. "Drive for Paid Family Leave Raises Cost Issues," *USA Today* (March 3):3B.

Pollitt, Katha. 1996. "Adoption Fantasy," *The Nation* (July 8):9.

14

The Nordic Countries:
Public Programs for Dealing
with the Consequences of Divorce

WILLIAM J. GOODE

The Nordic nations (Denmark, Norway, Sweden, and Finland) are expe-
riencing the same divorce rates as the rest of the industrialized world.
These Nordic countries are dealing with the effects of high divorce rates
(especially the special needs of the children of divorce) in a more suc-
cessful way than the United States or the other countries of Europe.

In the Nordic nations—Denmark, Norway, Sweden, Finland—the overlap of legal institutions over the centuries has been profound enough to justify considering them together.
For four centuries Norway was under the Danish crown, and for most of the nineteenth
century its legal system was continued within a personal union with Sweden. Finland
was under the Swedish crown for four centuries, and kept much of its internal autonomy
and Swedish law for more than a century after it was annexed by Russia in 1809. Iceland (not analyzed here) was under Danish rule from the fourteenth century until the end
of World War I. In addition, family law in all these countries was strongly shaped by the
dominance of the Lutheran church.

   As among other nations with closely intertwined destinies, stereotypes and counter-
stereotypes abound. Since Sweden has had more economic success in the outside world,
its "national character" has attracted more attention from both journalists and serious
students. Popenoe, for example, takes these stereotypes seriously enough to present confirming data for several of them: independence, personal privacy, social reserve, avoid-
ance of conflict, social rationality.[1] It is widely believed in addition that Sweden has a
high suicide rate while Norway does not, though in fact Sweden has a lower rate than
some other European countries. Perhaps because Norway developed industrially rather
late, it is sometimes thought to have a more conservative set of attitudes, especially with

Source: Excerpt from William J. Goode. 1993. *World Changes in Divorce Patterns* (pp. 79–83). New Haven, CT:
Yale University Press.

respect to family, but that is so only by comparison with other Nordic countries, not with other Western European countries.

Even if we leave aside such stereotypes, there are many differences among these nations. Nevertheless, they do seem to be moving in a common direction as they face the problems created by modern divorce trends.

Denmark not long ago seems to have become much freer in its sexual attitudes and with Sweden led the movement toward widespread unmarried cohabitation. As to the participation of women in the labor force, which in the view of many analysts is the major factor that has increased divorce rates generally in Europe, the percentage of women in Sweden's labor force was relatively low until the 1950s. It has, however, recently risen to among the highest among Western nations (for example, over 90 percent for mothers with one child).[2] On the other hand, 60 percent of women in the Swedish labor force work part-time. By contrast, a higher percentage of all Finnish women work full-time and have done so for many decades—indeed, since the turn of the century.

Norwegian women show a very different pattern: they were less likely to be counted in the labor force, but in fact far more of them were working independently in various forms of domestic skilled or artisan labor, since so many of the husbands were away from home for long periods of time, in forestry, fishing, and shipping.

But none of those stereotypes or real differences helps us to understand why all these nations have been moving toward family institutions that seem to be guided by a very different set of goals from those of the rest of Europe—or perhaps they are simply in the vanguard.

Whatever the reasons, the shared legal and moral background of these countries combined with continued joint planning to move them more closely together over the past four decades. They have looked to one another for counsel and cooperation for many years, probably in a more intimate and effective way than the European Economic Community has done up to this date. It also seems likely that some of their common social patterns have contributed to the strong upward movement in the divorce rates over the past two decades, above those of most other European nations.

It is not entirely clear why this rise, shared with other nations, has happened exactly in this period. It does not seem likely that any of the simple explanations used so widely in causal analyses of divorce trends is adequate. And Nordic citizens do not (in contrast with those of the United States and Europe generally) seem to judge their divorce patterns as evidence of a general breakdown of the family or of moral values.

Of course, all of these countries have been industrializing and urbanizing, and all show a rise in the percentage of women in the labor force, a higher educational level for women, a declining rate of marriage and fertility, and so on. As usual, Sweden is in the vanguard (though its fertility is higher than Germany's and, indeed, than that of many other European countries including Italy). But though the rise in the percentage of women in the labor force does generally correlate with an increase in the divorce rate, as early as 1910 some 39 percent of the Finnish labor force outside agriculture was female, and this appears to have had no effect on the divorce rate at all.[3] As Popenoe remarks of Sweden, "many of the typical U.S. explanations cannot be applied"—teenage pregnancy (it is very low), poverty, income instability, inter-ethnic marriage, or high residential mobility.

As it is too soon to be certain, I speculate that these countries are following a very different route from other Western nations, and thus the causal links seem somewhat different, though it is conceivable that other countries will also begin to move eventually toward the Nordic position. For although three trends are evident—cohabitation has risen along with divorce, the illegitimacy ratios (the percentages of births technically outside wedlock) have increased, and marriage has been postponed more and more (over one-third of Swedish women have not married by age 50)—the response to them has been unique. These countries have continued to fashion a complex set of socioeconomic supports for the inevitable problems these trends have generated. Sweden often takes the first new steps in such programs, but it should be noted that others are not far behind. For example, the 1987 Finnish Marriage Act expresses, albeit a few years later, the ideas that have shaped Swedish family programs as well.[4] By contrast, the United States especially—and other Western nations to a lesser extent—has expended far more moral indignation on these problems and far less thought and tax money on working out solutions for them.

As noted before, all Western countries have been moving toward a less familistic set of attitudes and behaviors and toward greater individual investments in self, career, and even personal growth and goals. But in the Nordic countries this shift has been accompanied by a steady attention to a *collective,* national sense of responsibility for mothers and children, illegitimate or not, divorced or not—in fact, for all citizens. They have also been more willing to accept the higher tax burden that decision necessarily creates.

If this interpretation is correct, the seemingly parallel curves in many of the family statistics of the Nordic and other Western countries conceal a very different direction of basic movement.

It is especially in these countries that cohabitation, because it is simultaneously unrecorded and so much accepted as a near-equivalent of legal marriage, creates real pitfalls for an adequate understanding of divorce data. Yet, precisely because there are so many supports for the problems that both married and unmarried couples face, their situations are very similar. We can often learn where and whether differences do exist because much research has been done on cohabitating couples.

Consequently it is often possible to de-emphasize the differences in marital status and focus instead on the dynamics of the family processes. Indeed it is one of the goals of the laws of the Nordic nations to pay less attention to family status and more to the individual's problem. For example, births out of wedlock (the illegitimacy *ratio*) comprised over 50 percent of the total births in Sweden in 1987, as they did in Iceland (in Norway, 31 percent; in Denmark, 44 percent). In almost all these cases, however, the father is publicly and socially known, and he is also held responsible. On the other hand, the *rate* of illegitimacy (the number of illegitimate births per 1000 women) among young women (including teenagers) is very low. (That is, the illegitimacy ratio is high because so many young women who bear children are not yet married, but their birth *rate* per thousand population is low.) That ratio is higher in both Denmark and Sweden than in the United States (except among Afro-Americans).

Similarly, the ratio of divorces per 100 marriages each year is high because so many in the younger years have not yet married and thus do not enter the divorce figures; but marriages are fragile. Over the two decades between the mid-1960s and the mid-1980s, the median age at first marriage rose almost five years.[5] In 1988, the official Swedish estimate of the total eventual divorce rate for that year's cohort was 41 percent, lower than that of the United States. If we add in all of the dissolutions of cohabiting couples the *total* rate was of course still higher but that step would also increase the total rate of dissolution in the United States as well, so that Popenoe's suggestion that the total Swedish rate may be the highest in the world seems unlikely.[6] To obtain such figures, of course, special surveys must be used, since neither the formation nor the dissolution of cohabiting households is officially recorded.

In general, the public stance of the commissions that formulate Nordic legal policies for family affairs is that these decisions are private and should not affect the standing or the rights of the people who enter or leave such relationships. Correspondingly, no one is to lose any state supports, job rights, parental allowances, or other economic privileges on account of cohabitation, because all these rights are assigned to the *individual*.[7] The compassionate effort to make sure that no one suffers because of domestic events such as divorce, having a child or being a child of divorce, or living with someone without the legal protection of marriage also makes the legal bonds of marriage much less relevant and much less binding. The child is protected because the father is known and can be made responsible. If he cannot meet these responsibilities, the state fills the financial gap. It should be repeated that these protections were generally put into effect earlier in Sweden and Denmark than in Norway and Finland, but the trends are the same. The mother receives the same help whether she is legally married or not. Then why marry?

Several ironies are evident in these new patterns. For example, it seems likely that these supports were created to strengthen the family, but as a collectivity they may well have weakened it. Family decisions are judged to be private, but state policies offer a collective safety net for such decisions. This is in contrast to the United States, where the official rhetoric as well as the law asserts that the state has a right to be concerned about family matters, but in fact the government does not create adequate programs for helping those who suffer disadvantages because of private family decisions.

In all countries, the husband's wages on average are higher than the wife's, but in the Nordic countries, the state support system, coupled with a more equitable wage distribution for all, compensates for that wage differential to some extent, and at a minimum reduces the losses the wife might otherwise have to experience when a marital dissolution occurs. It seems reasonable of course that as a consequence of this lowered threat of loss the divorce rates will be higher than elsewhere.

On the other hand, although such state programs doubtless help to decrease the marriage rate and increase the dissolution rates of both divorce and cohabitation, it can also be argued that since the other Western nations showed the same trends at the same time *without* such supporting programs, the Nordic programs may be no more than a wise response to problems that were arising anyway. That is, those programs may have had at most a minor causal effect.

NOTES

1. David Popenoe, *Distributing the Nest* (New York: Aldine DeGruyter, 1988), pp. 248–53.
2. Britta Hoem and Jan M. Hoem, "The Swedish Family," *J. Fam. Issues 9* (1988), p. 408. By U.S. standards this Swedish mode of calculation is somewhat inflationary.
3. Elena Haavio-Mannila and Riita Jellinoja, "Changes in the Life Patterns of Families in Finland," Vienna Center, *Current Research Reports,* vol. I, no. 1, ISSC (Vienna: European Coordination Center for Research and Documentation in Social Science, 1981), p. 6.
4. Matti Sovolainen, "Finland: The New Marriage Act Enters into Force," *J. Family Law 27:* 1 (1988–89), pp. 127–41.
5. Hoem and Hoem, "Swedish Family," p. 405.
6. David Popenoe, "Family Decline in the Welfare State," *Public Interest 102* (1991), p. 67.
7. Hoem and Hoem, "Swedish Family," p. 897.

15

It's About Time: Will Europe Solve the Work/Family Dilemma?

DEBORAH FIGART AND ELLEN MUTARI

The article examines the impact of paid family leave policies and shorter work hours on working women and parents. Unlike the United States, European countries long ago pioneered alternative programs aimed at helping working families. These programs have been unsuccessful, however, in reducing occupational sex segregation for women. The authors suggest combining public policies that shorten the work week with the social goal of shared responsibility between men and women for work in the home.

U.S. workers often gaze longingly at labor policies enacted across the Atlantic, especially in Sweden, a democratic socialist mecca. But all 15 European Union countries, including Sweden, offer a cautionary tale for those hoping paid family leave policies and a shorter work week will both help overworked parents and enhance women's position in the labor force.

In Europe, working mothers piece together their own solutions to the work/family dilemma based in part on national work time and family leave policies that are generous by U.S. standards. But these important policies seem to be reinforcing sex segregation of jobs as men fail to take advantage of them. Women, meanwhile, are finding it easiest to work part-time or take extended leaves, surrendering better-paying full-time jobs once they become mothers. This solution offers few answers for women supporting families on their own, who need full-time wages and time for family responsibilities.

Even worse, European women have been thrust into the center of a classic clash over work time between a male-led labor movement and management. Unions and employers in Germany and elsewhere are agreeing to work reorganization policies that limit the official work week while increasing overtime. Men have the social backing to stay late at the job or deal with increasingly erratic work schedules. But married women, with

Source: Deborah Figart and Ellen Mutari. 1998. *Dollars and Sense 215* (January/February), pp. 27–31.

their socially supported commitment to their families, are pushed even further into the part-time workforce.

That's why European feminists urge work redistribution schemes that combine a shorter work week with shared responsibility for work in the home. This approach offers more promise than policies implicitly or explicitly promoting overtime for men and part-time work for women. In particular, working women want a shorter work day, not "flexible scheduling" of the work week if that means unpredictable work hours or working four long, 10-hour days. But even far-sighted Sweden chose to emphasize family leave policies over shorter work days to solve the time crunch. And now that the debate over working time has moved to the level of European Union institutions, feminist proposals aimed at promoting gender equity once again are being eclipsed.

FAMILY LEAVE IN SWEDEN

Sweden is the poster child of alternative work schedules, including the shorter work week. Its family leave policy is one of the most generous in the world, allowing parents 18 months off—paid. Historically Sweden has been a leader in women's employment trends: Swedish women first entered the trades and sales occupations as early as 1810. In 1845 they secured the right to inherit property. Laws limiting married women from working were dropped in 1938. By the 1980s, the percentage of men and women in the labor force was almost identical.

In most EU countries, unions took the lead in backing shorter work weeks as a way to generate more jobs and reduce Europe's persistently high unemployment. In Sweden, gender equity, rather than job creation, has been central to the shorter work week movement. In the 1970s, the women's divisions of both the trade union federation and the Social Democratic Party (SDP) backed a six-hour day and 30-hour week for both men and women, explicitly as ways of achieving gender equity. Everybody—men, women, fathers and mothers—would work less. It was an attempt to thwart the traditional path of women who commonly reduce their ties to the labor market when they become mothers. The SDPs women's division has been leading the charge for this policy ever since.

Despite this support, both the SDP and nonsocialist governments chose to expand parental leave as a means of encouraging women's participation in the labor force. They paid little attention to proposals to reduce the work week. In 1974, the Swedish government began offering paid leave for the birth or sickness of a child, gradually extending the available leave time from six to 18 months. The government replaces the lost paycheck in full for a parent on leave in a two-earner household, while single earner households receive a low, flat rate. The policy encourages more women to join the labor force at least part-time because it does not require both parents to work full-time to receive the higher benefits.

In 1979, Sweden broadened its parental leave policies, allowing parents to shorten their daily hours (with a corresponding reduction in pay) until their child is ten to twelve years old. Despite the gender-neutral wording of the law and efforts encouraging men

Germany vs. France

While Germany and France have very different histories in reducing the work week and allowing flexible work schedules, they have ended up with similar gaps in men and women's work time. Men work an average of about 41 hours a week in both countries, and women work an average of about 33 hours a week in Germany and 35 hours a week in France.

Work time was reduced in Germany due to unions' bargaining, while in France work time was reduced due to government legislation. And while France has historically pressured EU institutions to incorporate policies in pursuit of gender equality, Germany lagged in this area.

The German union IG Metall negotiated a 1993 bargaining agreement with Volkswagen for a four-day, 28.8-hour week with a 20% cut in earnings. An industry-wide agreement in 1994 implemented a 30-hour week, also with a cut in pay. In exchange for shorter hours, the union conceded to employer demands for greater flexibility in organizing working time. Employers won the right to negotiate hours on a company-level based on firm and even individual plant needs—a radical departure from the traditional practice of negotiating hours in an entire sector. Other employer followed suit. The result has been increased overtime and weekend work (for men) and part-time jobs (for women).

France implemented the EU's Working Time Directive using a five-year plan, commonly called the Robien law, passed in December 1993. The French program includes direct government subsidies to employers to encourage worksharing, and the "annualization" of hours. Government assistance goes to employers who reduce work time (along with pay) by at least 15%, hire new employees to make up the work, and maintain the same size workforce for three years. After the Socialist Party, in coalition with other leftists, won a parliamentary victory in last June's elections, the French government newly committed itself to the goal of a 35-hour work week. In October, a National Conference on Employment devised a proposal for parliament to consider.

France, has pursued these policies entirely separately from it's five-year program "in favor of family life" that will be fully implemented by 1999. This law aims to "achieve a better reconciliation between family and working life through a reorganization of parents' working time." Most of its measures follow the Swedish model of encouraging, through subsidies, part-time employment for parents of young children. It also permits the parent of a sick child to take leave or to shift to part-time employment for 6 months to one year.

to take advantage of it, only 6% of leave-takers are men, a figure that has remained unchanged for 15 years. And women tend to take the full time allowed, while men use it for a much shorter time.

Encouraged by these policies, women in Sweden primarily use part-time jobs to balance work and family responsibilities. In the end, most Swedish women become part-time employees after their first child is born. Even women working in male-dominated fields tend to shift into part-time, dead-end jobs in female-dominated sectors once they become mothers. This way they avoid the penalties and discrimination that arise if they take leaves from their nontraditional jobs.

Many feminists support family leave and shorter hours for *both* parents as ways to maintain women's connection to paid work over their lifetime. Yet generous parental leave policies seem only to have reinforced women's occupational segregation in Sweden, which is worse than in many other European countries. Swedish policies have given women significant gains for their home life, but remain a mixed blessing at work.

SHORTER HOURS FOR ALL?

While Sweden accommodated traditional gender roles by emphasizing family leave, feminist-backed shorter work week policies try to change the "male model" of full-time employment. From this point of view, the only way to achieve gender equity in the workplace—and home—in the long run is to reduce the number of hours in everybody's standard work week. This is a position increasingly heard in countries with high proportions of women working part-time, not just Sweden, but the Netherlands and Germany as well.

The Social Democratic Union of Swedish Women was a pioneer of this position in the 1970s. Ylva Ericsson, a former staffer, pointed out that " . . . if everybody gainfully employed today were to work the same amount of time, Sweden would have a work week of just under thirty hours." The Dutch Emancipation Council, along with activists in the women's movement there, endorsed a shorter work week in 1989. In 1992, Frank Boddendijk, a member of the Dutch Council, claimed, "As long as men still have full-time jobs and women only part-time jobs, there will be no real equality, since in that case women have the full responsibility for domestic labour, including child care." You hear the same perspective from Friederike Maier, a consultant on women's issues to the European Commission.

Despite these feminist voices, gender equity has not been the driving force behind efforts to shorten the standard work week in Europe. Spearheaded by the European Trade Union Confederation, unions argued that a shorter work week would force employers to hire more workers; the goal was to share and redistribute employment, even if those with jobs had to sacrifice some income.

The first real breakthrough came in 1984, when a major industrial action by Germany's largest union, IG Metall, forced Volkswagen and other employers to reduce the work week from 40 hours to 38.5 hours in the male-dominated industries of printing and metalworking. This standard was extended to other sectors of the economy in 1985 and 1986. In 1987, IG Metall won a further cut to 37 hours by 1989; other industries again followed suit.

Inspired by these successes, British unions began to press for a 35-hour work week in 1989. By March 1990, over 50 companies, including British Aerospace and Rolls Royce, agreed to a enact a 37-hour work week.

That Germany gave rise to the strongest working time movement is not surprising. Germany has strong, centralized collective bargaining. Policies initiated by key unions tend to set standards for other workers. That the movement originated in male-dominated industries sensitive to the ups and downs of the economy is also not surprising. Working women have been more sheltered from the brunt of unemployment because they work largely in the service sector, where jobs are growing.

There's no fairy tale ending to these campaigns. What began in the 80's as a drive by unions to reduce working hours has been usurped in the 90's by employers seeking to improve competitiveness through "flexibility." Employers have won the right to shift

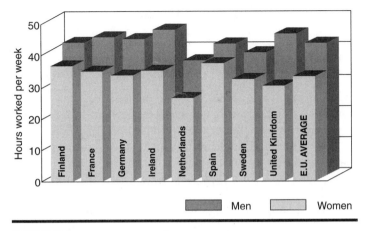

FIGURE 15.1

Usual Weekly Hours in the European Union by Gender, 1995

Not included: Austria, Belgium, Denmark, Italy, Luxembourg, Portugal, Greece.

Source: Eurostat, *Labour Force Survey*, 1995

schedules of workers at will and demand overtime, even as the official full-time work week becomes shorter. Flexibility will solve Europe's unemployment problem, employers claim, by enabling them to be more responsive to changes in demand for their products. They could increase the pace of work when demand is up, and ask for fewer hours from their workers when demand is down. The freedom employers have in setting hours in the United States, they say, is one of the reasons unemployment has dropped here. While the United States requires employers to pay overtime for wage workers working over 40 hours per week, in continental Europe (though not the United Kingdom) the limits on overtime have been stricter. European countries—including Austria, Belgium, Finland, France, Germany, Ireland, Italy, Luxembourg, Netherlands, Norway, Spain, and Sweden—should not restrict the amount of overtime that can be taken on a daily, weekly, or monthly basis, the employers insist. Nor should these countries require that employers give workers time off in exchange for overtime.

Along with expanded overtime, employers and policy-makers are selling part-time work to women workers. "Over a short period of time, part-time work has been transformed from the Cinderella in the kitchens of the labour force to the Prince Charming of new employment initiatives," say Ursula Barry and Pauline Jackson, two feminist writers from Northern Ireland. Part-time jobs do hold appeal for many working women. A Eurostat press release put an optimistic spin on the findings of their Labour Force Survey, headlining that "16% of EU Workers are Part-Time; Most are happy that way." But part-time work also suits employers' desire to adjust hours of work and hold down wage costs. Unfortunately, as long as men are pressured to work long hours and cannot participate equally in child care and domestic chores, women's desire to work part-time is not truly voluntary. They also will continue to take on most of the housework.

DIRECTIVES FROM EUROPE

In 1993, the Brussels-based European Union adopted a directive for its members to reduce the length of the work week and allow businesses to summon more overtime. This Directive on Working Time is silent on gender issues—at least on the surface. But by facilitating overtime, without dealing with issues of part-time employment (that will be in a separate directive), it reinforces the same division between male and female workers as did the national initiatives.

The Directive on Working Time is the result of efforts to harmonize employment conditions in EU countries and create a unified market. Constructing the policy was extremely controversial. Not only did the agendas of unions and employers differ, the governments of member countries had strong opinions on what the policy should look like. The British government, for instance, staunchly opposed any mandate regulating working time.

EU countries finally reached a compromise in 1992, after two years of discussion. To permit passage by a qualified majority (rather than unanimity) of the Council of Ministers under European Union rules, the directive was categorized as a health and safety issue. It established health and safety standards for the organization of working time, including minimum periods of daily rest, weekly rest, and annual leave; breaks; and maximum weekly working time. The Directive also addresses night work, shift work, and other work patterns.

Employer organizations managed to include provisions undermining what have been strong institutional constraints on overtime throughout the European continent. They won the flexibility in soliciting overtime they long sought. The cornerstone of their efforts was the so-called "annualization of hours." This policy—captured in "Article 6"—allows employees to work overtime so long as their weekly hours add up to a national standard that is no more than 48 hours, but averaged over a four month time period. That period is potentially expandable to six months. Moreover, the fine print of the directive allows member governments to permit employers to negotiate time periods of as much as twelve months—" annualization." Finally, member states have the option to ignore Article 6 completely, as long as they ensure that workers have acquiesced to the excess overtime in advance and employers do not subject a worker "to any detriment" for refusing long hours.

Negotiations for a European directive protecting part-time and other "atypical" workers—often women—finally reopened in 1996 after languishing for two decades following objections by the British and German governments. By June 1997, representatives of labor, employers, and European governmental institutions devised a tentative proposal. It would prohibit discrimination against part-time workers, giving them the same rights to training, holidays, and social security benefits as full-time workers. Emilio Gabaglio, President of the European Trade Union Confederation, hailed the agreement as guaranteeing "that part-timers can no longer be treated as second-class workers."

European feminists attribute unions' new defense of part-time workers to their desire to recruit them as members. It's a defensive tactic initiated after a long period of hostility. Kea Tijdens, a Dutch feminist economist, compares the shift to unions' sudden support of equal pay for equal work earlier in this century. Then too, unions wanted to prevent employers from replacing their male members with cheaper female workers. Gender equity was and is not their primary concern.

THE VIEW FROM THE MEMBER STATES

The European Union's 15 members enjoy considerable leeway in how they implement these EU directives. They need only stay within the standards set out in the directive. Despite this leeway, in country after country, observers are noting a similar trade-off. Unions are giving in to employers' desire for flexibility in exchange for work redistribution policies that save jobs. As part of this compromise, unions are accepting the expansion of both part-time and overtime work, giving control over work schedules to employers rather than individual employees and their representatives.

This compromise only reinforces a Europe in which gender roles are defined not by whether a man or woman has a job, but by the amount of time men and women spend on the job. Almost one of three working women in the European Union works part-time, compared with only one of 20 men. Male workers spend more time at their jobs than women (see Figure 15.1). The difference is greatest in the United Kingdom, where men's overtime is firmly established. It is also high in the Netherlands, where the majority of women work part-time. The gap is narrowest in Finland, Austria, and the southern European countries. Southern Europe generally has a more traditional gender division of labor; the relatively fewer women in the labor force are ones most in need of full-time jobs, such as the unmarried or poor. In twelve of the fifteen countries, men work over forty hours per week. Although men's usual weekly hours are less than the newly-legislated 48-hour threshold, overtime is concentrated in male dominated sectors such as manufacturing.

Increasingly, feminist and labor activists are accepting attempts to cushion rather than fight the expanding number of part-time jobs. They argue that upgrading the working conditions of part-time workers will concretely improve the lives of European working women. However, the proliferation of part-time work and overtime still encourages individual solutions to the problems of balancing work and family. As European countries adhere to the patterns established in the U.S. and U. K, new obstacles are being created to women's full and equitable integration into the workforce and men's sharing of domestic labor.

Public policy provides only a partial solution. Working women must demand that male members of their households contribute to the work of raising families, as well as pressure policymakers and employers. Unless that is done, there is no assurance that shortening paid work time for all will succeed in redistributing work between men and women.

REFERENCES

Eurostat, *Labour Force Survey: Results 1995. European Industrial Relations Review,* various issues.
Pacricia Hewitt, *About Time. The Revolution in Work and Family Life.* London: Rivers Oram Press, 1993.
Sara Horrell and Jill Rubery, "Gender and Working Time: An Analysis of Employers' Working-Time Policies," *Cambridge Journal of Economics,* Vol. 15, December 1991.
Gisela Kaplan, *Contemporary Western European Feminism.* New York: New York University Press, 1992.

16

Same-Sex Spouses in Canada

E. J. GRAFF

This article discusses the 1999 Canadian Supreme Court decision rec-ognizing same-sex partners as spouses for purposes of family law. Gay activists in Canada were successful in bringing about the change in law because they didn't argue that same-sex couples should be allowed to marry. The author discusses the possibility of adopting a similar strat-egy in the United States to gain legal recognition for same-sex partners.

On May 20, leaving its southern neighbor in the dust, Canada took a breathtaking leap forward in lesbian and gay rights. In what one advocate calls a "monumental" decision, Canada's Supreme Court declared 8 to 1 that for the purposes of family law, same-sex partners must be considered "spouses."

That doesn't mean Canadian lesbian and gay couples can now marry. Since 1978 Canada's provincial and federal family laws have recognized two categories for different-sex couples: full marriage, for which you register and exchange vows, and "common-law marriage," imposed on pairs who live together "conjugally" for several years. The deci-sion, which confers common-law status on cohabiting same-sex couples, is the cul-mination of Canadian activists' decadelong strategy of appealing to Canada's young Constitution and Equality Charter—which guarantees the right to "human dignity"—to win, one after another, "common law" responsibility and benefits for same-sex pairs.

M v. H started out as one of those cases: After M moved out of their ten-year rela-tionship, H changed the locks on their properties, took M's name off their joint busi-ness and warned their accountant and clients not to speak to M. Instead of the six months it would have taken to clear things up had H and M been male and female, it took six years in front of thirty judges for M to get the right to a family law judge's oversight. But now Canada's Supreme Court has ruled definitively that same-sex partners must be included under the term "spouse"—so for better or worse, Canadian lesbian and gay couples now have to worry about such things as alimony, child support, shared taxes and separation oversight, while gaining the rights to shared pensions, wrongful-death

Source: E. J. Graff. 1999. *The Nation* (July 12), pp. 23–24.

benefits, immigration, hospital visitation and much more. The decision's wording was so strong that every Canadian provincial government but Alberta—and the Canadian federal government as well—has agreed to open those second-tier spousal rights and responsibilities to same-sex partners.

How did Canada's gay activists bring this about? In part, by avoiding the veil-trailing, hymen-breaking, hysteria-inducing M-word. "We argued throughout the case that this had nothing to do with marriage," says Martha McCarthy, M's Toronto-based counsel. That meant the Canadian court could stay away from a word that turns out to be electrically charged, so dense with religious and historical symbolism that linking it with same-sex couples makes otherwise fair-minded people blanch. In fact, while the Canadian federal government agreed to amend its laws to count same-sex partners as common-law "spouses," it also voted to ban same-sex partners from "marriage"—despite a June 1999 *Globe and Mail* survey, which found that 53 percent of Canadians are willing to say "I do" to same-sex marriage.

That's what's happening in most of the West: Courts and legislatures are granting piecemeal or de facto or second-tier recognition—and then inching forward toward marriage. After a few years with a second-tier status, the Netherlands may soon be the world's first nation to offer same-sex couples full marriage—even use of the wedding-cake word. The Scandinavian countries have a special status for same-sex couples called "registered partnership," which includes almost every marriage responsibility and benefit, and which most citizens call "gay marriage." South Africa's ruling African National Congress formally endorses same-sex marriage, and its courts are steadily recognizing one right and responsibility after another. Hungary's common-law marriage includes same-sex couples. In early June, the legislature in New South Wales, Australia's most populous state, amended its De Facto Relationships Act to cover same-sex as well as different-sex couples. Finland, the Czech Republic, France, Spain and Germany are all seriously debating something similar. Other Western countries with specific same-sex partnership recognitions include England, Israel, Brazil, New Zealand and two Spanish provinces.

And the United States? Our country has passed laws—both at the federal level and in twenty-nine states—forbidding recognition of same-sex marriage, laws that are being used to threaten even the most toothless domestic-partnership statutes.

So should American lesbian and gay activists be adopting the Canadian strategy—delaying the push for full marriage, instead picking off individual rights and benefits in one suit after another? It might not be possible here; the United States is a much rougher playing field. We have no constitutional protection for "human dignity." Our states have spent this century dismantling—instead of creating—common-law marriage forms, so we have no recent legal history of recognizing families that don't start with wedding bells. And, perhaps most important, ours is the only Western country with a powerful obstractionist, fundamentalist bloc. The United Church of Canada (the country's largest Protestant denomination, which includes the Methodists, Presbyterians and Congregationalists) actually testified in favor of opening spousal recognition to same-sex partners. The Roman Catholic Archbishop of Toronto, Aloysius Cardinal Ambrozic, issued a statement saying that *M v. H* "cannot be good"—but added that Canada should offer "basic legal protections to individuals involved in non-traditional domestic relationships." Imagine that from John Cardinal O'Connor.

Besides, according to Evan Wolfson, director of the New York City–based Lambda Legal Defense and Education Fund's Marriage Project and co-counsel in the Hawaii marriage case *Baehr v. Anderson*, the piecemeal strategy has already been tried here. And every time lesbian and gay lawyers tried to win specific recognitions or benefits, judges and right-wing organizations all but spat, as if extending pensions to same-sex partners would sully the sacred territory of marriage. Says Wolfson, "We have not had the luxury of defining the battle." Only when Hawaii's Supreme Court made its surprise 1993 decision in the Hawaii case, then known as *Baehr v. Lewin*—and forced the country to debate the prospect of same-sex marriage—did the American public finally start telling pollsters it would be only fair to offer lesbian and gay couples such things as inheritance, pensions, hospitalization and so on.

In *M v. H,* Canada's Supreme Court wrote, "Certainly same-sex couples will often form long, lasting, loving, and intimate relationships." Says McCarthy, "The decision is carefully reasoned. It contains a lot of strong language. There are quite a few very moving passages. Other courts around the world are going to have to take notice."

Schools

THE UNITED STATES CONTEXT

Education in the United States has many problems. The following information is from Timmer and Eitzen, forthcoming. Foremost, schools are vastly unequal in resources because their finances depend largely on the local economy. This means, for example, that urban schools are the most poorly financed, yet they have the highest concentrations of poor children, minority children, and children of recent immigrants. Educational policy is not a federal issue; it is divided into fifty state programs and 15,000 local programs. Thus, there are wide differences in curricula, standards, and emphases depending on locality. It is estimated that school districts need $100 billion to repair or replace deteriorating facilities. Many high school graduates are barely literate. Twenty percent of American adults (25 million) are barely literate. Latinos, a majority in many school districts and soon (in 2010) to be the largest racial minority in the United States, have a 30 percent dropout rate from high school, compared to 12 percent for African Americans and 9 percent for whites. Colleges and universities, the most important gatekeepers, are so expensive that they are less and less available to children of the middle class, certainly less so to children of the working class, and even less so, if at all, to the working poor and the poor. This leads of course to a two-tiered society.

As a result, educational performance in the United States varies by locality and the social and economic background of students. Most notably, the country falls short on a number of indicators used to compare nations on education:

• The United States ranks second to last among twenty-nine nations in high school graduation rates (Bronner, 1998).
• U.S. teachers are paid less than teachers in other countries. An experienced U.S. high school teacher earns 1.2 times the nation's per capita gross national product. Only three of the twenty-nine nations studied (the Czech Republic, Hungary, and Norway) pay their high school teachers less than the United States in comparable terms (Henry, 1998b). Part of this salary difference is explained by the higher qualification standards for teachers in other countries.
• The longer U.S. students are in school, the lower their rank is on comparative test scores. Studies show, for example, that U.S. fourth-graders scored at or near the top tier in both science and mathematics, but below average by eighth grade (Sanchez, 1997).

High school seniors continued this downward trend, as they ranked in the bottom third (Henry, 1998a).

• Particularly troublesome are the internal disparities between the highest and lowest performing U.S. students. Other countries aim not only to encourage high performance but also to minimize internal disparities. Andreas Schleicher, one of the authors of a major study of comparative student performance by country, sponsored by the Organization for Economic Cooperation and Development (OECD), reached this conclusion: "The variation is too wide to attribute solely to the different abilities students bring to the classroom. U.S. schools and classrooms are key determinants of how students will perform. In Korea and Japan, the top performing countries, such disparities between schools amount to less than 6 percent of the overall variation. The variation runs up to 31 percent within the USA" (quoted in Henry, 1998c:10D).

• Measured by annual per pupil expenditures as a percentage of income per person, the United States ranks fourteenth out of sixteen industrialized nations. By this measure, Sweden invests 35 percent of per person income on education whereas the United States spends only 21 percent (Gluckman, 1998).

• The United States ranks ninth in early childhood education, with 56 percent of four-year-olds enrolled in preprimary programs. This compares to virtually 100 percent of French children and 98 percent of Belgian and Dutch children (OECD, 1990:107).

• The United States ranks fifteenth in days spent in school each year with an average of 180 days. At the upper end Japan averages 243 school days annually, Israel 216, Germany 210, and the Netherlands 200 (Shapiro, 1992:60).

• The U.S. curriculum is less demanding than that found in other industrialized nations. In most of the other countries, mathematics and science are required courses throughout high school. In the United States only half of high school seniors take a science course and a third do not take a math course. "American students spend about 1,416 hours studying subjects like math, science, and history during their four years in high school [according to a National Education Commission on Time and Learning study]. In stark contrast, Japanese, French, and German students spend 3,170, 3,280, and 3,528 hours, respectively" (Manegold, 1994:13A).

REFERENCES_____

Bronner, Ethan. 1998. "Long a Leader, U.S. Now Lags in High School Graduation Rate," *New York Times* (November 24):A1, A18.

Gluckman, Amy. 1998. "Tests and Money: Where Does U.S. Public Education Stand?" *Dollars and Sense,* No. 216 (March/April):11–13.

Henry, Tamara. 1998a. "Top U.S. 12th-Graders Lag Foreign Peers in Math, Science," *USA Today* (February 25):2D.

Henry, Tamara. 1998b. "Teacher Salaries Get Low Grades," *USA Today* (November 24):10D.

Henry, Tamara. 1998c. "U.S. Losing Ground in the Race toward Education Equality," *USA Today* (November 24):10D.

Manegold, Catherine. 1994. "41% of School Day Is Spent on Academic Subjects, Study Says," *New York Times* (May 5):13A.

Organization for Economic Cooperation and Development (OECD). 1990. *Education in OECD Countries 1987–88.* Paris: OECD.

Sanchez, Rene. 1997. "Good Marks for Fourth-Graders," *Washington Post National Weekly Edition* (June 16):35.

Shapiro, Andrew L. 1992. *We're Number One: Where America Stands—and Falls in the New World Order.* New York: Random House Vintage.

Timmer, Doug A., and D. Stanley Eitzen. (Forthcoming). *Where the Welfare State Works.* Lanham, Maryland: Rowman and Littlefield.

17

Teaching Our Teachers:
Lessons from Abroad

RICHARD P. McADAMS

The author surveyed teacher education programs and policies in the United States, Canada, Denmark, England, Japan, and Germany. The findings revealed that teachers in these other countries were better grounded in academic fields and more confident in their knowledge and abilities in their subject matter than those in the United States. The main differences are as follows: (1) teachers in the other countries had higher salaries and status; (2) the training that prospective teachers receive is more vigorous in the other countries; and (3) the teacher training institutions in the other countries had higher standards for admission.

The common sense truism "You can't teach what you don't know" is taken seriously by countries that are our major competitors in the world economy. In a recent survey of teacher education in the United States, Canada, Denmark, England, Japan, and Germany, I found that most of the other countries have teacher education policies that produce teachers well grounded in their academic fields. Particularly in Germany, Japan, and Denmark, aspiring teachers typically receive a more rigorous academic training than their American counterparts.

This difference in training is reflected in a recent international study (Poppleton 1990) of teachers' perceptions of their qualifications to teach their assigned subjects. In the area of physical science, for example, only 47 percent of American teachers assigned to teach this course felt qualified to teach it. The corresponding numbers for the other countries surveyed were 80 percent of teachers in England, 95 percent of Japanese teachers, and 91 percent of German teachers. Forty-two percent of American teachers felt qualified for their math teaching assignments. Corresponding percentages for the other countries were 81 percent for English teachers, 77 percent for Japanese teachers, and 89

Source: Richard P. McAdams. 1995. "Teaching Our Teachers: Lessons from Abroad," *The Clearing House 68* (July/August), pp. 353–355.

percent for German teachers. Clearly, a large proportion of America's teachers of math and science believe that their academic training is deficient. Similar levels of concern are expressed by American teachers of other subjects such as foreign languages, history, and language arts. My survey (McAdams 1993) revealed other major differences between the United States and the other six countries studied.

EDUCATIONAL DIFFERENCES

Teacher Salaries

Supply and demand factors influence the quality of persons selected as new teachers. Japan has five to six applicants for each vacant teaching position. Teaching is a high-status occupation in Japan, with one-fourth of all university graduates becoming qualified to teach. Denmark, Germany, and Japan pay their secondary school teachers on a higher scale than elementary teachers, a further incentive for academically qualified persons in those countries to pursue a teaching career. Teacher salaries in those countries also compare more favorably with salary levels in the country overall, unlike teacher salaries in many regions of the United States.

In the early to mid-1980s, American teacher salaries were about equal to the average salary of American factory workers. During the same period, teachers in Canada earned 40 percent more than factory workers in their nation. Danish teachers earned 28 percent more than Danish factory workers, and Japanese teachers earned 77 percent more than Japanese factory workers (Nelson 1991). In more recent years, the national push to raise teacher salaries has somewhat improved the position of American teachers relative to American factory workers. Nonetheless, it is still fair to say that the relative economic status of American teachers is not as secure as that of teachers in many other countries.

Requirements for Elementary Teachers

Educational requirements for elementary teachers are similar in all six countries surveyed. Common practice is for elementary teachers to attend a teachers' college or a university for three or four years, followed by a student teaching experience varying in length from a few weeks in Japan to a year or more in Germany. The major difference between the academic training of future teachers in the United States and that of future teachers in other countries is the intensity and rigor of their secondary school education. American elementary teachers are the product of American comprehensive high schools where they are likely to be B-level students, pursuing a general academic program that is often of only modest rigor.

Their counterparts from many other economically advanced nations pursue a more academically challenging secondary school program. Elementary teachers in Denmark are typically graduates of the academic *gymnasium* and have successfully passed the difficult *Studentereksamen* examination. German elementary teachers have passed the *Abitur* exam, which entitles them to go on to higher education.

English elementary teachers are graduates of the academically rigorous sixth form of English secondary education. Japanese elementary teachers all attend academically challenging Japanese secondary schools. Only in Canada, among the foreign nations surveyed, does a less rigorous level of precollege academic training for future teachers prevail. The academic rigor of secondary schooling experiences for elementary teachers from most other countries surveyed makes these teachers better equipped academically to pursue challenging university-level work. Not surprisingly, these teachers ultimately become better-educated classroom teachers than their American counterparts, who often enter college without a solid secondary school academic experience.

Raising the academic rigor of American high school programs—in particular, by requiring students to take college entrance exams similar to those of other major world economic powers—would improve the general academic preparation of students entering teacher training programs after high school. Currently, many teaching candidates are drawn from the less academically able members of entering college classes, the type of student presently ill served by undemanding coursework at the high school level.

A national sample of college graduates who took the Armed Forces Qualifying Test confirmed that graduates with lower IQ scores were more than twice as likely to choose a career in education than were graduates with higher IQ scores (Murname et al. 1991). A more challenging high school program would lead to a dramatic improvement in the general knowledge and skill levels of future teachers.

Secondary School Preparation

A closer look at secondary education in the countries surveyed for my book, *Lessons from Abroad: How Other Countries Educate Their Children* (1993), reveals dramatic differences between current practices in American secondary schools and those of secondary schools abroad. Secondary school aged students in most of the other survey countries face rigorous academic challenges beginning as early as seventh or eighth grade. By age twelve or thirteen, students in Germany and Denmark must determine whether they will seek admission to the academic high schools or pursue a technical or vocational education. By age fifteen, English students need to perform well on their school leaving examination to qualify for attendance at the sixth form schools, which will prepare them for later university admission. In many Canadian provinces, examinations are being reinstated to ensure that a high school diploma represents a definable standard of achievement.

Japanese students experience the most extreme pressures in preparing for an academic high school. Students in Japan must take competitive exams in ninth grade to determine which high schools they will be able to attend. Schools in each region are rated according to academic excellence, with acceptance at certain high schools offering a better chance for later acceptance at a prestigious university. In their senior year of high school, Japanese students must again take competitive exams to win placement at a university. In Japan the national public universities are the most prestigious and also the least costly. Therefore, the competition for the limited places available is intense.

Over 90 percent of Japanese students attend *juku* tutoring schools for five to ten hours each week to prepare for these competitive entrance examinations. The student is relieved of all household chores during the year or two preceding the examination, and the mother makes a special effort to accommodate meal schedules to her student's study schedule. Japanese high school students involved in the intense competition for admission to the top public universities may spend five or six hours each day on homework for regular classes as well as juku school.

Entry into Higher Education

Academic high school students in Denmark, Germany, and England invest considerable effort in mastering the material necessary to pass required university admission tests in their countries. English students generally take the General Certificate of Education Advanced Level (GCE A-level) in two or three subjects to apply for university admission. These national tests determine whether a student will be selected for a university of his or her choice or whether a student will even be admitted to any university.

In Germany, students must earn the Abitur at the end of gymnasium to qualify for admission to a university. The Abitur consists of a written test in two main subjects and one optional subject. There is also an oral exam in one optional subject. Required subjects to be tested include German, a modern foreign language, and either mathematics or a natural science.

Danish students must successfully pass a combination of ten written and oral tests during their final two years at the gymnasium, the Danish academic upper secondary school. Students must score satisfactorily on these tests, collectively known as the Studentereksamen, before being considered for admission to a university. Both Germany and Denmark now have more students meeting the Abitur and Studentereksamen requirements than there are places available at the universities. This has created an intense competition among students to receive the higher scores on these university admission tests.

Canada and the United States essentially offer an open admissions policy to higher education. Both countries have a multitude of two-year community colleges and a variety of private colleges that accommodate even poorly prepared high school graduates. Although most U.S. colleges require students to submit scores on the SAT (Scholastic Aptitude Tests) or the ACT (American College Testing Program Assessment), only the more selective private and public universities use these scores as meaningful screening devices. A telling statistic on the extent to which many American students are ill prepared to enter college is the astounding fact that only about half of the students who enter a four-year college earn a bachelor's degree within a six-year period (National Center for Education Statistics 1991). Significantly fewer college-bound seniors earn a bachelor's degree within the traditional four-year period.

The ease of entry into American higher education, as well as the lack of generally accepted entrance examinations, conspires to lull typical teenagers, including future teachers, into a state of complacency regarding their level of academic achievement. There is little external pressure to motivate a student to excel academically. In the spring of 1988, about 2.9 million students graduated from high school. Three months later about 2.4 million students enrolled as first-time freshmen in institutions of higher education

(National Center for Education Statistics 1991). Allowing for a fair proportion of adult students among this number, clearly there is no shortage of college places for America's high school graduates.

The laws of supply and demand ensure that all but the most marginal students can gain entrance to higher education in the United States. A recent group of forty-six Rochester-area college administrators and professors, when asked to discuss admission standards, responded "that they have no requirements, only preferences" (Tucker 1991).

Also, academic credentials are more directly related to financial and social status in countries such as England, Germany, Japan, and Denmark than they are in the United States. Americans, both students and their parents, are less likely to perceive academic excellence as critical to their future success and security than are their counterparts in other countries surveyed.

Open access to higher education, an accepted fact in the United States, has yet to be achieved in the other survey countries, although Denmark, Germany, and Japan have dramatically increased the proportion of their citizenry enrolled in higher education. Germany and Denmark have increased the proportion of their students attending the university from 5 to 10 percent in the 1950s to close to 30 percent today (McAdams 1993). The proportion of Japanese college-aged students attending colleges and universities has increased from 17 percent in 1970 to 28 percent in 1987. The proportion of American students of college age attending colleges and universities in 1987 was 65 percent (National Center for Education Statistics 1991). Each of these foreign nations appears determined, however, to maintain academic standards even as they expand opportunities for higher education.

RECOMMENDATIONS FOR U.S. EDUCATION

What lessons might we learn from the nations surveyed in order to improve our teacher education programs? Following are several recommendations.

The good news is that the foundation for a better-educated college graduate, including future teachers, can be laid at the secondary school level. It is within our power and financial means to develop more rigorous academic programs for all of our secondary school students, including the next generation of teachers. Once these programs are in place, relatively minor adjustments at the college level will lead to a cadre of much better educated teachers. Recent national initiatives such as Goals 2000 and the drive for national teacher certification standards are welcome signs of a growing interest in raising academic standards in the United States.

Elementary teachers should continue to be educated in teacher education programs in four-year colleges and universities. Better preparation of students at the high school level will allow for increased depth of the academic component of these programs. A rigorous academic achievement test should be required of teacher education graduates as a part of their initial certification.

Secondary teachers should be required to graduate with a major in the academic subject that they will teach. Permanent certification regulations should require that a secondary teacher earn a master's degree in a field relating to his or her teaching assignment within the first five years of teaching. Secondary teachers would also be required to pass rigorous subject area tests as a condition for initial certification.

Most important, better-educated teacher candidates at the beginning of the formal training period will allow colleges to raise their academic expectations, thus producing better-educated, more self-confident teachers for the classrooms of America.

REFERENCES_____

McAdams, R. P. 1993. *Lessons from abroad: How other countries educate their children.* Lancaster, Pa.: Technomic.

Murname, R. J., J. D. Singer, J. B. Willett, J. J. Kample, and R. J. Olsen. 1991. *Who will teach.* Cambridge, Mass.: Harvard University Press.

National Center for Education Statistics. 1991. *Digest of education statistics 1990.* Washington, D.C.: U.S. Government Printing Office.

Nelson, F. H. 1991. *International comparisons of public spending on education.* Washington, D.C.: American Federation of Teachers.

Poppleton, P. 1990. The survey data. *Comparative Education* 26(2/3): 187.

Tucker, M. 1991. Many U.S. colleges are really inefficient high priced secondary schools. *Chronicle of Higher Education* (June 5): A36.

18

U.S. and German Youths: Unemployment and the Transition from School to Work

ROBERT J. GITTER AND MARKUS SCHEUER

Compared with the United States, Germany has a lower youth unemployment rate and is more successful in transitioning young people into the labor market. This article examines differences in the U.S. and German educational systems and discusses the impact of apprenticeship training on youth employment in Germany. The article ends with a discussion of the applicability of the German model to the United States.

Unemployment among young people is a serious problem facing the United States today. The labor market difficulties of youths cause the members of this cohort economic hardship now, as well as hinder their future economic success. Moreover, the difficulties youths face impinge on the Nation as a whole: a well-trained work force is vital to the U.S ability to compete in the international market as a high-productivity, high-wage country. Youths who gain work experience and receive on-the-job training will reduce both the chances of future labor bottlenecks and the burden that might be imposed on others to pay for their support.

It can be argued that U.S. youth unemployment results from inadequate labor market preparation in schools, as well as an especially difficult school-to-work transition for young Americans. The comprehensive German apprenticeship system is often seen as a model for an improved school-to-work transition. As James J. Heckman, Rebecca L. Roselius, and Jeffrey A. Smith state:[1]

> *A new consensus has emerged in influential policy circles that the American labor market and educational system are unable to equip workers with sufficient skills. American youth are said to experience a disorderly transition from school to work characterized by too much job turnover and too little training on the job. In contrast, the German apprenticeship system has been held up as a model of order that produces smooth school to work transitions and provides workers with human capital directly related to their career interests in a format especially helpful for workers poorly served by formal schooling.*

Source: Robert J. Gitter and Markus Scheuer. 1997. *The Monthly Labor Review 120* (March), pp. 16–20.

This article explores the school-to-work transition and youth unemployment in the two nations[2] and the lessons the United States might learn from Germany, but with an important cautionary note about the limited potential for transferring the German model. We begin with a discussion of some of the differences in the unemployment rates of various demographic and educational groups within the youth population of both countries. We then explore the reasons behind the lower German youth unemployment rates in terms of the vocational preparation of the two school systems and discuss the potential for transferring parts of the German model to the United States. We show that the key to Germany's success is the country's social consensus on the importance of work force training for youths. Whether Germany's methods could be successfully transferred is a direct function of another nation's likelihood of adopting such a social consensus.

YOUTH UNEMPLOYMENT

We define the youth unemployment rate as the unemployment rate for youths 16 to 24 years of age in the United States and 15 to 24 years in Germany; we define the overall unemployment rate as the rate for all individuals 16 years of age and older in the United States and 15 years and older in Germany. Substantial differences exist in the youth unemployment rates of Germany and the United States. Table 18.1 presents a detailed comparison of youth unemployment in the two nations. The figures are for 1993, a year in which the overall U.S. unemployment rate was less than that of Germany.

In 1993, the youth unemployment rate in the United States was roughly double the overall unemployment rate, in direct contrast to Germany, where the youth unemployment rate was equal to the overall rate. The unemployment rate for U.S. youths 16 to 19 years of age was substantially higher than the comparable German rate, but there was a much smaller difference for 20- to 24-year-olds.[3] Thus, unemployment has a much younger face in the United States, with almost 1 in 3 unemployed Americans being between the ages of 16 and 24. The figure is only 1 in 7 for German youths between 15 and 24.[4]

Youth unemployment is most severe among minorities in the United States, where racial composition is more heterogeneous than in Germany. Black American youths had an unemployment rate of more than 27 percent in 1993, compared with 11.2 percent for white youths. Further, the group with the most labor market difficulty, 16- to 19-year-old black men, has an unemployment rate of 38.9 percent. Hence, to the extent that those youths who experience unemployment have less labor market success as adults, minority youths will experience disproportionately more labor market problems in the future.

EDUCATION AND UNEMPLOYMENT

The difference in unemployment rates between the two countries suggests that the initial entry of young workers into the labor force is more difficult in the United States than in Germany. To what extent this is related to the educational systems and levels of educational attainment of youths in the two nations may be gleaned from the following tab-

TABLE 18.1 Youth Unemployment in the United States and Germany, 1993 (in percent)

AGE, SEX, AND RACE	UNITED STATES	GERMANY
UNEMPLOYMENT RATE		
Total, 15 or 16 years and older[1]	6.8	7.7
Total, 15/16–24[1]	13.4	7.7
Men	14.3	7.7
15/16–19[1]	20.4	5.4
20–24	11.3	8.6
Women	12.2	7.7
15/16–19[1]	17.4	5.3
20–24	9.6	8.5
White	11.2	—
Black	27.3	—
Other	13.3	—
15- OR 16- TO 24-YEAR-OLDS[1]		
Proportion unemployed:		
Men	10.0	3.3
Women	7.6	3.7
Proportion unemployed long term:		
Men	1.1	1.1
Women	5	1.4
Proportion of total unemployment:		
Men	31.1	14.4
Women	31.1	15.2
Proportion in population 15/16–64:		
Men	19.3	14.4
Women	18.7	13.8

[1]Lower limit of 15 years for Germany and 16 years for the United States.

Note: Dash indicates data not differentiated by race because Germany has almost no races other than white.

Source: U.S. data, *Employment and Earnings* (Department of Labor, January 1994); German data, EUROSTAT.

ulation, which presents unemployment rates for youths 20 to 24 years of age, by educational attainment, in both countries in 1991:[5]

EDUCATION LEVEL	UNITED STATES	GERMANY
Total	12.2	6.6
Less than secondary	21.8	10.1
Upper secondary	13.2	5.5
Postsecondary	5.9	5.9

Two important conclusions emerge from the data. First, in both nations, youths with less than a secondary education fare worse in the labor market than those who have completed their secondary schooling. Second, with the exception of those with a postsecondary education, the unemployment rates in the United States are more than double those in Germany for groups with a comparable level of education.

Not only do American youths with lower levels of education fare worse than their German counterparts, but also, they constitute a greater share of the youth cohort. The OECD study cited in [note] 4 showed that 16.6 percent of U.S. youths aged 20 to 24 had not completed a secondary education, much larger than the figure for the same group in Germany. Furthermore, only 36 percent of 20- to 24-year-olds in the United States were currently employed in the year they left school.[6] In short, U.S. youths without a secondary school diploma fare worse in the labor market than their German counterparts, and there are relatively more of them in the youth population.

U.S. AND GERMAN EDUCATIONAL SYSTEMS

In light of the greater degree of difficulty in integrating youths into the labor force in the United States, an examination of the educational systems of the two countries might shed some light on the causes of this unemployment disparity. The curriculum of U.S. high schools can be divided into three broad categories: college preparatory, vocational, and general (defined by the U.S. Department of Education as a "program of studies designed to prepare students for the common activities of a citizen, family member, and worker").[7] For the most part, these categories can be found in high schools throughout the Nation. The following tabulation of the percentage of 17-year-olds in each of the three programs in 1982 and in 1990 reveals an increase in students electing the college preparatory curriculum, with a decline in the other two areas:[8]

PROGRAM	1982	1990
College preparatory (academic)	43.8	54.4
Vocational	12.2	8.7
General	44.0	36.9

Although the share of high school students undertaking a general curriculum has declined in recent years, more than one-third of American youths still pursue this course of studies. From a labor market perspective, the problem is that the general curriculum is designed to provide students neither with vocational preparation nor with the ideal background for college. Students can, of course, pursue employment or further education with this background, but their preparation will not be focused on the skills that are required for labor market success either upon graduation from high school or after college.

Table 18.2 shows that slightly more than half of U.S. youths enroll in college, and approximately one-quarter of U.S. youths will receive at least a 4-year (bachelor's) degree. From an international perspective, this is a relatively large share of youths with a college degree. But for the 20 percent of Americans who leave college without even

TABLE 18.2   Postsecondary Education and Training in the United States, 1985

LEVEL OF EDUCATION TRAINING AS OF 1985	PERCENT OF THOSE WHO LEFT SCHOOL IN 1972, 1973, OR 1974
College	52
Attained college degree	32
Attained master's degree	7
Attained bachelor's degree	17
Attained associate's degree	8
Dropped out of college	20
Received certificated vocational training	7
Did not receive certificated vocational training	13
Did not enroll in college	48
Received certificated vocational training	15
Did not receive certificated vocational training	33
Received some postsecondary education or training, but no certificate or degree	2
Received no postsecondary education or training at all	31

Note: Percentages are from Christoph F. Buechtemann, Juergen Schupp, and Dana Soloff, "Roads to Work: School-to-Work Transition Patterns in Germany and the United States," *Industrial Relations Journal,* vol. 24, no. 2, 1993, pp. 97–111, based on data from United States Panel Survey of Income Dynamics.

an associate's degree, two-thirds of them (13 percent of all youths) do not receive any vocational training in a program that leads to some type of certification.

Turning to the 48 percent of high school leavers who did not enroll in college, we find that roughly one-third of them (15 percent of all youths) obtained vocational training that led to a certificate, but two-thirds (31 percent of all youths) did not. Hence, the higher youth unemployment rates of the United States should not be surprising in light of the fact that 31 percent of U.S. youths received no postsecondary education or vocational training whatsoever, and another 13 percent attended college but failed to obtain even an associate's degree and also received no vocational training.[9]

The situation in Germany is quite different. (See Table 18.3.) There, 84 percent of youths pursued a postsecondary vocational or educational certificate. Currently, two-thirds of German youths have passed through an apprenticeship program.[10] By contrast, in the United States, the figure is approximately 3 to 5 percent.[11]

Apprenticeship training in Germany combines classroom instruction with employment, a so-called dual system. For each of the more than 300 occupations that have apprenticeships, there is a nationally standardized curriculum. Students must pass an examination administered by external bodies (chambers of crafts and chambers of industry and commerce) in order to be awarded a journeyman certificate.

The employment portion of the apprenticeship typically lasts between 2½ and 3½ years. Apprentices are trained on the actual machines and equipment they will later use.

TABLE 18.3   Postsecondary Education and Training in Germany, 1990.

LEVEL OF EDUCATION OR TRAINING AS OF 1990	PERCENT OF THOSE WHO LEFT SCHOOL IN 1978 OR 1979
Postsecondary vocational education or apprenticeship training	84
Received apprenticeship certificate	46
Received full-time vocational education certificate	23
Did not receive vocational certificate	15
Higher Education[1]	16
Attained college degree	11
Attained master's degree	9
Attained technical degree	2
Dropped out of college	3
Still enrolled in college	2

[1]Two percent of sample was enrolled in postsecondary vocational education or apprenticeship training, as well as in higher education.

Note: Percentages are from Christoph F. Buechtemann, Juergen Schupp, and Dana Soloff, "Roads to Work: School-to-Work Transition Patterns in Germany and the United States," *Industrial Relations Journal,* vol. 24, no. 2, pp. 97–111, based on data from German Socio-Economic Panel.

The apprenticeship will teach the apprentice not only the skills needed for the profession, but also broader work skills, as well as an appreciation for what is needed in general to succeed in the world of work. Although the German Government builds vocational schools and provides some public sector apprenticeships, the overall success of the dual system depends on ensuring that private firms employ a sufficient number of apprentices.

Although unemployment is worse for youths with lower levels of education and training, there are relatively fewer of these people in the population of German youths. In 1990, among German students who left high school in 1978 or 1979, 80 percent either completed vocational education (through an apprenticeship or in some other form) or graduated college.[12] By contrast, among U.S. youths who left high school in the 1972–74 period, only 54 percent received either a college degree or a certificate for vocational training.

THE GERMAN SOCIAL CONSENSUS

The so-called German dual system tries to combine practical training in an economic enterprise with an education in vocational schools. Generally speaking, the aim of vocational training in Germany is twofold: to enable the individual to acquire the skills and knowledge judged to be necessary for employment; and to ease the person's entry into the labor market. German apprenticeship cannot be fully understood, or its potential transferability to the United States examined, without keeping in mind the fact that German society has a long historical tradition of a social consensus on providing young people with good initial vocational training.

This social consensus can be summarized by the slogan, "First of all, vocational training for everybody."[13] In other words, vocational training in any field is said to be better than no training at all. The Germans believe this to be the case even if the apprenticeship will not result in employment in the field for the young, qualified worker now or anytime in the foreseeable future. Germans consider vocational qualifications as having value in themselves, as the training will result in skills that can transfer to other occupations.[14] Not only does apprenticeship confer broadly transferable skills on the individual, but also, it socializes the person into the work force—that is, it results in an understanding of the rules and values of the workplace, such as punctuality, discipline, and the acceptance of hierarchies. In addition, there is a perceived value in the feeling of belonging to a group of coworkers and sharing their common language and values. The German social consensus is that vocational training is important and should be provided to all youths.

A recent incident illustrates that this social consensus regarding vocational education is shared by employers, workers, and the German Government. A restructuring in the German economy had resulted in a shortage of apprenticeship placements in both the private and public sector. The shortage was made even more severe by a recession. The number of apprenticeships dropped from 500,000 in 1992 to 450,000 in 1994.[15] There was a consensus that the latter number was insufficient. The German chancellor, Helmut Kohl, invited the leaders of employers' associations and major trade unions, as well as the ministers of labor, the economy, training and science, and finance, to his office. A communiqué was issued stating that all parties agreed that both vocational training and further training appropriate to the qualifications of the person or to the current labor market situation would attract investors and be of the highest importance to the economic and social future of Germany.[16] An agreement was reached whereby the employers' associations promised that their members, together with the public employers, would create enough apprenticeships to raise the total to 600,000 by 1996. The Government pledged to aid in the implementation of the plan by increasing training subsidies if needed. Based on earlier, similar situations, it is extremely likely that the increase in promised apprenticeships will occur.[17]

The German dual system of apprenticeship training is a key factor in the more successful school-to-work transition in Germany than in the United States and helps explain the low level of German youth unemployment. The system is dependent, however, on a sufficient number of apprenticeship employment opportunities, particularly in the private sector. If the number of apprenticeships is too low, the Government can summon forth an increase with some financial incentives (for example, by awarding more procurement contracts or by allowing business leaders to accompany the chancellor on State visits abroad), but primarily through moral suasion. The Government's ability and even obligation to get firms to increase the number of apprenticeships is deeply rooted in the idea of a social consensus on training, namely, that training will be made available to all qualified youths and that private enterprises regard it as a social obligation to ensure that enough employment openings exist. Without this social consensus, Germany would not be able to create enough apprenticeship opportunities for the system to function well.[18]

APPLICABILITY TO THE UNITED STATES

There is a substantially higher youth unemployment rate and more difficult school-to-work transition in the United States than in Germany. The rate is especially high for U.S. youths who lack a secondary school diploma, vocational training, or both. A greater share of U.S. youths fall into this category than do German youths. Germany's heavy reliance on an apprenticeship system both trains youths and eases their transition into the labor market. The German system is based on a social consensus that results in private firms providing an adequate number of apprenticeship placements at any given time.

The United States could copy some aspects of the German system with relatively little difficulty—for example, increased occupational certification, more vocational schools, and the use of common national curricula and external examinations. However, the success of any U.S. effort to use apprenticeship as a primary vehicle for reducing youth unemployment and easing the school-to-work transition is more problematic. The German system is heavily dependent on an adequate number of apprenticeship employment opportunities in the private sector. In Germany, the social consensus on the value of apprenticeships will result in firms providing training slots.[19] To the extent that there is a weaker consensus in the United States, the success of increased apprenticeship training would be limited, and without such a consensus, the prospects for a transfer of the German model are questionable at best.

NOTES_____

ACKNOWLEDGEMENTS. The authors gratefully acknowledge the help of Helmut Rudolph of the IAB, Nuremberg, for data on the German labor market.
1. James J. Heckman, Rebecca L. Roselius, and Jeffrey A. Smith. *U.S. Education and Training Policy: A Re-evaluation of the Underlying Assumptions behind the "New Consensus,"* Working Paper #CPSE 94–1 (Chicago, Center for Social Program Evaluation, University of Chicago, 1993).
2. Unless otherwise indicated, all references to Germany are to unified Germany.
3. On the face of it, one might view the situation of falling unemployment rates with age as meaning that there is no lasting effect from teen unemployment and that American youths are just taking longer to find a permanent job. A closer look, however, leads one to a different conclusion: a sizable number of youths– especially those with lower levels of education—are not able to attain stable employment in later years. Jacob A. Klerman and Lynn A. Karoly ("Young men and the transition to stable employment," *Monthly Labor Review,* August 1994, pp. 31–48) found that almost one-quarter of male high school dropouts had never held a job of even as little as 2 years' length by their late twenties. From this, one might argue that the longer run job prospects of this group may not be good either.
4. The U.S. figure is even more surprising, given the fact that in the United States, over the period 1983–92, the number of 16- to 24-year-olds fell by 14.3 percent, while the overall population 16 years and older increased by 13.8 percent. With a decreasing supply of young workers, one might have expected a decline in the youth unemployment rate.
5. Data from Organization for Economic Cooperation and Development, *The OECD Employment Outlook,* July, 1994 (Paris, OECD, 1994), p. 23. For the most part, youths 15 to 19 years had not yet completed their secondary schooling; hence, they are omitted from the tabulation.

6. National Center for Education Statistics. *Youth Indicators, 1993* (Washington, Department of Education, 1993).

7. Digest of Educational Statistics, 1995 (U.S. Department of Education, National Center for Educational Statistics, 1995), p. 493.

8. Ibid. p. 60.

9. Christoph F. Buechtemann, Juergen Schupp, and Dana Soloff found that one-tenth of U.S. youths received no postsecondary training whatsoever and were working at a job that required less than three months of on-the-job training. Because replacements for these workers can easily be hired and trained, it is once again not surprising that a substantial number of U.S. youths will be facing difficulties in the labor market. (See Christoph F. Buechtemann, Juergen Schupp, and Dana Soloff. "Roads to Work: School-to-Work Transition Patterns in Germany and the United States," *Industrial Relations Journal,* vol. 24, no. 2, 1993, pp. 97–111.)

10. See Hilary Steedman, "The Economics of Youth Training in Germany," *Economic Journal.* September 1993, pp. 1279–91.

11. See Lisa M. Lynch, "The Economics of Youth Training in the United States." *Economic Journal.* September 1993, pp. 1261–78; and Robert J. Gitter, "Apprenticeship-trained workers: United States and Great Britain," *Monthly Labor Review,* April 1994, pp. 38–43.

12. Substantially fewer German youths (16 percent) pursue higher education than do American youths (52 percent). Those German youths who do enroll, however, have a higher probability of completing their degree.

13. Authors' translation of quote from Klaus Daweke, spokesperson for training policies of the governing Christian Democratic Union party in the *Bundestag,* the German lower House of Parliament.

14. See Myriam Campinos-Dubernet and Jean-Marc Grando. "Formation professionnelle ouvrière: Trois modèles européens," *Formation emploi,* no. 22, 1988, pp. 5–29, especially p. 9. One example of the transferability of training occurred in the early 1960s. There was a shortage of trained workers in the chemical industry, and the industry was forced to employ people trained in other areas. One firm sought out cooks and bakers. As one manager explained, bakers and cooks had acquired a sense of timing in the food production process, and that skill is important in the chemical industry as well.

15. The figures are for western Germany only. The situation in eastern Germany is unique due to the region's ongoing transformation from a planned economy to a market economy.

16. See the *Frankfurter Allgemeine Zeitung,* Mar. 17, 1995, p. 18.

17. In fact, there was a small increase in apprenticeship placements from 1994 to 1995; see Rudolf Werner. "Rückgang der Ausbildungsplätze betrifft Kernbereiche des dualen Systems—eine statistische Analyse," in *Berufsbildung in Wissenschaft und Praxis,* vol. 25, no. 3 (1996), pp. 14–20.

Arguably, the best known display of the social consensus on apprenticeship training was in the early 1980s, when Chancellor Helmut Kohl made the shortage of apprenticeship training positions a major issue in his election campaign. He promised to induce enterprises to fulfill their "duties" to training. Following his election, Kohl gathered together representatives of employers' organizations and chambers of industry, commerce, and crafts. After deliberations, the employers guaranteed an apprenticeship to every young German who was willing and able to assume one. With financial assistance from the Government, more than enough apprenticeships were created.

18. Note, however, that although the social consensus exists, it does require the efforts of the Government to keep it intact. Recently, concern has arisen about the availability of an adequate number of training places in core industries (see Werner, "Rückgang der Ausbildungsplätze"), and Chancellor Kohl has already begun efforts to ensure a sufficient number of places for 1997 (see "Kohl fordert mehr Lehrstellen," *Handelsblatt,* no. 120, June 25, 1996, p. 4).

19. This consensus is not universal to all European nations. France, for example, lacks it. (See Odile Benoit-Guilbot, Helmut Rudolph, and Markus Scheuer, "Youth Unemployment in France and Germany." paper presented at the European Association of Labor Economists, Maastricht, the Netherlands, Sept. 30–Oct. 3, 1993.)

Work

THE UNITED STATES CONTEXT

As noted elsewhere in this text, pay for work is highly skewed in the United States. The chief executive officers of the 365 largest companies in 1998 were paid 419 times the pay of the average blue-collar worker. In 1998 alone, the pay for top executives rose 36 percent compared with a 2.7 percent increase for the average blue-collar employee (Smart, 1999). This gap is actually understated because it does not include the stock options, paid insurance, travel subsidies, country club memberships, huge retirement settlements, and other perks commonly provided to corporate executives but not to blue-collar workers. This gap between the pay and benefits of corporate executives and their workers is much higher in the United States than in any other industrialized nation.

Public policy in the United States actually accentuates the gap between the rich and the poor. For example, blue-collar workers cannot write off their lunches at work but executives get a tax break for their business meals. The tax code also gives breaks for "business travel" and even for owning second homes, advantages available only to those in the upper tier. Moreover, while wages are taxed fully, profits made from the sale of stocks, bonds, land, houses, and other property are taxed at a lower rate. Also, Congress recently made it easier to pass wealth on to heirs by increasing the amount exempt from estate taxes. At the same time Congress has chosen *not* to provide universal health insurance, an adequate minimum wage, subsidized child care, universal preschool for four- and five-year-olds, or free public education through college as found in other industrialized nations.

The gap between the executives and workers is unusually harsh when companies decide to trim the workforce. Common laborers are given modest severance packages, if any, while executives receive "golden parachutes." Consider the case of the former head of Apple Computer, Gilbert Amelio. During Amelio's seventeen-month tenure at Apple, the company lost nearly $2 billion, and 3,600 employees lost their jobs. Amelio's golden parachute included $6.7 million in severance pay plus other compensation (Sklar, 1998a). Occasionally during hard times workers are laid off while corporate executives are rewarded. In 1997, for example, American Express laid off 3,200 workers while giving CEO Harvey Golub a 224 percent pay increase, bringing his total annual compensation to $33.4 million (Sklar, 1998a).

American workers, when compared to their peers in other industrialized societies, work more hours. According to data from the International Labor Organization, the average number of hours worked annually per person in the United States was 1,966 in 1997, seventy hours more than the Japanese and 350 hours more (almost nine full work weeks) than Europeans (cited in Greenhouse, 1999; Grimsley, 1999).

A major difference between the United States and the other industrialized nations is that it has a relatively weak and declining labor union movement. The proportion of workers in unions fell from 27 percent in 1978 to 13.9 percent in 1998. This erosion in the numbers of union workers, coupled with the rise of international competition and accelerated capital mobility, has weakened their bargaining power (Brecher, 1998).

To conclude, on Labor Day 1999, two observers noted that despite low inflation and low unemployment and the longest uninterrupted economic growth in U.S. history, the situation for workers was anything but rosy:

> *Americans are working longer hours than their counterparts in any other industrialized nation; a growing share of the workforce has no pension and health benefits; and the income gap between the rich and the rest of society continues to widen. From these crosscurrents emerges a snapshot of a divided society in which the middle class is running harder and harder to support a bountiful lifestyle while the wealthiest can afford unimaginable luxuries and the poor find work but little security in a world that appears to be leaving them behind (Williams and Otto, 1999:1E).*

REFERENCES_____

Brecher, Jeremy. 1998. "New Tactics for Labor," *Z Magazine 11* (March): 33–39.

Greenhouse, Steven. 1999. "Leisure Time Flattened as the Good Times Roll," *Rocky Mountain News* (September 12), 1G, 13G.

Grimsley, Kirstin Downey. 1999. " . . . U.S. Workers Keep Going and Going," *Washington Post National Weekly Edition* (September 13):19.

Sklar, Holly. 1998a. "CEO Greed Is Out of Control," *Z Magazine 11* (June):30–32.

Sklar, Holly. 1998b. "Let Them Eat Cake," *Z Magazine 11* (November):29–32.

Smart, Tim. 1999. "It Pays Even More to Be the Boss," *Washington Post National Weekly Edition* (September 6):20.

Williams, Larry, and Mary Otto. 1999. "Mild Unrest Marks Modern Labor Day," *Denver Post* (September 6):1E, 5E.

19

Jobs versus Wages: The Phony Trade-Off

PHINEAS BAXANDALL

The recent high incidence of unemployment in the European social democracies has been blamed on expensive social welfare policies. The dominant U.S. argument is that in today's global economy it is no longer possible to maintain both high wages and a low rate of unemployment. Baxandall argues that this notion is a myth. Low wages relegate a large part of the working population to poverty or near poverty, which becomes costly to society in the form of various social problems. The other point is that the low U.S. unemployment rate is much higher than stated, since the United States does not count as unemployed those who no longer are looking for work, or those who are working part-time but want to work full-time. Finally, he argues, low wages are accompanied by rising profits, mounting productivity, and escalating salaries for management and owners.

People used to point to Sweden, France, Germany and other European social democracies to show how markets could be organized in a kinder, gentler fashion. We used their lower unemployment rate, universal social benefits and high wages to say that things could be better at home and to counter the many economists who insisted that increasing our wages would lead to large increases in unemployment.

But that was then, this is now. Before the 1980s, Europe consistently had lower unemployment rates than the United States. Since then European unemployment has been almost double the American rate.

Now we hear from the mainstream press that Europeans just can't seem to harness the political will to get their high wages and expensive welfare states under control. They tell us that in today's global marketplace, Europe's generous wages and social programs just aren't competitive enough to generate enough jobs. "Insiders" such as Europe's powerful unions have pressed for wage demands and job benefits but in doing so, the story

Source: Phineas Baxandall. 1996. "Jobs versus Wages: The Phony Trade-Off," *Dollars & Sense 206* (July/August), pp. 8–11, 42.

goes, they have indirectly put others out of work by slowing the creation of new jobs. This story is said to illustrate an unavoidable trade-off between jobs and wages. When U.S. workers and poor communities push for higher wages or stronger social programs, naysayers invoke the specter of European levels of unemployment.

Readers of the business press will be familiar with charts like the one labeled "Mirror Images." While American wages have stagnated, employment has steadily increased. Meanwhile the Europeans have maintained steady growth in wages and benefits, but their employment has fallen far behind the growth of the population, yielding persistently high numbers of unemployed, many of whom remain unemployed for alarmingly long periods.

But this picture is misleading. There is probably some trade-off between more low-wage jobs and higher total employment, but that trade-off is not as large as typically portrayed. Nor is it really the point. Even with double-digit unemployment the bottom half of Europe's labor market is better off than ours. The bottom 10% of American workers earn only about half as much as does the bottom 10% in Germany, Norway, or even Italy. By law, European workers have extensive vacation, sickness leave, maternity leave, advanced notice before dismissals, severance pay and longer lasting unemployment benefits. Even Europe's unemployed are mostly better off than America's working poor, and certainly less stigmatized than jobless Americans. In short, Europeans with jobs, and most without, are free from poverty. If only the same were true here.

TRADE-OFF? WHAT TRADE-OFF?

To start with, country-by-country comparisons raise serious doubts about the jobs–wages trade-off. Harvard economist Richard Freeman, a skeptic about the trade-off, notes that according to many mainstream economists, solving Europe's unemployment problem is a simple matter: "Remove labour-market regulations, eliminate job protection laws, reduce unemployment benefits, weaken unions, decentralize wage setting, and presto! European unemployment would vanish." But this has been tried. In the 1980s, Margaret Thatcher's government made Britain more like Reagan's America: wages were slowed, unions beat back, industries deregulated and privatized. But the result was that unemployment, which stood at 5% in 1979, rose to almost 12% before falling to the current 9% rate. Also, countries such as Spain and Ireland, which have some of the lowest wages in Europe, also have some of the highest unemployment rates. Canadian wages are lower than U.S. wages but Canada has the higher unemployment rate.

In fact, the U.S. and Canada generally have similar labor markets and job programs, at least compared to Europe. Their unemployment rates were generally in step up until the early eighties, with Canada's rates lower during the late 1970s. But the early 1980s ushered in harsher treatment of the unemployed in the United States, as state governments slashed unemployment compensation and pushed the jobless to take any available job. Since then, Canadian jobless rates have persistently been two or three points higher than in the United States.

WHAT THE UNEMPLOYMENT RATE COUNTS

Now consider the unemployment rate itself. First of all, the federal government explicitly designed the unemployment rate *not* as a measure of social misery but as an indicator of business conditions. According to a U.S. Bureau of Labor Statistics booklet, *How the Government Measures Unemployment,* "Unemployment statistics are intended to provide counts of unused, available [labor] resources. They are not measures of the number of persons who are suffering economic hardship." When, on the other hand, the government tries to measure social misery, it uses the poverty rate. In this category the U.S. far exceeds Europe.

Unemployment statistics can be deceptive. The unemployed are not equivalent to those "without work" or those "out of work." The measurement defines an unemployed person as a person who is actively seeking work but unable to get it. That may seem simple enough, but a great deal then depends on exactly what the government includes as the official labor force, what it requires for "active job search," and how much paid work it defines as enough to count as "employment."

Small differences in labor force surveys can make big differences in the unemployment rate. While many European countries count the underemployed as out of work, Americans working a mere hour a week do not get counted as unemployed. What is required for an "active job search" also varies greatly between countries. In some countries— including Denmark, Ireland, the Netherlands and the UK—a recent look through the want-ads counts as an active job search. In some countries one must only register at a public employment center, often lured by the promise of free medical benefits and pension contributions even after their unemployment benefits have run out. Other countries, especially the U.S., count people only if they have directly contacted potential employers.

LOCKED OUT OF UNEMPLOYMENT STATS

Many of America's hard-core unemployed are literally locked out of the unemployment statistics because they are put behind bars. Part of America's "success" in combating unemployment in the 1980s came from a 9% jump in our imprisonment rates each year of that decade. In the U.S., people were in jail instead of on the unemployment rolls.

Imprisonment in the United States is, as of 1993, roughly ten times the European rate. And U.S. prisons are filled disproportionately with the same groups of people who would otherwise be unemployed in large numbers: blacks, youth, and the least skilled.

As Harvard economist Richard Freeman shows, the number of U.S. men incarcerated in 1993 was almost 2% of the total number of men in the labor market—more than 1.3 million American men were incarcerated out of a male workforce of less than 70 million. That's one man in prison or jail for every fifty in the workforce. One in three young African-Americans who dropped out of high school is in prison rather than counted in the official workforce where a majority are already counted as unemployed. While this alone does not account for America's lower unemployment rate, it cannot be ignored.

America's low unemployment rate also reflects much larger public employment in criminal justice and corrections. Public jobs for police, judges, prison guards and related jobs account for around 2% of U.S.'s full-time employment. In fact, the total cost of arresting, prosecuting and locking up so many people is now around $100 billion annually. There are certainly cheaper ways to keep unemployment down. Expenditures for a prisoner average about $30,000 yearly, an amount sufficient to pay for food and shelter, community college tuition and the regular attention of a social worker.

CAN YOU KEEP THEM DOWN ON THE FARM?

Perhaps the most important reason for Europe's higher unemployment has nothing to do with the continent's supposedly rigid labor markets: it lies with the timing of European agricultural decline. Europe's unemployment used to be lower than ours in part because our agricultural sector was shrinking while European policies traditionally protected employment in farms and livestock. But in recent years Europe has been lifting many of these protections, sparking farming employment losses. On both sides of the Atlantic manufacturing employment is slumping, but Europe has had to deal with the double problem of a belated slump in agriculture.

As economist Andrew Glyn has shown, in the 1980s the difference in the number of new jobs per capita between the European Community (EC) and the United States was almost entirely due to the greater number of jobs lost from agriculture in Europe. On both sides of the Atlantic the service sector has been the main source of new jobs. Since 1973 the service sector in the EC has been growing almost as fast as in the United States (1.2% per year versus 1.5% between 1973 and 1990). But while U.S. agricultural employment has fallen only 1.6% annually, in the EC it has been dropping at a yearly rate of almost 4%. While unemployment due to agricultural downsizing is as painful as any other kind of unemployment, it certainly does not point to a jobs-wages trade-off.

WHO SUFFERS MORE?

Simply comparing unemployment rates overlooks another important fact: the jobless in the U.S. suffer far greater economic deprivation than their European counterparts. A recent OECD study shows dramatic differences between the portion of unemployed that receive benefits in different countries, and the amount of benefits they receive. . . . The researchers found that while most countries of Western Europe offer unemployment compensation to essentially all of their unemployed, only about a third of the American jobless receive any unemployment benefits. Separate studies by the U.S. Department of Labor show that in staunchly conservative states such as New Hampshire the ratio is even worse, especially since the 1980s.

Keeping unemployment benefits low and making it difficult to receive them, as the United States does, helps keep unemployment rates down by discouraging potential recipients from applying for benefits. It is similar to the way eliminating hospitals and making them more miserable places to stay keeps hospitalization rates down, without improving health. The average U.S. unemployment benefit in 1993 was only $180 per week, and unlike Europeans, the American unemployed are pushed quickly into new jobs, even if the new job won't support their family or make use of their skills. Since unemployment compensation provides for neither child care nor health care, many people are forced onto welfare to receive these benefits, and they are dropped from the unemployment statistics if they stop searching for work. Economists agree that the significant differences between nations' unemployment rates come not from how many enter unemployment, but from how quickly people leave.

WHAT IS AT STAKE

What's at stake in arguing about the "jobs-wages trade-off" is what we can do about the lack of jobs with decent wages and benefits. Policy wonks and the media alike hold up the picture of Europe to convince us that we are helpless victims in the face of the abstract forces of globalization and post-industrialism. Deceptive unemployment statistics suggest that there is a finite amount of total wages to be divided among either more or less workers, implying that battles for decent wages can only help a shrinking number of privileged jobholders at the expense of a growing pool of unemployed. We must confront this false choice between equally unattractive alternatives because it narrows the possibilities for political action.

Low wages have come on the backs of rising profits, stock prices and CEO salaries. Corporate downsizers are emboldened by victories over organized labor and a rightward turn in government. Today layoffs are a boon for upper management as the stockmarket—smelling higher future profits—bids up the stock options of CEO's. If layoffs and wage cuts were met with enough resistance, we might break the cycle. We need more efforts such as the Baltimore and Milwaukee ordinances that require businesses receiving city money to pay wages that at least bring a family of four up to the poverty line. Policies that encourage reductions in the work week could also spread around the number of jobs while decreasing inequality. In our current era of increasing inequality we shouldn't be fooled into thinking that the only choices of redistribution are between bad wages and not enough jobs.

20

Jobs for Life:
Why Japan Won't Give Them Up

EAMONN FINGLETON

Fingleton dispels the myth that because of global competition Japan will no longer be able to maintain its system of lifetime employment. To the contrary, he argues, that type of job security actually has positive effects for Japanese industry (e.g., increased productivity, the use of new technologies in the workplace, greater innovation, a more highly trained workforce, and a focus on research and development).

No aspect of Japan's remarkable economy has been so consistently underestimated as its employment system. Because the system's three main principles—lifetime-employment, company unions, and seniority pay—flout free-market ideals, Westerners consider it self-evidently incapable in the long run of withstanding global competition from the "more efficient" hire-and-fire labor system of the U.S. and Europe. Thus, every time Japan's economy slows down, influential foreign observers can be counted on to write the system's obituary. Such reports reached a peak during the recession of the early 1990s, when Western publications, led by the *Wall Street Journal* and the *Economist,* vied with one another in printing comments from anonymous sources suggesting that lifetime employment was doomed.

The truth is precisely the opposite. Lifetime employment makes more sense now than ever, and the system's continuing strength is a key reason why Japan, with an unemployment rate of just 3% at its peak during the last recession, has been the one major industrial country to buck the global trend of ever-rising rates of structural unemployment.

Why have Western observers constantly been blind-sided on this point? In part, because they misunderstand a not-quite-what-it-seems system that contains several hidden elements of flexibility, as we shall see later. More important, though, is the widely held and mistaken belief that lifetime employment is deeply rooted in Japanese culture. This is pure myth. In fact, in the early days of Japan's industrialization, employers

Source: Eamonn Fingleton. 1995. "Jobs for Life: Why Japan Won't Give Them Up," *Fortune 131* (March 20), pp. 119–125.

generally operated by hire-and-fire rules, and as a result suffered many of the same labor problems that we think of as peculiarly Western.

Although absenteeism is virtually unknown in Japan today, a century ago it was so common after payday that employers paid different workers on different days to stagger the disruption of output. In the 1920s, Japan suffered a series of bitter strikes in steel, shipbuilding, and mining, and labor turnover in some industries was as high as 100% a year. As recently as the late 1940s Japanese labor relations were notable for widespread confrontation, chaos, even violence.

The employment system in its present form has existed only since World War II. It was consciously invented as Japan's answer to a Western labor regime that Japanese business leaders and bureaucrats concluded was inappropriate for an advanced economy. One vital element was the formation of informal employment cartels in many industries. These restrict competition for labor by requiring rival employers to refrain from hiring from each other. This practice immediately explains one of the most puzzling aspects of the present-day system, Japanese workers' apparent lack of interest in changing jobs. The key reason is not loyalty, as Westerners often imagine, but lack of opportunities.

Via the Employment Security Law of 1947, government officials also won case-by-case powers to block employers from advertising for labor and from hiring any worker whose job change required a change of residence. While these comprehensive curbs strengthened the hand of employers in resisting demands for wage increases, they were balanced by a regulation making it illegal for employers to fire workers. Here stands revealed the reason why Japanese employers persistently refuse to break with the lifetime employment system: They provide job security not because they want to but because they have to.

Despite such legal coercion, however, Japan's employment system offers a host of advantages, many of which are not widely recognized in the West, and only one clear disadvantage—the fact that employers cannot cut labor costs as fast as their Western counterparts when demand turns down.

Consider Japanese corporations' well-deserved reputation for the speed with which they introduce productivity-enhancing new technologies. A big reason is that since Japanese workers enjoy lifetime job guarantees, they see no downside risk in helping employers improve productivity. In fact, they embrace new technology because they know it will enhance their company's future and their own jobs.

One notable example: automation. Japanese workers are delighted for robots to take over dirty, dangerous, and repetitive jobs such as pressing and painting. These machines are often treated as part of the corporate family, to the point where they are named after favorite female singers and movie stars. By contrast, American workers are naturally suspicious of such new labor-saving technology because they know from experience that U.S. employers often use it to cut jobs. It is not surprising, then, that with only half America's work force, Japan has three times as many robots in operation.

If a corporation is to innovate, it must also train its workers to handle ever more sophisticated tasks. Here again the Japanese labor system provides a vital advantage because companies can undertake expensive training programs confident that their enterprise will reap the rewards. By contrast, American employers increasingly consider training a dubious investment, since in the U.S. system trained workers are free to take their skills to rival employers. A recent survey found that U.S. corporations are only one-seventh as likely as their Japanese counterparts to provide new recruits with formal training.

Another major strength of Japan's labor system is the way it encourages corporations to invest in research and development. The key factor here is that thanks to the no-poaching rule, Japanese companies know that their expensively acquired R&D secrets will not leak to competitors via the job market. Such losses are a major problem for American corporations, particularly in the case of innovative new production techniques that are hard to patent but easy for a rival employer to acquire by headhunting a key employee. And since Japanese corporations can expect to keep more of the rewards from R&D than their American competitors, they naturally do more of it. As of the early 1990s, Japan's commercial R&D spending was running at about 3% of GDP, vs. just 2.2% for the U.S.

Now consider the high quality of Japanese management, which is rightly considered a major source of Japan's success. Why are Japanese managers so good? The answer lies mainly in the long-term accountability built into the lifetime employment system. A Japanese executive knows that the decisions he makes today will remain permanently on his record, and he may be asked to account for them many years from now. He cannot simply sweep problems under the carpet.

Japan's employment system also reinforces the labor peace that has generally prevailed in that country in the postwar era, despite the bizarre (at least to Westerners) ritual of the annual wage negotiation. Each year, in many Japanese industries, demonstrating workers fill the sky with red Marxist banners. Labor leaders use language so fiery they would risk arrest in many countries. Sometimes a mob of slogan-chanting workers will corner a top executive in his office and hold him hostage for hours.

If management still has not gotten the message, a union will have no hesitation in resorting to the ultimate weapon—the strike. But at this point things take a distinctly Japanese turn. A Japanese union's idea of a strike is a one-hour work stoppage timed for the lunch break: Workers indignantly put down their tools at noon and don't report back for work until one! If the union has planned things right, the "strike" will not have cost the company a single unit of lost production.

Underneath this theater of the absurd lies a great deal of uncommon common sense. Because the Japanese corporate system has been deliberately arranged to align workers' interests with their employers', a striking Japanese employee generally feels he's striking against his own long-term future. He knows the company will be left weakened and may not have the capital to stay the course in the technology race, which in turn means lower pay raises and less in the kitty for retirement benefits.

What has helped reinforce Japan's latter-day labor peace is that by the late 1950s workers began to recognize that the old them-and-us divide between management and workers had truly begun to disappear. Because workers had been given lifetime job security, they, more than shareholders, had become the real beneficiaries from an enterprise's existence.

Indeed, that stock enemy of American labor, the grasping chief executive officer who is "incentivized" by huge stock options, is unknown in Japan. Top Japanese executives are, generally, salaried employees like everyone else and do not have stock options—a fact that probably reflects an informal prohibition imposed by the Finance Ministry. Thus, they are under no pressure to make penny-wise, pound-foolish cuts in staffing to manipulate short-term profits. And when they call for pay restraint from the work force, as they do in bad times, they act in the role of the workers' leaders, not the workers' opponents.

Top executives in Japan are also modestly compensated by international standards. On an after-tax basis, a typical Japanese CEO is paid only about ten times the earnings of the most junior staff member and just four times the salary of middle-aged workers. The norm in corporate America is close to 100 times, a gap that Fujitsu Chairman Takuma Yamamoto has characterized as "absurd."

It is sometimes assumed that Japan's low executive compensation is simply a manifestation of the strong egalitarianism that runs through East Asian culture. In fact, this policy of keeping a tight lid on top salaries is the linchpin of a highly systematized salary structure in which managers and workers are generally paid and promoted according to seniority rather than competence. In the Japanese promotion race, merit becomes a decisive factor only in the case of senior positions that become available toward the middle or end of a manager's career.

This systemization extends beyond individual corporations. Major companies in the same industry typically pay nearly identical salary scales. In the auto industry, for example, the starting salary for graduates recruited in 1993 was $1,700 a month at all five of the biggest companies—Toyota, Honda, Nissan, Mitsubishi, and Mazda. Every Japanese corporation discloses its starting pay rate in public financial reference books, providing a useful signaling system for young graduates as they size up prospective employers.

All this saves Japanese companies the enormous transaction-cost burden of setting salaries on a person-by-person basis. And given the no-poaching rule of Japanese cartels, Japan's egalitarian salary system is easy to maintain.

The primary rationale of the salary system is to foster teamwork among managers and to eliminate a possible source of friction and jealousy between close colleagues. The system also makes it easy for top management to win workers' cooperation for postings in different departments, a factor that explains not only the speed with which Japanese companies can restructure themselves in a crisis but also the generally high level of communication and cooperation that exists between different departments.

Promotion by seniority rather than competence is to Western eyes one of the strangest aspects of the Japanese employment system. But it has its advantages. One is that it provides a powerful force for cooperation between the generations. Although Westerners argue that competent young people are blocked from reaching their potential in such a system, the truth is generally the opposite. Because senior managers are fully protected against being leapfrogged in the promotion race, they are much more likely than senior managers in the West to mentor their staff.

Perhaps the biggest misconception about Japanese labor economics in the West is that it gives workers a free ride for life. Nothing could be further from the truth. Since seniority pay is, in effect, a form of deferred pay, one of the most persuasive disciplinary tools in the Japanese system is early retirement. Generally, the poorer a person's long-run performance has been, the more likely he is to be asked to take retirement in his 50s or perhaps even in his late 40s. This is a much feared penalty because it means that he misses out on the best earning years of his life.

Officially, early retirees leave voluntarily, but in reality, most do so under threat of coercion. They know that if they resist, their employer has ways of making things uncomfortable. But if they go quietly, they can expect to get a significant termination payment and, more important, vital help in establishing a second career elsewhere. In most cases, large corporations find jobs for their early retirees in closely associated, if less prestigious, companies.

Peer pressure also serves to enforce labor discipline. Workers in a Japanese corporation generally function as part of a clearly identified team, and assignments are given to the team rather than to individuals. Persistent offenders of the team ethic risk ostracism by their peers. This pressure helps explain the apparently irrational behavior of Japanese workers in, say, not claiming their vacation entitlements: An individual worker feels obligated not to claim his rights if this would impair the group's chance of gaining a large salary bonus.

For the worst cases, companies find ways to harass a habitual shirker into resigning. Typically offenders are assigned to the *mado giwa zoku*—the tribe by the window. This denotes a special dunce's corner in which Japanese companies place certified pariahs. The term's significance derives from the fact that in Japan's huge open-plan offices, the further away one is from the center of the floor, the less important one's position or section.

The Japanese labor system contains several other hidden checks and balances without which it would not be an effective tool for employers. Corporate Japan's system of paying large twice-yearly salary bonuses, for instance, is an important shock absorber. In bad times these can be cut or even eliminated, allowing corporations to reduce annual pay levels by as much as 40%.

Another hidden element of flexibility: If a company can convince the authorities that without layoffs its whole future will be jeopardized, it can usually gain exemption from the no-layoff law. Ordinarily this loophole is available only to small employers, which means that companies lower down in the *keiretsu* system operate with employment practices closer to American-style hire-and-fire. Thus, big employers at the top of the *keiretsu* can count on their suppliers' labor flexibility as a swing factor in maintaining their group's viability in tough times.

A final nuance of the system is that many corporations maintain a large pool of low-grade, mainly white-collar workers who are specifically denied employment security under a legal, loophole providing for "temporary" employment. Although in practice such workers are rarely fired, the fact that they can be affords corporate planners a further insurance policy against bad economic conditions.

Such safety valves apart, Japan's labor system aims to provide stable long-term employment for virtually all higher-grade workers. It is backed by tough laws requiring employers to pay significant compensation to any permanent staff member who is involuntarily terminated. The strength of these laws can be gauged from the fact that some staffers at Japan Airlines recently were paid as much as $600,000 each to leave.

Perhaps the most ingenious aspect of Japanese labor economics is the extent to which the main elements of it are mutually reinforcing. The lifetime employment system, for instance, bolsters the company union system. Because employees don't expect to be fired, they have no need for industrywide unions and are content to entrust their negotiating power to company unions.

Similarly, the employment cartels' requirement that companies not hire from each other is a hidden support for the lifetime employment system: It protects employers against the loss of their most talented and productive workers. By contrast, in the modern American employment system, where aggressive employers are allowed to hire away their rivals' best people, any company that offers career-long employment security finds its payroll gradually silts up with subpar performers.

The most profound self-reinforcing effect of the Japanese labor system is the way that lifetime employment helps stabilize the economy in times of recession. To an individual employer, the no-firing rule may seem undesirable but, from the nation's point of view, the rule pays off in damping the downswing in the business cycle. In the Western system, by contrast, workers fired in a recession necessarily cut back their consumption, which throws other workers out of a job and thus further burdens the national welfare system. Japanese planners believe, not unreasonably, that workers contribute more to national output if they are in jobs rather than in dole queues.

When we add up all the fine print, a picture emerges of a highly organized and quite self-sustaining employment system—a system that is the antithesis of the cultural hangover it has long been portrayed as in the West. Jobs for life may be on the way out elsewhere in the industrialized world. But in Japan, at least, they are a central part of a labor system with a bright and stable future.

Health Care and Delivery

THE UNITED STATES CONTEXT

The United States spends more for health care, both in total dollars and percentage of gross domestic product, than any other industrialized nation (the following is taken from Eitzen and Baca Zinn, 2000:411). It also has the most technologically sophisticated health care with the best-trained practitioners. Why, then, when compared to other advanced industrial societies, does the United States have a relatively high infant mortality rate, record the highest percentage of low-birth-weight babies, and rank low in overall life expectancy? The answer to this contradiction is that health care in the United States is rationed on the basis of ability to pay; that is, the system is superb for people who can afford it and falls woefully short for those who cannot. For those with adequate health insurance, the system works. Among the impoverished and near-poor, however, approximately 44.3 million people (1998) are uninsured, including more than 11 million children, which means that they are essentially left outside the health care system. Another 50 million are underinsured, which leaves them exposed to large financial risks or excludes coverage for certain medical problems. In short, the health delivery system in the United States and the health of people in the country are maldistributed on the basis of economic resources.

This has serious consequences, endangering the lives of millions of adults and children on the economic margins. "When people lack health insurance, they often receive substantially poorer health care. The uninsured are more likely to delay health care, receive less preventive and primary care, have illnesses in more advanced stages, and have higher mortality rates [25 percent higher]" (Miringoff and Miringoff, 1999:93).

The problem of inadequate or nonexistent health insurance is increasing. Over the past two decades the proportion of Americans without health insurance has risen from 10.9 percent in 1976 to 16.3 percent in 1998. This increase in the uninsured results from our reliance on obtaining insurance through employment. The problem is that fewer employers are providing coverage for their employees or are limiting their coverage in order to increase or maintain their profits. Also, when workers change jobs, their previous insurance generally is not portable. Of course, workers who are laid off lose their health insurance. Economist Robert Kuttner argues that the United States must change its health care system, in line with what other industrialized nations have:

> *The only way to cut through this mess is, of course, to have universal health insurance. All insurance is a kind of cross-subsidy. The young, who on average need little care, subsidize the old. The well subsidize the sick.*

With a universal system, there is no private insurance industry spending billions of dollars trying to target the well and avoid the sick, because everyone is in the same system. There is no worry about "portability" when you change jobs, because everyone is in the same system. And there are no problems choosing your preferred doctor or hospital, because everyone is in the same system. (Kuttner, 1998:27)

REFERENCES

Eitzen, D. Stanley, and Maxine Baca Zinn. 2000. *Social Problems,* 8th ed. Boston: Allyn and Bacon.

Kuttner, Robert. 1998. "Toward Universal Coverage," *Washington Post National Weekly Edition* (July 20):27.

Miringoff, Marc, and Marque-Luisa Miringoff. 1999. *The Social Health of the Nation: How America Is Really Doing.* New York: Oxford University Press.

21

Primary Care and Health:
A Cross-National Comparison

BARBARA STARFIELD

Ten Western industrialized nations are compared on the basis of three characteristics of their health care systems: (1) the extent of their primary health service, (2) their levels on twelve health indicators, and (3) the satisfaction of their populations regarding the overall costs of their systems. Ratings for the United States were low on all three measures. In contrast, Canada, Sweden, and the Netherlands had generally high ratings on all three measures.

A persisting sense of crisis in the US health services system is responsible for a new willingness to consider experiences from abroad. Debates focus on the relative advantages of various other systems, with the leading contenders for emulation emerging as the Canadian and West German models.[1,2]

Arguments for and against these and other national systems focus largely on their philosophical underpinnings, especially concerning the appropriate balance between the private sector and government and on the costs associated with the different systems. Little of the debate centers on the value of the systems as reflected by indicators of health that are amenable to medical care.

This article presents the results of an analysis of the characteristics of the systems of primary care in 10 Western industrialized nations and the relationship to the attitudes of the populations toward their health services systems and to levels of health as reflected by 12 indicators.

Since primary care is the place of entry (the "gatekeeper") into health services and the locus of continuing care for most of the health problems that occur in the population, it is an appropriate point of departure for an examination of the relationship between the health system and levels of health.

Source: Barbara Starfield. 1991. "Primary Care and Health: A Cross-National Comparison," *Journal of the American Medical Association 166* (October 23), pp. 2268–2271.

METHODS

Ten Western industrialized nations that have comparable data on characteristics of their primary care health systems and health status indicators for the same years were chosen for comparison. Information concerning the characteristics of primary care in the 10 countries was obtained from six major sources.[3-8] Where particular items of information were lacking in these six sources, information was sought from individuals who were from the particular country and who either had access to published data in their country or were experts concerning their country's health services system. Information from the published sources was also confirmed by these individuals or updated where necessary.

Characteristics of primary care were of two types: those related to the overall system and those related to the mode of practice. The former category comprised five characteristics: the type of system (in particular the extent of regulation on place of practice of primary care practitioners); the type of physician who provides primary care (family physician, internist, pediatrician, or specialist); financial access to care (national health insurance sponsored by government, by nongovernmental agencies, or no national health insurance); percentage of active physicians who are specialists; and income of primary care physicians relative to that of specialists.

Six characteristics of primary care were considered to be related to the mode of practice: the extent to which the primary care physician acts as the point of entry into the system; the extent to which that physician provides continuous (longitudinal) care over time; the comprehensiveness of the care provided; the extent of coordination of services by the primary care physician; the extent to which the physician is "family-centered"; and the community orientation of the physician. All of these characteristics have been considered essential or, at least, important in primary care practice.[9-11]

Possible scores for each of the characteristics ranged from zero (where the level of achievement was not conducive to primary care) to two (where the level of achievement was most conducive to primary care). Intermediate levels of achievement were given a score of one. Table 21.1 describes the method of scoring. The score for each country was the average of these 11 scores.

A satisfaction-expense ratio was obtained from a study conducted by Blendon et al.[12] These investigators conducted a telephone survey of a random sample of individuals in 10 countries, seven of which are countries in this analysis. Three statements were posed to people who were asked to indicate which came closest to expressing their overall view of the health care system in their country: "On the whole, the health care system works pretty well, and only minor changes are necessary to make it work better"; "There are some good things in our health care system, but fundamental changes are needed to make it work better"; and "Our health care system has so much wrong with it that we need to completely rebuild it." Hellander and Wolfe[13] used the data from that study to calculate a ratio. The numerator of the ratio is the percentage of people who said that their system needed only minor changes divided by the percentage of people who said that the system needed to be completely rebuilt, and the denominator is the per capita cost of the health care system in thousands of dollars.

TABLE 21.1   Rating Criteria

CRITERIA FOR RATING OF HEALTH SYSTEM CHARACTERISTICS RELATED TO PRIMARY CARE

---

1. **Type of System.**—Regulated primary care or public health centers are considered to be the highest commitment to primary care. Regulated primary care implies that national policies influence the locations of physician practice so that they are distributed throughout the population rather than concentrated in certain geographic areas. Public health centers are also assumed to represent the equitable distribution of physician resources. Intermediate scores connote systems where incentives for equitable distribution are present and moderately effective.

2. **Type of Primary Care Practitioner.**—Generalists (family or general practitioners) are the prototypical primary care physicians because the nature of their training is exclusively devoted to primary care practice. General pediatricians and general internists are considered intermediate primary care practitioners because their training has a major subspecialty focus. Other specialists are not considered primary care physicians because their training is focused on subspecialty issues.

3. **Financial Access to Care.**—Universal government-sponsored national health insurance or a national health entitlement is considered most conducive to access to primary care services. National health insurance sponsored by nongovernmental agencies is considered intermediate because of the absence of uniform benefits. Absence of national health insurance is not considered conducive to access to primary care.

4. **Percentage of Active Physicians Who Are Specialists.**—A value below 50% is considered indicative of an orientation toward primary care. Values of 50% to 75% are considered intermediate, and values above 75% are considered to indicate a specialty-oriented system.

5. **Salary of Primary Care Physicians Relative to Specialists.**—A high ratio (0.9:1 or above) of average salary of primary care physicians to specialty physicians is considered an incentive toward primary care. A low ratio (0.8:1 or less) is considered an incentive toward a specialty-oriented system. Ratios between 0.8 and 0.9 are considered intermediate.

System characteristics not scored for primary care are where care is provided (since there is not evidence that one type of site is better than another), the type of reimbursement of generalists and of specialists (since the impact of type of reimbursement on incentives for primary care practice is unknown), whether or not generalists care for patients in hospitals (since there is little evidence on the impact of this feature of a health services system), and whether or not specialists are restricted to hospitals (since consultations with primary care physicians might be enhanced by limited specialty practice in the community). Even though the assignment of primary care services to a defined geographic area is considered conducive to community orientation and hence potentially pursuant to high level primary care, no points are assigned since community orientation is assessed directly.

CRITERIA FOR RATING PRACTICE CHARACTERISTICS RELATED TO PRIMARY CARE

---

6. **First Contact.**—First contact implies that decisions about the need for specialty services are made after consulting the primary care physician. Requirements for access to specialists via referral from primary care are considered most consistent with the first-contact aspect of primary care. The ability of patients to self-refer to specialists is considered conducive to a specialty-oriented health system. Where there are incentives to reduce direct access to specialists but no requirement for a referral, an intermediate score is assigned.

7. **Longitudinality.**—Longitudinality connotes the extent of relationship with a practitioner or facility over time that is not based on the presence of specific types of diagnoses or health problems. Highest ratings are given where the relationship is based on enrollment with a source of primary care, with the intent that all nonreferred or nondelegated care will be provided by the practitioner. Lowest rates are given where there is not an implicit or explicit relationship over time and intermediate scores are assigned where this relationship exists by default rather than intent.

(continued)

TABLE 21.1   Continued

8.   **Comprehensiveness.**—The extent to which a full range of services is either directly provided by the primary care physician or specifically arranged for elsewhere is the measure of comprehensiveness. Highest ratings are given to arrangements for the universal provision of extensive and uniform benefits and for preventive care. Intermediate ratings are given to arrangements for the provision of either extensive benefits or preventive care, or for concerted efforts to improve these for needy segments of the population. Low ratings are given when there is no policy regarding a minimum uniform set of benefits.

9.   **Coordination.**—Care is considered coordinated where there are formal guidelines for the transfer of information between primary care physicians and specialists. Where this is present for only certain aspects of care (such as long-term care), intermediate ratings are given. Low ratings reflect the general absence of guidelines for the transfer of information about patients.

10. **Family Centeredness.**—High ratings are given to explicit assumption of responsibility for family-centered care. Only one point is assigned to this characteristic, however, since it is related (although not necessarily identical) to the type of primary care physician.

11. **Community Orientation.**—High ratings are given where practitioners use community data in planning for services or for the identification of problems. Intermediate values are assigned where clinical data derived from analysis of data from the practice are used to identify priorities for care. Low ratings are given when there is little or no attempt to use data to plan or organize services.

Twelve indicators of health obtained from reliable sources[14-17] were used to compare the countries: neonatal mortality, postneonatal mortality, total infant mortality, age-adjusted death rate, average life expectancy at age 1 year for males and females separately, average life expectancy at age 20 years for males and females separately, average life expectancy at age 65 years for males and females separately, years of potential life lost, and percentage of birth weights below 2500 g. All of these indicators are relatively standard indicators of health. The only one that may require special explanation is years of potential life lost, because it may not be widely known. It reflects that component of mortality occurring before age 65 years that is considered preventable.[16,17] All data on health indicators were from the mid-1980s except for average life expectancy at ages 1 year and 20 years (1980) and low birth weight (1983 or 1984). The data on each indicator were almost always from the same year for every country. Greater detail regarding each indicator is in Starfield.[18]

To summarize the findings for the health indicators, each country was categorized as being in the upper third, middle third, or lower third of the distribution for all 10 countries. Sometimes there were three countries and sometimes four in the bottom third, depending on whether the adjacent countries had very similar values. In the case of the top third, there were sometimes only two countries because they had values far better than the middle group, which had values very close together. For example, the rates of infant mortality ranged from 5.85 to 10.35 per 1000 live births. Finland and Sweden had values of 5.85 and 5.93 per 1000 live births, respectively, whereas the countries in the middle third had values of 7.76, 7.88, 8.19, 8.54, and 8.85 per 1000 live births. The countries in the bottom third had values of 9.55, 9.69 and 10.35 per 1000 live births.

All characteristics reflected the situation existing in the middle to late 1980s.

Additional details concerning the components of the items, the methods of scoring, and the raw data on the scoring of the primary care components and the levels of each of the health indicators can be found in Starfield[18] or obtained from the author.

RESULTS

The primary care scores ranged from 0.2 in the United States to 1.7 in the United Kingdom. Scores for the other countries were as follows: West Germany, 0.5; Belgium, 0.8; Australia, 1.1; Canada and Sweden, 1.2; and the Netherlands, Denmark, and Finland, 1.5.

The satisfaction-expense index ranged from 0.2 in the United States to 9.0 in the Netherlands. Intermediate values were obtained for the United Kingdom and Australia, 2.1; West Germany, 2.9; Sweden, 4.3; and Canada, 7.6. These data were not available for Belgium, Denmark, and Finland.

Table 21.2 summarizes the position of each country with regard to the health indicators. The United States was in the top third of the distribution for only one indicator—life expectancy at age 65 years for men, in the bottom third for seven of the 12 indicators, and in the middle third for four—life expectancy at ages 1, 20, and 65 years for females and age-adjusted death rate.

West Germany was in the top third for one indicator (neonatal mortality rate), in the bottom third for seven indicators, and in the middle third for four indicator conditions (infant mortality, age-adjusted mortality, years of potential life lost, and the percentage of infants born at low birth weight).

Canada ranked in the top third for five indicators: age-adjusted death rate and life expectancy at ages 1, 20, and 65 years for females and at age 65 years for men. For the remainder of the seven indicators, Canada ranked in the middle third.

TABLE 21.2   Health Indicator Status by Country

| | Health Indicators* | |
| | TOP | BOTTOM |
COUNTRIES	THIRD	THIRD
Australia	3	0
Belgium	0	9
Canada	5	0
Denmark	0	3
Finland	5	6
West Germany	1	7
Netherlands	10	0
Sweden	10	0
United Kingdom	0	8
United States	1	7

*These columns present the number of indicators for which the country falls in the top (best) third of the distribution and the number for which it falls in the bottom (worst) third. Sometimes there were three and sometimes four countries in the bottom third, depending on whether or not the countries had very similar values on the indicator. In the case of the top third, there were sometimes only two countries because they had values far better than the middle group which had values very close to each other. Although there were 31 indicators in all (including separate breakdowns by age and sex), comparable information was available for all countries for only 12 of the indicators (excluding death rates from injuries and natural causes by individual child age group, and immunization rates). Similar ratings are obtained, however, where the other indicators are added and used for comparisons among countries for which they were available.

The Netherlands and Sweden ranked in the top third for all 12 indicators; only Australia, Canada, the Netherlands, and Sweden had no conditions for which they were in the bottom third of the distribution for the 10 countries.

The United Kingdom had no indicator conditions in the top third of the distribution and eight in the bottom third. The only conditions in the middle third of the distribution were neonatal mortality, life expectancy at age 1 year and 20 years for males, and years of potential life lost.

Figure 21.1 summarizes the relationship between the ranking for the primary care score, the satisfaction–expense index, and the health indicators of the seven countries for which all three were available. There is a general tendency for the three indicators to relate to each other. That is, where the primary care score is high, so are the satisfaction–expense index and the number of indicator conditions in the top third of the distribution, while the number of indicator conditions in the bottom third of the distribution is low. The major exception was the United Kingdom which had the highest primary care score

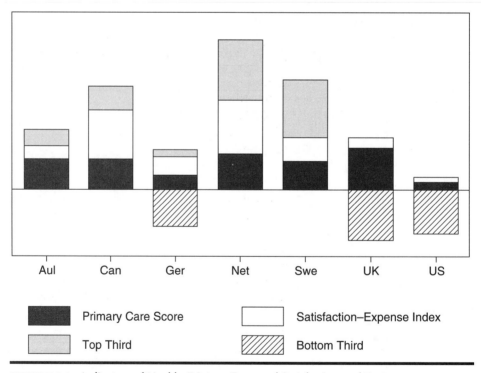

FIGURE 21.1   Indicators of Health, Primary Care, and Satisfaction and Expense

The top third and the bottom third of the distribution contain the number of indicators for which the country was in that third. The ratings for the primary care score were multiplied by 4 to make their ranges comparable with the other two indicators. The satisfaction–expense ratio for the United States was 0.2. Aul indicates Australia; Can, Canada; Ger, West Germany; Net, the Netherlands; Swe, Sweden; and UK, the United Kingdom.

but a low satisfaction–expense index, no conditions in the top third of the distribution, and a large number of conditions in the lowest third of the distribution.

COMMENT

There are several potential limitations of these analyses. The findings are from one point in time only, during the middle to late 1980s. The analyses are descriptive and, in part, based on judgments rather than precise measurements of primary care. The data concerning the health indicators assume accuracy of those indicators and the divisions of the indicators into thirds could only be roughly accomplished.

Nevertheless, the data stem from multiple independent sources, which confirm each other. The ranking of the countries on those indicators for which more recent data are available (such as infant mortality) remain the same. The data on health indicators are from reliable published sources, such as the World Health Organization, the Organization for Economic Cooperation and Development, the National Center for Health Statistics, and the Centers for Disease Control.[14-17] The characterization of the countries as high, middle, or low for each of the health indicators was essentially the same when they were characterized by having clearly extreme values on the top or bottom of the distribution or when the countries were ranked and arbitrary cuts were made so that four countries were always in the top third and four in the bottom third of the distribution. That is, the United States, the United Kingdom, and West Germany were low in their standing, whereas the Netherlands, Sweden, and Canada were high in their standing.

The anomalous position of the United Kingdom, with its high primary care score and low ranking on the health indicators, bears comment. The United Kingdom has the lowest per capita spending on health of all of the countries studied. However, per capita spending does not guarantee high performance on the health indicators, as the United States has by far the highest level of spending of all of the countries. Another possible explanation derives from the observation that the United Kingdom and the United States are the only two countries of the 10 studied that are in the lowest third of the distribution both for the percentage of central government expenditures for housing, social security, and welfare, and for education.[19] Although the United Kingdom, the United States, and West Germany are in the top third of the distribution for the percentage of central governmental expenditures for health, there appears to be little relationship between this indicator and levels of health. Access to primary care services may have little impact on health when other social services are underdeveloped and where resources for public education are relatively inadequate.

The findings of this study have implications for the public debate on appropriate models for modifying the financing and organization of health services in the United States. The specialty orientation of the system and underdevelopment of the primary health care system in this country are well recognized.[20] Financial barriers to services in the absence of national health insurance and restrictions in coverage of many existing health insurance policies exacerbate the limitations on access to primary care.

Alternative explanations for the apparent relationship between the level of health indicators and the extent of development of the primary care sector are not readily evident.

One commonly expressed view is that the heterogeneity of the US population is responsible for its relatively low health levels when compared with the more homogeneous populations of many other industrialized countries. Other analyses have shown that most of the other countries in this study also have substantial minority populations, including the Lapps in Finland, the native American population in Canada, and the foreign workers who have immigrated into many central and northern European countries.[21] At the very least, the findings of this study should indicate the need for consideration of both health levels and the adequacy of the primary care sector when competing systems are debated as possible models for this country.

NOTES

1. Letter from Sen. John Heinz to the General Accounting Office. February 12, 1990.
2. The Pepper Commission (US Bipartisan Commission on Comprehensive Health Care). *A Call for Action.* Washington, DC: US Senate; September 1990.
3. Stephen WJ. *An Analysis of Primary Medical Care: An International Study.* New York, NY: Cambridge University Press; 1979.
4. Swedish Health Services. *Primary Healthcare Today: Some International Comparisons.* Stockholm, Sweden: Swedish Health Services; 1981. Publication HS90.
5. Schroeder S. Western European responses to physician oversupply: lessons for the United States. *JAMA.* 1984;252:373–384.
6. Fry J, Hasler J. *Primary Health Care 2000.* New York, NY: Churchill Livingstone Inc, 1986.
7. Weiner J. Primary care delivery in the United States and four northwest European countries: comparing the "corporatized" with the "socialized." *Milbank Q.* 1987;65:426–461.
8. Iglehart J. Germany's health care system. *N Engl J Med.* 1991;324:503–508.
9. Millis JS. *The Graduate Education of Physicians: Report of the Citizens Commission on Graduate Medical Education.* Chicago, IL: American Medical Association; 1966;37.
10. Alpert J, Charney E. *The Education of Physicians for Primary Care.* Rockville, MD: Public Health Service, Health Resources Administration; 1974. US Dept of Health, Education, and Welfare publication HRA 74–3113.
11. Institute of Medicine. *A Manpower Policy for Primary Health Care.* Washington, DC: National Academy of Sciences; 1978. IOM publication 78–02.
12. Blendon R, Leitman R, Morrison I, Donelan K. Satisfaction with health systems in ten nations. *Health Aff.* 1990;9:185–192.
13. Hellander I, Wolfe S. Which countries are satisfied with their health care? *Health Lett.* 1990;6(8):9–10.
14. World Health Organization. *World Statistics Annual.* Geneva, Switzerland: World Health Organization; 1986.
15. Organization for Economic Cooperation and Development. *Living Conditions in OECD Countries.* Paris, France: Organizations for Economic Cooperation and Development; 1986. Social policy studies No. 3.
16. Centers for Disease Control. Premature mortality in the United States. *MMWR.* 1986;35:29–31.
17. Centers for Disease Control. Mortality in developed countries. *MMWR.* 1990;39:205–209.
18. Starfield B. *Primary Care: Concept, Evaluation, and Policy.* New York, NY: Oxford University Press Inc. In press.
19. World Bank. *World Development Report 1990.* New York, NY: Oxford University Press Inc; 1990.
20. Beeson P. Too many specialists, too few generalists. *Pharos.* 1991;54:2–6.
21. Williams B, Miller. A *Preventive Health Care for Young Children: Findings from a 10-Country Study and Directions for United States Policy.* Arlington, VA: National Center for Clinical Infant Programs; 1991.

22

The Health Care System in Sweden

SWEDISH INSTITUTE

This article describes the health care system in Sweden. Fundamental to the Swedish system is the belief that it is a public sector responsibility to provide and finance health care for everyone in the country. Good health and equal access to health services for everyone are the goals of the Swedish health care system.

A fundamental principle of the health care system is that it is a public sector responsibility to provide and finance health services for the entire population. Responsibility for these services rests primarily with the county councils, which levy taxes to raise the financial resources required and also operate almost all the services provided. Thus it is mainly local politicians, in 21 geographical areas, who are responsible for health services in Sweden. Two characteristics of the Swedish system are that it is decentralised and it is run on democratic principles.

THE HEALTH SITUATION

By international standards, health in Sweden is relatively good. Infant mortality is low, at 4.1 deaths per 1,000 in the first year of life. Of the predominant diseases, cardiovascular conditions account for half of all deaths. However, deaths attributable to these diseases diminished substantially during the 1980s, and this has contributed to an increased average life expectancy. For men average life expectancy is 76.5 years and for women 81.5 years. Over a long period of years, mortality from injuries, alcohol-related diseases and suicide has also declined. The proportion of the population with allergic conditions doubled during the 1980s. More than one third of all Swedish residents say that they suffer some form of allergy or over-sensitivity. Another public health problem is the growing proportion of overweight individuals among children and young people as well as the middle-aged. The number of elderly people has risen substantially—with the greatest rise in the age group 80 years and older. Sweden is seen as having the world's oldest population, with 18% aged 65 or over. There are marked differences in health between different social groups, and these differences are growing.

Source: Swedish Institute. 1999. *Fact Sheets on Sweden* (May).

THE HEALTH SERVICES

The primary level is the level of the health care system to which people shall be able to turn with all their health problems. The primary care sector has the aim of improving the general health of the people and treats diseases and injuries that do not require hospitalisation. This sector employs many different professional categories—physicians, nurses, auxiliary nurses, midwives and physiotherapists. Their work has been organised in health centres, which has facilitated teamwork. During recent years there has been a structural change in the work of the doctors in primary care—today everyone may choose a doctor who has qualified as a general practitioner as their own family doctor.

In addition to local health centres and family doctor surgeries, primary care is also provided by private doctors and physiotherapists; at district nurse clinics; and at clinics for child and maternity health care. At the children's clinics, vaccinations, health checks and consultations as well as certain types of treatment are provided free of charge to all children under school age. At the maternity clinics there are both midwives and doctors. These clinics are visited by expectant mothers for regular check-ups, which are free of charge during the entire pregnancy. The district nurses give medical treatment as well as advice and support, both at their clinics and when visiting patients in their homes. Industrial health services and school health services are also available to specific groups.

By adapting housing, using technical aids, and providing medical services and nursing in the homes of patients, it is both possible and easier for elderly and disabled people to stay in their own homes. People in hospitals for long-term patients, in nursing homes and those living in service apartments have access to nursing services 24 hours a day. Great importance is attached to making these places as much like home as possible. Most of the patients in nursing homes, for example, have their own room.

For conditions that require hospital treatment, medical services are provided at county level and regional level. County medical services are available at some 80 central county hospitals and district county hospitals. Here, somatic care is provided in a number of specialist fields, partly as inpatient care and partly at clinics (outpatient care). The county medical services also include psychiatric care, which is provided to an increasing extent in outpatient forms. The regional medical system is operated at nine regional hospitals, which have a greater range of specialist and sub-specialist fields than at county level, for example neurosurgery, thoracic surgery, plastic surgery and highly specialised laboratories.

In Sweden a relatively large proportion of the resources available for medical services has traditionally been allocated to the provision of care and treatment at hospitals. This can be seen, for example, in the low number of visits per person and year to doctors in the primary care services. The number of general practitioners is also low in relation to the total number of doctors (approximately 20%).

The number of days of short-term care per person and year has decreased during the last few years for all age groups. In long-term care, too, the number of inpatient days has decreased per person per year in most age groups. Extensive changes have been made in the area of psychiatric care during the last ten years. People with mental handicaps have, to a great extent, left institutional care and now live in the community. At the same time as reductions have been made in inpatient care, more outpatient care has been established.

The changes that have taken place in inpatient care must be seen in relation to the deliberate emphasis given to various forms of outpatient care. An increasing proportion of visits to doctors is made outside the hospitals and the nature of these visits has also changed. An increasing amount of treatment is given and operations performed without the patient needing to be taken into hospital. The introduction of day surgery, for example, can illustrate the changes that are taking place. The deliberate emphasis on outpatient forms of care also means that visits to medical staff other than doctors is encouraged.

MANAGEMENT AND PLANNING

In Swedish society there are three political and administrative levels—central government, county council and local authority. All these levels have important roles in the welfare system and are represented by directly elected political bodies that have the right to finance their activities by levying taxes and fees.

One important role for central government is to lay down basic principles for the health services through laws and ordinances. The most important of these is the Health and Medical Services Act of 1982, which lays down that the people shall be offered health and medical services of good quality which shall be provided on equal terms and be easily accessible to all. The services provided shall be based on respect for the patient's integrity and his right to make his own decisions. They should also, as far as possible, be organised and performed in consultation with the patient. Other laws regulate the obligations and responsibility of personnel, professional confidentiality, patients' records and the qualifications required by personnel to practise in the health professions. The number of detailed rules has diminished during recent years. Today central government is more interested in the results and performance of the services rather than how they are organised. It is chiefly by means of systems for follow-up and evaluation that central government can exercise control over the health services.

The Ministry of Health and Social Affairs (*Socialdepartementet*) is responsible for developments in areas such as health care, social insurance and social issues. The Ministry draws up terms of reference for government commissions, drafts proposals for Parliament on new legislation, and prepares other government regulations.

The National Board of Health and Welfare (*Socialstyrelsen*) is the government's central advisory and supervisory agency in the field of health services, health protection and social services. The key task of this agency is to follow up and evaluate the services provided to see whether they correspond with the goals laid down by central government.

Another government agency that is engaged in evaluation work is the Swedish Council of Technology Assessment in Health Care (*SBU*). The SBU shall contribute towards the efficient utilisation of the resources allocated to the health services by evaluating both new and established methods from medical, social and ethical perspectives. Reviews of current knowledge in the field and syntheses of existing scientific material are produced with the aid of experts. Information on the SBU's findings is then disseminated to central and local government officials and medical staff to provide basic data for decision-making purposes.

Under the Health and Medical Services Act the county councils are responsible for providing health services and for striving to achieve a good standard of health in the population. In Sweden there are 20 county councils. One local authority (Gotland) also has the same responsibilities as the county councils where health care is concerned. In addition to health services, the county councils are responsible for certain issues related to education, culture, public transport and regional development. In the latter field, the county councils in Skåne and Västra Götaland have a wider range of tasks and are referred to as regions. The population of these 21 areas varies between 60,000 and 1.7 million people. County council elections are held at the same time as parliamentary elections—every fourth year. The county councils decide on the allocation of resources to the health services and are responsible for the overall planning of the services offered. It is also the county councils which own and run the hospitals, health centres and other institutions, even if these institutions are supplemented by those of private organisations which, in most cases, have contracts with the county councils.

The total domination of the county councils in the provision of health services enables them to make decisions on structural issues in the health services. During recent years considerable changes have taken place in this area, particularly the reduction in the number of beds but also where other hospital activities are concerned, such as the cutbacks in the number of casualty wards open 24 hours a day. The reduction in the number of beds has been achieved by increases in productivity generated by new medical technology, shrinking financial resources, and incentives resulting from the development of financial management systems.

One significant change introduced by the county councils in recent years is the freedom for patients to choose where and by whom they wish to be given medical attention. Patients can choose the health centre and/or family doctor and even which hospital they wish to attend. If a patient wishes to receive medical care at a hospital outside the county council in which he or she resides, a referral may be required. A patient does not usually need a referral to obtain specialist hospital care—he/she can go directly to the hospital without going via the primary services. The primary level therefore does not always have a referral function; the way in which the county councils can influence patients' decisions about which part of the health care system to approach first is to differentiate consultation fees.

Where highly specialised care is concerned, and, to a certain extent, research and the training of doctors, the county councils co-operate in six medical care regions. The population of these regions varies from 900,000 to 1.9 million and in each region there is at least one university hospital. This collaboration is based on agreements between the county councils in the region, for example on the prices that shall be charged for highly specialised care. The county councils also collaborate at national level through the Federation of County Councils (*Landstingsförbundet*).

One example of the management of the health services is the introduction of a care guarantee for patients which has been in force since 1992. This guarantee was the result

**EMPLOYEES IN THE COUNTY COUNCIL
HEALTH SERVICES (SELECTED PROFESSIONAL
CATEGORIES, 1997)**

Doctors	23,000
Nurses	70,000
Auxiliary nurses	64,000
Physiotherapists	5,000
Occupational therapists	4,000

Note: SEK 1 (Swedish krona) = USD 0.12 or GBP 0.07
(May 1999)

of an agreement concluded at national level by the Ministry of Health and Social Affairs and the Federation of County Councils to reduce the waiting time for certain forms of treatment for which there were long queues. The nature of the agreement has changed, and it is now chiefly concerned with accessibility for patients. The primary care services shall offer help the same day that the patient contacts them, with a medical consultation within eight days. Where necessary the patient shall be able to see a specialist within three months, or within one month if his or her medical condition has not been clearly diagnosed. The aim of these new criteria for accessibility is to reinforce the position of the patient vis-à-vis the care services. This aim is to be further emphasised by the extension of the care guarantee to patients with severe chronic illnesses, such as diabetes, who will be ensured an agreed standard of care.

The local authorities also have their own area of responsibility within the field of health services, namely the care of elderly and disabled people in the places where they live. In 1992 the responsibility for, among other things, nursing homes was transferred to the local authorities from the county councils. At the same time the local authorities also assumed the obligation to pay for patients who had been treated in a hospital and who were obliged to remain in hospital since the local authority could not offer a suitable place in, for example, a nursing home. A similar change in responsibility came into force in 1995, this time concerning the living arrangements, employment and support for those suffering from long-term mental illnesses.

FINANCES

Sweden's costs for its health services amounted in 1996 to SEK 128 billion. This figure includes costs for pharmaceutical preparations and dental care. This corresponded to 7.6% of GNP. About 90% of the costs were spent on care provided or financed by the county councils.

The health services account for some 85% of the operations of the county councils. Most of these operations, or 77% (1997), are financed by tax revenues. The county councils are entitled to levy a proportional tax on the incomes of their residents. On average the tax rate is 10.2%. Other revenue sources of significance to the county councils are

DISTRIBUTION OF PUBLIC HEALTH CARE COSTS, 1997

Somatic short-term care	60%
Geriatric care	4%
Psychiatric care	13%
Primary care	17%
Dental care	4%
Other	2%

grants and payments for certain services received from central government, in total 9%. Patients' fees amount to 4% of county council revenue.

The revenues of the county councils, and thus the health services, have diminished in recent years due to reductions in the tax base. To counteract this deterioration in their finances, the county councils have reduced their expenditure in real terms by 1.5% per year between 1992 and 1997. Patients have spent less time in hospital and have been treated more often as outpatients. The number of beds in short-term somatic care has been reduced from 4.4 per 1,000 inhabitants in 1985 to 2.7 per 1,000 inhabitants in 1997. The corresponding figures for psychiatric care are 2.5 in 1985 and 0.7 in 1997. It is possible that patients will become more aware of the reductions in the future, when the potential for further streamlining of the health services has been exhausted.

In the early 1990s, most county councils introduced some form of purchaser–provider model in their medical services. Under this model the traditional system of fixed annual allocations to hospitals and primary care services has partly been abandoned. Instead, payment is made according to results or performance. In some county councils, competition with the private sector has been encouraged. Special purchasing units, normally under the leadership of a committee of politicians, have been formed with the task of formulating the requirements which should be made of the hospitals by the county councils and of evaluating quality and prices. The hospitals, for their part, have become more independent in relation to political bodies.

PATIENTS' FEES

Those entitled to use the Swedish health services at subsidised prices are all residents of Sweden regardless of nationality, as well as patients seeking emergency attention from EU/EEA countries and some other countries with which Sweden has a special convention.

The fee charged for a stay in hospital is SEK 80 per day.

Each county council sets its own fees for outpatient care. The fee for consulting a doctor in the primary health services, that is to say a family doctor or a district doctor, varies between county councils from SEK 100 to SEK 140. For consulting a specialist at a hospital or a doctor in private practice, the fees vary from SEK 120 to SEK 250.

The county councils also set patients' fees for other medical treatment—for example for visits to physiotherapists, occupational therapists and nurses, both in the public health services and, should the occasion arise, in private care. The fees vary from SEK 50 to SEK 120 per visit, depending on the county council.

To limit the expenses incurred by patients there is a high-cost ceiling. A patient who has paid a total of SEK 900 in patients' fees is entitled to free medical care for the rest of the twelve-month period, calculated from the date of the first consultation. Children and young people under 20 do not need to pay any patients' fees.

Sweden has an extensive system of benefits for the sick. The main component of this system is sickness benefit, but it also includes compensation for participation in labour market rehabilitation schemes, compensation payable to persons with infectious diseases who are obliged to stay in quarantine, and benefits payable to expectant mothers who are unable to work due to pregnancy.

PHARMACEUTICAL PREPARATIONS

Before a medicine may be sold in Sweden, it must be registered at the Medical Products Agency (*Läkemedelsverket*), which is a government authority responsible for the control of pharmaceutical preparations. The activities of this authority are regulated in a new law governing medical products that has been adapted to EU regulations. The number of registered pharmaceutical preparations is approximately 3,800. The prices of pharmaceuticals are set by means of negotiations between the central government and pharmaceutical companies.

Under the terms of the social insurance scheme, the patient pays the entire cost of prescribed pharmaceutical preparations up to SEK 900. Above this a rising scale of subsidy operates, with a high-cost ceiling, which means that the patient never has to pay more than SEK 1,800 in any twelve-month period.

The responsibility for financing the pharmaceutical subsidy previously rested with the central government, but on 1 January 1998 it was taken over by the county councils, which have traditionally borne most costs of health services in Sweden. The financing is based on annual negotiations between the Federation of County Councils and the central government.

The National Corporation of Swedish Pharmacies (*Apoteket AB*), in which the state is the majority shareholder, has the sole and exclusive right to retail medicines, both to the general public and to hospitals. This is done via 885 pharmacies. The pharmaceutical companies have insurance coverage that provides compensation to patients who are harmed by a medicine.

DENTAL CARE

The county councils are responsible for ensuring that all children and young people up to the age of 19 years receive free dental care. Here the emphasis is placed on preventive care. The dental health of this group has improved considerably since the 1970s and continues to improve steadily. Adults receive an economic subsidy from the national dental insurance system for basic dental care. The pricing of dental care has been deregulated, which means that providers set their own fees for each form of treatment. There is also an option to sign two-year agreements on the provision of basic dental care at a fixed price. For certain more extensive dental procedures, there is a special high-cost protection system, aimed at limiting patients' outlays. Approximately half of all dentists work in the national dental service, which is run by the county councils; the others are private dentists. The county councils are responsible for ensuring that sufficient specialist dental care is available to meet the needs of both children and adults.

STAFF

Just over 225,000 people are employed in the health services, i.e., about 6% of all employees in the country. This number has diminished in recent years, partly due to the financial squeeze and changes in the work done by the services. There is a tendency for the numbers of doctors and nurses to increase at the expense of less qualified staff. There is a certain shortage of nurses, especially nurses with specialist training. It is also difficult to recruit doctors to certain geographic areas and to certain specialist fields. In Sweden there is one physician (under the age of 65 years) per 320 inhabitants.

In addition to the above, there are some 1,700 physicians and 2,200 physiotherapists working in private practices. They are paid by the county councils per visit/call in accordance with a fee scale determined by the central government.

The average salary of a hospital doctor with a specialist qualification is SEK 38,000 per month. The salary of a nurse is approximately SEK 17,000 per month.

The head of a department is, almost without exception, a doctor with the overall responsibility for the management of the clinic. This includes responsibility for medical services as well as administration, finance and personnel.

TRAINING AND RESEARCH

Doctors are trained at the universities of Lund, Gothenburg, Linköping, Stockholm (Karolinska Institute), Uppsala and Umeå. The training programmes are linked to the operations of the university hospitals and other relevant parts of the health services, for example the primary health service. To become a registered doctor, a student must successfully complete a study programme of five and a half years and an 18-month pre-registration period as a house officer. On registration a doctor is authorised to practise medicine, but almost all doctors continue their studies in order to qualify as a specialist after five years' service in one of the 62 recognised specialist fields. Every year some 900 students start medical training programmes. The study programme for nurses lasts three years and is available at some 30 colleges of nursing, which admit some 3,500 new students each year.

Swedish medical research has a prominent international position in many fields. It is characterised by strong links between basic research and clinical research and by the integration of research and development into the health services, particularly at the university hospitals. Medical research is mostly financed by government funds, but the county councils also provide resources for clinical research that is closely connected to patient care. The strong position occupied by medical research in Sweden is demonstrated by the fact that about 25% of university research spending goes to the medical field.

QUALITY AND SAFETY

During the 1990s, quality-oriented development work has gained a stronger position in the Swedish health services. The aim of this work is to generate value-added for the people these services are intended for—patients, their relatives and the public in general— and to improve the health care system's ability to meet their needs.

Important target areas are the availability and client focus of health services and the degree to which they are knowledge-based. Special agreements between the central government and the Federation of County Councils have established that this is a desirable orientation for the development efforts that are underway in the Swedish health care system.

In 1994, the National Board of Health and Welfare issued a set of regulations on quality issues, which it reworked in 1997. These regulations state that all health services in Sweden shall include a system for continuous quality improvement. The new regulations embody a changed approach to quality assurance work—from an emphasis on monitoring and quality-improvement measures that focus on technical quality to covering the full range of health services in a continuous, target-oriented development process focusing on the people for whom health services are intended.

One expression of this increased activity is that since 1996, there has been a Swedish instrument for analysing the ability of the health services to achieve systematic quality improvement, known as QUL. Developed by the Federation of County Councils, this instrument is linked to the Swedish Health Services Quality Award, presented annually to an organisation that, after an evaluation procedure, can be considered to provide a model for the Swedish health care system.

The Swedish health services have access to another invaluable asset: the clinical improvement efforts represented by some 50 national health care quality registers, each containing data on health care outcomes and treatment measures in an equal number of illness categories. These registers serve as a knowledge base for continuous improvement efforts.

To build up a broader knowledge base in the health care system, evidence-based diagnostic and treatment guidelines are being developed at the national level for such major categories of chronic illness as diabetes, stroke and coronary artery disease.

If, in connection with medical care or treatment, a patient suffers a serious injury or illness, or is exposed to the risk of injury or illness, the institution providing the care or treatment is obliged to report this fact to the National Board of Health and Welfare. Where faults or negligence are attributable to members of staff, the matter can be referred to the National Medical Disciplinary Board (*Hälso-och sjukvårdens ansvarsnämnd*), a government authority whose organisation is somewhat similar to that of a court. A patient or a relative of a patient can approach the Board if he considers that health service staff members have acted incorrectly. The Board can decide on disciplinary measures (warning or admonition) or remove the person from the professional register.

The Board does not deal with the matter of financial compensation for a patient who has suffered an injury. There is a patient' insurance scheme which covers such claims. The issue of holding staff responsible for their actions and deciding on sanctions is therefore kept separate from the issue of financial compensation for the patient.

Since the mid-1970s, the county councils and other institutions providing health care services have voluntarily assumed responsibility to grant financial compensation to patients who have suffered injuries during treatment. A patient who has been injured, infected or has met with an accident in connection with an examination or treatment can be compensated, regardless of whether it is the responsibility of the medical services or not. From 1997, every institution organising health care will have a legal obligation to provide compensation for injuries that occur in the course of these services. The institutions are insured to meet demands for compensation from patients.

CURRENT ISSUES

Responsibility for subsidising pharmaceuticals was transferred in 1998 from the central government to the county councils. The background was sharply rising pharmaceutical costs over a period of years, but so far the reform has not slowed these cost increases to the extent desired. Meanwhile new, expensive drugs are being introduced, leading to an intensive discussion of prioritisation—pharmaceuticals are, after all, financed from the total county council budgets for health services and thus compete with other forms of treatment. Letting patients pay a larger share of drug costs or eliminating all subsidies on drugs mostly related to lifestyles are examples of measures under discussion.

Throughout the 1990s, the position of patients has gradually become stronger. This includes expanded options for choosing care providers (hospitals, local health centres, doctors' surgeries, etc.) and maximum waiting times for visits and treatment. Another aspect is stronger patient influence in health services, for example improved and individually tailored information on patients' health condition and treatment alternatives, as well as greater opportunities to influence the choice of treatment. But the issue of patient influence and availability of health services remains controversial. Above all, this focuses on the issue of whether patients should be given a guarantee that they will receive all treatment within a certain period, maximised at three months.

The hottest topic, however, is the issue of overall health care resources. The financial resources of the Swedish health services have been shrinking throughout the 1990s. Altogether, this represents cost reductions of nearly 10% in real terms. Meanwhile health care needs have risen, due to both demographic trends and medical progress. There are two opposing viewpoints on the issue. One says that there is still room to meet growing health care needs by means of continued efficiency-raising measures. The other side argues that further cost reductions are not possible without severe consequences, both for patients and for employees in the health care system.

23

Long-Term Care:
A Comparison of Policies and Services in Israel and the United Kingdom and Implications for the United States

CAROLE COX

The issue of long-term care continues to be a main concern in the United States. As the country wrestles with the development of policies and services, the experiences of Israel, whose system rests upon national insurance, and that of the United Kingdom, which is based on grants to local authorities, can act as valuable teaching aids in the development of programs in the United States. Although both countries focus on community care with virtually universal access, concern over resources is forcing each to target their services increasingly to the most frail. The findings underscore the necessity for accurate planning and adequate resources if services are to meet the needs of the frail elderly population.

More than 12 million Americans, due to chronic physical impairments, report a need for nonmedical assistance with the routines of daily living (U.S. Government Accounting Office, 1995). The continued growth of the elderly population in the United States has meant that increased attention is being given to the area of long-term care and the most effective ways of meeting the needs of those persons with reduced capacity for self-care. Although the majority of assistance is provided by the informal system, the capacity of caregivers is often sorely taxed by the demands of work and family, their own aging, and the increasing frailty of their relatives. Formal services that can relieve and assist them in maintaining these frail elderly in the community and prevent institutionalization are essential. As discussion and debate continue about how to best and most effectively meet the needs of this population, the experiences with long-term care in other countries can act as valuable teaching aids in the development of U.S. policy and program reforms.

Source: Carole Cox. 1997. "Long-Term Care: A Comparison of Policies and Services in Israel and the United Kingdom and Implications for the United States," *The Journal of Aging & Social Policy 9* (2), pp. 81–99.

This article examines long-term care in Israel, a centralized system benefiting only older persons and funded through national insurance, and in the United Kingdom, a decentralized system open to all persons with long-term care needs and funded largely through grants to local authorities. Government documents, reports, and papers in each of the respective countries in conjunction with information obtained by the author in interviews with policymakers and service providers in Israel and the United Kingdom provide the basis for the review.

In both Israel and the United Kingdom, a key impetus for the development of long-term care reforms has been the prevention of unnecessary and costly institutionalization of older persons by providing community care services. Prior to reform, both countries maintained systems of care that were fragmented and biased towards institutional care. Consequently, in both countries, the reforms focused on developing a continuum of community-based services.

ISRAEL

Israel's population, as the populations of the United States and the United Kingdom, is rapidly aging. Since the founding of the country in 1948, the elderly population has more than doubled, increasing from 3% to 4% of the total to 9.4% in 1993, Accompanying this change has been a substantial increase in the number of old-old, those 85 years and older. whose numbers expanded by 100% between 1970 and 1990 (Habib & Factor, 1994). Between 1980 and 1990, the number of functionally disabled elderly increased from 31,500 to 44,800, composing 12% of the elderly population in 1995.

This shift in the age structure of the population, with its concomitant demands for care, resulted in an expensive system of community and institutional services in Israel. Concern over the rising costs of this system and its adequacy in addressing the needs of the growing older population contributed to the enactment in 1988 of the Community Long Term Care Insurance Law (CLTCI). This legislation sought to assure that all of the state organizations involved in long-term care of the aged would be integrated into one system through which the needs of the disabled elderly would be addressed.

Services available under the law were intended to provide alternatives to more costly institutionalization. Estimates were that approximately 60% of the disabled elderly on waiting lists for institutional care could be cared for in their homes at substantially lower costs than those of institutions (Habib, Factor, Naon, Brodsky & Dolev, 1986).

The Community Long-Term Care Insurance Law (CLCI)

The CTCLI Law defines the government's role in providing services to the severely disabled elderly on the basis of personal entitlement and eligibility criteria. The law is funded through long-term care insurance contributions paid by workers (0.2% of wages) and contributions from the government. Responsibility for program administration, monitoring of benefits, and determining eligibility was given to the National Insurance Institute. In this way, the stigma often associated with services given through welfare departments was avoided. In addition, as the program is an entitlement, it does not have a capped budget. Everyone meeting the eligibility criteria is entitled to receive benefits.

The legislation was intended to supplement rather than supplant the informal care system. Similar to the situation in other countries, the majority of care to the disabled elderly is provided by family members who provide an average of 20 to 45 hours of assistance per week (Brodsky & Naon, 1993). Through a "basket" of in-kind services, home care, personal care, day care, incontinence supplies, and alarm systems, the aim has been to relieve the burden placed on the family and thus reduce the need for nursing home placement.

About 10% of the elderly population receive services under the law (Bar-Giora & Kerem, 1995). This amounts to a five-fold increase in the amount of home care provided to this population since the law's implementation in 1988. In the first year of the Law's implementation alone, the number of elderly receiving personal services quadrupled, rising from 5,000 to 20,000 persons (Korazim & Kahan, 1993). The number of persons receiving benefits, 58,000 in 1995, far exceeded the original projected number of 10,000. Factors responsible for this unanticipated demand for care include the increase in the number of older persons and especially in the population aged 80 and over, as well as a massive influx of immigrants, many of them older and disabled, from the Soviet Union.

Indicative of the impact of the new legislation on community care is the dramatic shift that occurred in the budgeting of services. Prior to 1988, community services received 17% of the government's funds for long-term care; in 1990, this had increased to 55%.

Assessment and Eligibility

Approximately 20,000 assessments for services are made each year with half of those assessed found eligible for services. Anyone can request an assessment from the local community care committee. It is conducted by a public health nurse in the person's home. The examination focuses on the activities of daily living (ADLs) and requires the person to attempt to dress, eat, get in and out of the shower or bath, and to move about the house. The need for supervision is assessed separately and is an area in which the nurse has more flexibility and can be more subjective in scoring.

Eligibility for services is based on age, severity of disability, and income. Men over 65 years and women over 60 who are severely dependent in their mobility, bathing, dressing, feeding; are incontinent; and have a need for supervision are eligible. Single elderly persons are eligible if their income is not higher than the average wage (approximately $US 1,200 per month); for couples the ceiling is 1.5 times the average wage (approximately $US 1,800 per month). Single persons with incomes less than 1.5 times higher than the average wage and couples with incomes less than 2.25 times higher are eligible for half the benefits. Houses and other capital and savings are not included in determining financial eligibility. As only about 10% of the elderly are ineligible due to income, the program is considered to be a universal entitlement.

There are two levels of disability. Those less disabled are eligible for service benefits equivalent to 25% of the average wage, or about $US 300 per month and those who are more disabled are eligible for service benefits equal to 37% of the average wage, or $US 450 per month. These benefits cover between two and three hours of personal care in the home per day, to a maximum of 16 hours per week, or six hours a day, five days a week at a day care center.

In determining the amount of disability and services required, persons living alone receive an additional 2 points on the assessment instrument. Persons requiring constant supervision automatically receive 6.5 points. Scores ranging from 2.5 points to 6 points entitle one to 10 to 11 hours of home care per week. Scores above 6.5 points make the person eligible for the higher level of service or 16 hours of care per week. Although a "basket" of services (which can include day care, occupational therapy, and personal response systems) is available, the majority of recipients receive only home care.

The wide range of points that can be obtained on assessments has made targeting of services difficult. In order to relate benefits more closely to the disability, a third level of care of four to six hours per week is being considered for those with lower levels or impairment. Introducing greater flexibility into the system and assuring a better match between needs and resources is viewed as necessary to increase the sensitivity and effectiveness of the program (Morginstin, Baich-Moray, & Zipkin, 1993).

Assessments are reviewed by a committee composed of a representative of the national insurance fund, clinic nurse, and social worker at the local district health office. There are 200 committees in Israel, each responsible for its own mode of operation, services, and providers. The committee formulates the care plan, selects the care manager, usually a social worker, and selects the home care agency with little involvement of the client in the decisions. Any changes in services or the care plan must be approved by the committee. All home care must be provided by certified agencies. However, within the Arab communities, if the older person is reluctant to have a stranger in the home, trained family members may act as providers.

Services must begin within two weeks of the assessment, with special provisions for immediate services for those requiring urgent help. Although the Law mandates reassessments, there is no requirement regarding their timing. Thus, given average caseloads of over 200, reassessments are given little priority by case managers. Unfortunately, as needs change, underservice and overservice are likely to occur.

In addition to actual services, older persons living with a family caregiver in an area without any formal services may be eligible for cash benefits. Older persons living alone are not eligible for cash benefits but are given priority for entrance into residential or nursing homes. The cash benefits are intended to provide some financial assistance to the families as well as offer recognition of their involvement. These benefits are given only until services in a community can be developed.

The preference of the government is to offer in-kind services, such as home care and day care, which are viewed as more effective in reducing the burden experienced by informal caregivers as well as in stimulating the development of formal service agencies (Factor, Morginstin, & Naon, 1991). On the other hand, proponents of cash benefits have argued that they would help to compensate family caregivers. Cash benefits would also empower the elderly by enabling them to choose their own services and providers.

Ministry of Labour and Social Affairs

Community care services are also offered under the Ministry of Labour and Social Affairs to frail elderly with low incomes who require assistance but do not meet the criteria for services under the CTCLI. Eligibility is restricted to those whose incomes are 25% of the average monthly wage or approximately $400 per month. Persons receiving only a pension and a supplement are automatically entitled to services. The requirements for services are standardized throughout the country and are based on limitations in functioning and mobility problems, with priority given to those living alone. Because the Ministry does not use a strict scoring system, there is greater flexibility with regard to eligibility than is found under the CTCLI.

The amount of assistance given is less than that offered under the CTCLI. Recipients are limited to 25 hours of care per month, averaging about 4 hours per week, and are entitled to either home care or day care as well as meals-on-wheels. All services are provided by certified agencies which must have nurses or social workers supervising home care workers. Recipients are not charged for home care but are expected to pay for day care. These payments, approximately $5.00 per day, may be subsidized by the Ministry.

Each local welfare department receives 75% of its funds for services from the Ministry according to a formula that takes into account the number of elderly persons in the community, the number receiving pension supplements, the number who received services in the previous year, and current government priorities. The municipality is responsible for raising the remaining 25%. The Ministry decides on the proportion of funds to be distributed to each service, such as home care, day care, and meals.

By July of each year, most municipalities are experiencing a deficit and rely upon the Ministry to cover their costs. The strain to meet the demand for services is particularly acute in poorer areas where needs can far exceed the available funds. Consequently, even though the program is an entitlement, waiting lists for services often develop. In 1995, 25,000 older persons received services through the Ministry.

Residential Care

There are three types of institutions for older persons in Israel, each operated by a separate agency. Nursing homes are administered by the Ministry of Health and are for the very frail and cognitively impaired. The sick funds or Health Maintenance Organizations have responsibility for institutional care for those with chronic illnesses requiring complex skilled care, and the Ministry of Labor and Social Affairs is responsible for residential care for those with moderate dependency.

Eligibility for entrance to a nursing home is determined by a committee in the district health office. In contrast to community care, there are no standardized assessment forms or criteria for placement. Consequently, the decision is usually based on the availability of beds, the severity of the older person's disability, and whether or not care can be adequately provided in the community. These assessments are made without the committee having seen the older person and are based solely on reports from doctors and the district nurse. They are independent of reviews for community care.

Both the income of the resident and that of all of his or her children, regardless of whether or not the older person had lived with the child, are assessed for payments for care. These payments range from zero to approximately $US 2,000 per month with the average payment approximately $US 1,500. Regulations require children to contribute on the premise that they are responsible for their parents. However, this requirement may, in some instances, also act as a financial incentive to maintain older relatives at home who might be more appropriately cared for in an institution.

Impact of the CTCLI

The assurance of funding under the CTCLI Law has resulted in a phenomenal expansion of home care agencies. Whereas in 1988 there was one large nonprofit agency providing the bulk of all home care throughout the country, in 1995 there were more than 300 agencies. Although this multitude of agencies guarantees competition, it also makes monitoring and regulation extremely difficult. In order to rectify this situation, the Ministry of Labor and Social Affairs introduced specific criteria in October, 1995, which agencies must meet in order to be certified as eligible providers. The aim is to reduce through elimination the number of agencies to approximately 50 throughout the country.

The primary goal of the law was to reduce unnecessary institutionalization through the provision of community services. Indicative of its success is the dramatic increase in the number of elderly persons receiving home care and, for some years, the decreasing demand for institutional care.

At the same time, it appears that this objective has been more clearly achieved for the less disabled elderly. The current waiting list of 2,000 persons for institutional care suggests that the needs of the more disabled are not being met through existing community care services. Whether this is a temporary situation or a trend is not clear, but it does indicate problems with the current system. (It is important to note that the waiting list results from a shortage of funds to staff the beds rather than a lack of beds.) Neither the community or nursing homes appear able to meet the needs of this very vulnerable population.

Summary of Israel's Long-Term Care System

By placing long-term care services under National Insurance, Israel has developed a universal system of benefits for which the large majority of older persons are eligible, based on need, without any social stigma. By focusing on services rather than cash benefits, the system has encouraged the development of a vast community care system with a well-developed home care program and an array of services.

However, the demand for services has exceeded and is expected to continue to exceed earlier projections and resources. Meeting the needs of the most impaired elderly is a challenge to both community and institutional resources. Increasing community care hours and accessibility to nursing home beds are possible solutions, but both depend upon increased resources.

Refining the criteria for determining eligibility for assistance could act as an intermediate measure to improve the effectiveness of community care. By assuming that a specific score reflects a need for specific service hours, the present system does not recognize individual variations which may require more or less assistance. Grouping disabilities together eases the administration of the program but is not necessarily sensitive to unique problems and living situations.

Similar to Medicare-Medicaid programs in the United States, a two-tiered program of services exists with the low-income elderly not meeting the disability criteria under the CTCLI Law possibly eligible for services through the Ministry of Labor and Social Affairs. The gap between the programs undermines the comprehensive nature of community care as it leaves a group of impaired elderly persons, who because of their incomes or disability levels, are ineligible for either program. Until their financial or physical resources are exhausted, these persons, similar to those just above the poverty line in the United States, must manage without any government assistance.

UNITED KINGDOM

Present policies for the care of older persons in the community in the United Kingdom can be traced to the National Assistance Act of 1946, which gave local authorities the duty of providing for older persons needing care, and to the Local Authority Social Services Act of 1970, which gave social service departments the responsibility of offering services such as domestic help, meals and recreation, accommodation, and social work support. Notwithstanding this history of involvement in community care, the tendency until 1993 was to place those in need of assistance in residential care under an open-ended social security entitlement. Skyrocketing costs, coupled with the realization that many could function in the community with appropriate services, led to a renewed interest in community care. This interest was fueled by the dramatic increase in the numbers of elderly in the United Kingdom. In 1990, 15.7% of the total population was 65 and older, and 7.5% of this age group was 85 and older (Askham, Barry & Grundy, 1992).

The National Health Services and Community Care Act of 1990

Building upon the recommendations of the 1988 review of the then existing system of long-term care, *Community Care: Agenda for Action* (1988), and the subsequent government white paper, *Caring for People: Community Care in the Next Decade and Beyond* (1989), the National Health Services and Community Care Act of 1990, implemented in April, 1993, established the current policy for the organization and provision of health and social services throughout the country. The focus of the new system, similar to Israel, was on the development of community care services as alternatives to institutionalization. The underlying tenets of the reforms were that elderly persons prefer to remain in their own homes as long as possible and that community care is less expensive than institutional care.

In order to promote community care, the Act highlighted the importance of multi-disciplinary assessments of need, the central role of the care manager, and a mixed economy of care. Care managers would have responsibility for assuring that needs are accurately assessed and reviewed, that resources are managed effectively, and that each user has a single point of contact and entry into the care system, Under the new system, care managers were expected to be creative in their design of care packages, developing them according to the individual client's needs.

The Community Care Act instituted a major shift in social policy. Since 1948, the public sector had been the major provider of services, but under the new system of care, local authorities were expected to purchase services from the private sector. They were advised to separate their roles as service providers from that of needs assessors. They could continue to offer services but the two functions, assessments and arrangement of services, had to be separated from actual service provision.

Financing of Services

The Community Care Act shifted primary responsibility for the funding of both community and residential services to local governments. Grants from the central government fund these services along with local taxes and user charges. However, the central government continues to control overall spending at the local level as it caps the amount that can be raised through local taxes.

Two types of grants are allotted to the local authorities for services. The revenue support grants are based on standard spending assessments (SSAs) which take into account the budgets for education, personal social services, and other major services provided at the local level. Although the central government estimates the amount to be designated for social services, each local authority has the right to determine its own allocation.

Beginning in 1992, special transition grants (STGs) were distributed to local authorities to further assist them in assuming the costs of community care and the continuing support of those already in residential homes. The majority of the STG funds came from the residential care sector of the social security budget. A complex formula, based upon each authority's standard spending assessment (SSA), is used to determine the amount of STG grants. As a transitional program, STG funding will end in 1997, forcing community care to compete with other social service sectors for funds. Providing services when these grants cease is a pressing concern among many local authorities.

Stipulations for the receipt of STG funds required that local authorities have joint agreements with health authorities on strategies for placing persons into nursing homes and on arrangements for hospital discharges. In addition, 85% of STG grants must be spent on services provided by the private sector—services not under the ownership or control of the local authority. Given the paucity of privately owned home care agencies, the majority of these gains are spent on private residential and nursing home care.

Community care introduced another major policy change. Since 1948, residents in Britain have been accustomed to receiving services free of charge. Now, almost all local authorities are charging for community services. In fact, the government expects that 9%

of the costs of nonresidential community care will be covered through local charges (Age Concern, April, 1995).

Charges are discretionary and are set by each local authority, but must be reasonable. Moreover, persons cannot be denied services if they refuse to pay. Those on income support programs usually pay nothing or a very small amount. Most authorities' charges are based on a flat rate or on a means test which tends to use the same criteria as that for residential care. However, as persons residing in the community have more expenses than those in residential care, critics claim that it is inappropriate to use the same means test criteria. The law is vague with regards to the assessment of a spouse's income and in the treatment of capital in determining charges for community services. In addition, respite care, which falls under the category of residential care, may or may not be charged.

According to a survey of local authorities conducted in 1994–95, the demand for community care exceeded available resources in at least 30 of the 116 social services departments throughout the country (Community Care, 1995). This gap in care is attributed to the planners' lack of awareness of community care needs and the interest in receiving services on the part of community persons. Local authorities continue to maintain that there are still insufficient resources for community care and that the numbers of people seeking assistance have been underestimated by the government (Association of County Councils & Association of Metropolitan Authorities, 1995). Without additional resources, local authorities predicted there would be a shortfall between spending and resources of £100m in 1994/95 ($240m) and £290m in 1995/96 ($696m). In order to cope with the demands for services, many authorities reported having to tighten their eligibility criteria in order to keep within their budgets.

In addition to insufficient resources to meet demand, poor planning for community care is at least partially responsible for the budget difficulties. In the first funded year of operation, it was not unusual for enthusiastic care managers to develop elaborate and expensive care packages based on the needs of the individual with little regard for costs. Once initiated, these packages tend to be maintained and continue to absorb funds that could be allocated for new cases.

The Purchaser/Provider Split

The Community Care Act sought to promote the creation of a flourishing independent or private sector alongside good quality public services. Prior to the Act, local authorities were the main providers of services. With the changes in community care, social service purchasers were encouraged to be separated from service providers as a means of improving service quality and choice and providing better value for the money (Sharkley, 1995). However, a lack of suppliers, an unwillingness by local authorities to consider alternative providers and their preference for in-house providers as well as political uncertainty have meant that this split frequently does not occur (Knapp, Wistow, Forder, & Hardy, 1993).

The "flourishing" independent sector is more likely to be found in residential and nursing homes, where the majority of the required spending on the independent sector occurs. In contrast to Israel, the U.K.'s policy reforms have not resulted in the growth of home care agencies. Uncertainty over contracts and concerns regarding future funding when the STG's terminate have deterred the development of private independent agencies. Although some authorities prefer private agencies because of their lower overhead and less expensive rates, private services are primarily used to fill in gaps in other services, such as overnight and weekend care, not covered by local authority home care.

Assessment and Eligibility

Local authorities are required to assess people requesting assessments whom they think may require community care services and to decide on the basis of the assessment what, if any, services in accordance with available resources, are needed to meet these needs. In contrast to assessments made prior to 1993, assessments must now also take into account the caregiver's ability to continue providing care on a regular basis. Of interest is that the Carers Recognition and Services Act of 1996 gives caregivers a right to an assessment of their needs.

Assessments are intended to be needs-led, that is they start with the needs of the user, not with the services available (Tinker, McCreadie, Wright, & Salvae, 1994). But, as government guidance only states that needs be met within available resources, assessments are increasingly dictated by the amount of available money (Age Concern, 1995). The result is that assessments are needs-led but resources-constrained. Local authorities determine their own priorities for assessment and eligibility criteria. The tightening of resources has meant that services are now increasingly targeted to the most needy cases with little priority given to prevention. Thus, most authorities are unable to provide services such as cleaning and assistance with home chores to the less frail. Under community care, many elderly persons accustomed to receiving these services found that they are no longer eligible for assistance.

The urgency of targeting was underscored in my visits to five local authorities, Tameside, Wiltshire, Hampshire, Lewisham, and Bradford in October, 1995. All five authorities were found restricting services to the most needy. Moreover, two of the departments had no resources to open new cases until other cases had been closed. One was reassessing existing cases to determine if they continued to meet the criteria for care. All of the five local authorities faced an increasing demand for assessments and services. Even those authorities whose initial funding was adequate are concerned with their ability to meet future needs.

Once services are started, they cannot be reduced or stopped without a reassessment that finds that they are no longer appropriate. However, services may be altered if the local authority changes the criteria for services and the user does not meet the new eligibility requirements.

Community and Residential Care

The community care reforms were aimed at encouraging growth in the community care sector, which would take the burden off residential care, reduce costs, and offer individuals more options and opportunities for staying at home. These aims were at least partially achieved in that day care and home care provided by local authorities increased by 25% between 1993 and 1995. The use of private day and home care increased from 4% to 17% of the total services provided (Department of Health, 1995). There is no absolute cost limit in terms of money to the package of community services but in most instances, service packages are not permitted to exceed the cost of residential care. It is noteworthy, though, that even if the cost is excessive by this standard, all authorities attempt to maintain younger disabled persons at home.

Prior to 1993, admission into residential care was determined primarily by a person's finances, with less attention given to the level of functioning and need for assistance. With local authorities now responsible for funding placements, the criteria for eligibility include an assessment of needs and whether or not they can be met in the community. There are no standardized forms for assessments or criteria for admissions. However, local authorities are required to assess anyone requesting an assessment.

For those accepted into residential care, fees are determined through national guidelines. Persons with £8,000 or more in savings ($US 18,000) are liable for the total payment. A graduated level of payments is required for those with smaller incomes and savings, with the government responsible for paying the balance. All income, savings, and property not occupied by a spouse or close elderly relative are included in determining the amount of payment. If the person's home is not occupied, it is expected to be sold with the proceeds going towards the payment for care.

Although the community care reforms stress providing services in the community, there remains a financial incentive to place dependent persons in residential care. In contrast to community care services in which local authorities are responsible for total costs except for the charges they may impose, local governments receive both public and private pension benefits for persons in residential care. This reimbursement substantially reduces the amount the authority actually pays. In addition, local authorities receive additional reimbursements from the central government for those persons placed in private-sector homes. Thus, depending on the availability and costs of services, it can be easier and more cost effective to place persons in residential care than to develop community-care packages.

Care Management

Care management, or the coordination of services, including the ability to purchase services according to the user's needs, was a cornerstone of the reforms and was implemented in almost all local authorities. The process is intended to enable skilled practitioners to put together creative, individually tailored care packages, purchasing services when appropriate.

The success of care management in reaching these aims is closely dependent upon resources. Without sufficient funds, the ability of managers to purchase services and develop specialized care packages is sharply curtailed. Resources are also closely tied to the quality of care management services, which itself is related to the sheer number of cases. In many areas of the country, the demand for assessments and services that accompanied the new legislation resulted in an unexpected expansion of caseloads. In each of the areas visited, a common complaint by managers was that they had insufficient time for care planning and monitoring.

The effectiveness of care management is further affected by the fact that many authorities were initially assessing every older person requesting an assessment and each person received care management. Consequently, many managers continue to be responsible for individuals whose needs are slight in comparison to others in the community. Authorities that had started planning for community care earlier had an advantage in implementing care management as they had guidelines for assessments and services in place. In addition, implementation of care management was easiest among stable local authorities that were prepared for the changes and had adequate budgets.

Care plans tend to be service driven rather than needs driven as service plans are determined primarily by the services available rather than individual needs. There is an overriding tendency to interpret client needs in terms of concrete tasks and services with less attention given to emotional problems and counseling interventions. In addition, care managers are often struggling with the basics of care planning rather than being innovative in developing care packages. The more creative packages tend to include a mix of services such as day care, night care, bathing help, and respite, and they may also include support from neighbors and local businesses, such as restaurants that can provide meals to the homebound.

In contrast to services for children, in the United Kingdom there are no standards for care management for the elderly. The Social Security Inspectorate attempts to maintain a degree of quality assurance through its standards-based approach for monitoring and inspecting local authorities. But, although there is some guidance for assessments, none exist for monitoring or care reviews. Given the key role of care management in maintaining people in the community, further efforts to assure quality are essential.

Summary of Community Care in the United Kingdom

The effectiveness of community care in the United Kingdom may be severely undermined by a shortage of resources, which makes it difficult to achieve the intended aims of the reforms. The budgets of local authorities are frequently insufficient to meet the demand for assessments and services. Waiting lists, targeting the most needy, and reassessments of existing clients have become common strategies for local authorities as they struggle to provide community care.

One of the primary aims of the community care reforms was to discourage institutionalization and to offer greater choices for care. However, the anomaly of offering financial reimbursements to local authorities for institutional placements but not for providing community services appears to be a direct contradiction. These financial incentives, coupled with the greater availability of residential care in comparison to home care, continue to indicate a bias towards institutionalization.

DISCUSSION

Israel and the United Kingdom have managed to develop almost universal systems of care with services based primarily on needs rather than income levels. In Israel, this system is restricted to the elderly with younger disabled persons covered under general disability insurance. In contrast, the system in the United Kingdom is available to all persons with long-term care needs. It has yet to be determined if long-term care policy in the United States will seek to merge the needs of the younger and older disabled into one program.

As assistance in both Israel and the United Kingdom is perceived as a right, stigmas are not attached to requesting care or receiving benefits. In both countries, the result of this policy reform was an unexpected demand for assessments and services which exceeded original expectations and has subsequently stretched resources. Funding is a major concern in both countries.

The issue of matching resources to needs has direct implications for program development in the United States. As the country turns towards block grants as the most effective way for states to address social needs, the effectiveness of the system will be largely determined by the extent to which local budgets are sufficient to meet the needs of the population. The concern voiced by British local authorities regarding the future of community care services when the present STG grants end may be duplicated in the United States when under block grants community care for the elderly will be forced to compete with other programs for funds.

Scarcity of resources to meet the needs of the frail elderly is a concern in both Israel and the United Kingdom. In Israel, the demand for residential care suggests that the needs of the most disabled older persons may not be adequately met in the community. In the United Kingdom, community services are becoming increasingly targeted to the most impaired. The issue of balancing the needs of those who could benefit from a little assistance (which could assist them in maintaining their independence and perhaps prevent further deterioration) with those who require a great deal of care is a major policy and program concern in both countries. The decision as to whether to offer a little service to many or a great deal of service to a few is a pivotal one which programs in the United States will also have to make. How Israel and the United Kingdom fare with that decision should be of great interest to the United States.

In each country, care managers play key roles in enabling access to the system, determining eligibility, and designing care packages. However, in each, the effectiveness of the care management system is compromised by large caseloads which limit the manager's role and involvement. With the focus on opening cases and designing care plans, monitoring and reassessments to determine if services are congruent with needs are given little priority. The exception to this is in areas of the United Kingdom where the closing of cases is essential if new ones are to be opened.

Long-term care policy advocates in the United States have recommended that care managers play a major role not only in coordinating services, but also in assuring that they were compatible with the older person's needs and desires. Findings from the study reported on here indicate that the sizes of caseloads must not overwhelm managers to the extent that they are unable to monitor clients sufficiently to assure that services remain congruent with changing needs. To be most effective, case managers will require training and the authority and resources to develop individualized care plans based on client needs.

Community care depends to a large extent upon a viable and accessible system of home care. Israel's current interest in reducing the number of home care agencies highlights the success of its system of nationally guaranteed payments in promoting their development. With funding of services assured through National Insurance, programs have flourished. This has not occurred in the United Kingdom where the growth of home care has been restricted by uncertainty regarding contracts and what will happen when grants to local authorities terminate.

The United States has in place an enormous network of home care agencies able to provide varying levels of assistance, ranging from help with home chores to personal care. However, the roles of these agencies remain limited by stringent Medicare restrictions on eligibility and the amount of care. If community care becomes a reality and these restrictions are eased, these agencies should be able meet the needs of the frail elderly in the community.

Both countries recognize the major role played by informal supports in the care of the frail elderly. Israel's system depends upon this care, as it views the formal services it provides as supplementing the support of these caregivers. However, there remains an absence of services, such as respite care, which can offer critical relief and support to caregivers.

Service providers in the United Kingdom attempt to address both the needs of the older person and the caregiver by involving both in the development of care plans. Moreover, the United Kingdom underscores the important role of caregivers by giving them the right to their own assessments. In addition, services such as respite care and overnight-sitting are readily available. In contrast to this involvement with families, care plans in Israel are made by committees without the active participation of the older person or the caregiver. Given the key roles which informal caregivers have in maintaining the impaired elderly in the community and in recognition of the interests and concerns of the older person, programs in the United States should assure that both participate in the planning process.

Israel and the United Kingdom both offer a wide range of services, including alarm systems and home modifications, to assist the elderly to remain in the community. These "baskets of services" mean that community care has the potential of being tailored to meet the specific needs of the individual client. In the United Slates, too, increasing the availability of a wide range of services could help to reduce the need for most costly care.

Data as to whether the programs are really preventing institutional care are lacking. In Israel, community services do appear to be supporting the less frail but it is not known if, without such assistance, these persons would have entered residential care. Moreover, the current waiting list for nursing home placement suggests that the program is failing to meet the needs of the more disabled. Data from the United Kingdom are not yet available but, according to the directors in each of the local authorities I visited, services were helping many elderly to stay at home who would have otherwise required residential care. As found in Israel, those entering residential care now tend to be more frail and disabled than those who did so before the reforms.

Given the resistance in the United Slates to national health insurance and the interest in block grants, the system of the United Kingdom appears to be the most adaptable approach to long-term care. However, in developing long-term care policy, the United States may also benefit from Israel's use of a uniform criterion for assistance that guarantees all older persons throughout the country the same services. This type of uniformity would assist in reducing the gaps in service provision that are likely to occur if states are completely autonomous in developing their own programs.

Finally, as indicated by the experiences of both countries, the effectiveness of long-term care in meeting the needs of the elderly is dependent upon accurate planning and sufficient resources. Without adequate funds, the result is increased targeting, with those requiring lesser amounts of assistance in danger of being denied care. Perhaps one of the strongest lessons for policymakers in the United States is the dual necessity of careful planning, which accurately assesses the needs of the long-term care population, and assuring levels of funding, which can adequately meet these needs.

REFERENCES_____

Age Concern (1995, April). *Inquiries into long-term care: Evidence to the Health Select Committee.* London: Author.

Askham, J., Barry, C., & Grundy, E. (1992). *Life after 60: A profile of Britain's older population.* Gerontology Data Service, Age Concern Institute of Gerontology. London: Kings College.

Association of County Councils and Association of Metropolitan Authorities (1995). *Who gets community care?* London: Her Majesty's Stationery Office.

Bar-Giora, M., & Kerem, B.Z. (1995). *Services for the elderly in Israel.* Jerusalem: Ministry of Labour and Social Affairs.

Brodsky, J., & Naon, D. (1993). Home care services in Israel: Implications of the expansion of home care following implementation of the community long term care insurance law. *Journal of Cross-Cultural Gerontology, 8,* 375–390.

Carer's Recognition and Services Act of 1996. London: Her Majesty's Stationery Office.

Community Care (January 26, 1995). Hard Times: Community care: Funding crisis, pp. 16–18.

Department of Health and Social Security (1988). *Community Care: Agenda for action.* London: Her Majesty's Stationery Office.

Department of Health and Social Security (1989). *Caring for people: Community care in the next decade and beyond.* London: Her Majesty's Stationery Office.

Department of Health, Social Security Inspectorate. (1995). *Implementing caring for people: Community care packages for older people.* London: Her Majesty's Stationery Office.

Factor, H., Morginstin, B., & Naon, D. (1991). Home care services in Israel. In A. Jameison (Ed.). *Home care for older people: A comparison of policies and practices* (pp. 157–187). Oxford: Oxford University Press.

Habib, J., Factor, H., Naon, D., Brodsky, J., & Dolev, T. (1986). *Adequacy of care for elderly receiving community services and for elderly awaiting institutionalization.* Discussion Paper D-133-86. Jerusalem: JDC-Brookdale.

Habib, J., & Factor, H. (1994). Services for the elderly: Changing circumstances and strategies. In *Aging in Israel: Selected research papers from the JDC-Brookdale Institute* (pp. 1–30). Prepared for the World Conference of Jewish Communal Service, Jerusalem, July 3–7, 1994.

Knapp, M., Wistow, G., Forder, J., & Hardy, B. (1993). *Markets for social care: Opportunities, barriers and implications,* London: Department of Health, Her Majesty's Stationery Office.

Korazim, M., & Kahan, P. (1993). *Meeting the training needs of home care workers: Evaluation of a training program.* Paper presented at the XVth World Congress of Gerontology, July, Budapest.

Morginstin, B., Baich-Moray, S., & Zipkin, A. (1993). Long-term care insurance in Israel: Three years later, *Ageing, International,* XX, 27–31.

National Health Service and Community Care Act (1990). London: Her Majesty's Stationery Office.

Sharkley, P. (1995). *Introducing community care.* London: Collins.

The National Insurance (Amendment No. 61) Law, 1986. *Laws of the State of Israel,* April 25, 1986.

Tinker, A., McCreadie, C., Wright, F., & Salvae, A. (1994). *The care of frail elderly people in the UK.* London: Her Majesty's Stationery Office.

U.S. General Accounting Office (1995). *Long term care: Current issues and future directions.* GAO/HEHS-95-109. Washington: Author.

PART FOUR

Problems of People, Resources, and Place

Cities

THE UNITED STATES CONTEXT

There were two dramatic population movements in the United States during the twentieth century—from rural areas and small towns to the cities and then outward from the central cities to the suburbs. The latter represents an exodus by predominantly young and middle-aged upper-middle-class and middle-class whites as well as business and industry to the outer rings of metropolitan areas. This movement of people and jobs to the suburbs has resulted in many urban problems (Timmer, 2000):

• The central cities are faced with shrinking economic resources for schools, infrastructure, and other essential city services (e.g., recreation, crime control, fire protection, snow removal). This is the result of loss of their tax base to the suburbs. The suburbs then, generally, can afford better schools, parks, and the like than found in the cities.

• The predominantly white flight to the suburbs leaves the central cities with a disproportionate concentration of minority (including recent immigrants) and poor people. Thus, suburbanization has meant the geographic separation of the social classes and races.

• The move of warehouses, factories, and other businesses to the suburbs has left inner city residents with fewer job opportunities. For example, in the neighborhood of Woodlawn on the South Side of Chicago, the number of commercial and industrial establishments plummeted from over eight hundred in 1950 to about one hundred now, most of them with no more than one or two employees (Wilson, 1996:5). The resulting high unemployment and hopelessness has led to a social deterioration of ghetto neighborhoods that were once stable.

• Related to the job loss is disinvestment in urban centers as banks, savings and loans, and insurance companies have redlined metropolitan areas (i.e., the practice of not providing loans or insurance in what are defined as undesirable areas). These "undesirable areas" are almost always in city centers highly concentrated with racial minorities. This practice, technically prohibited by federal law but commonly used, results in a self-fulfilling prophecy—individuals and businesses in the "undesirable areas" do not receive loans and insurance, which results in failed businesses, relocation of businesses, and further social disruptions, thus "proving" the negative label by banks and insurance companies.

• Policies by the federal government have contributed to further deterioration of the central cities. Federal aid to cities has declined ever since the Reagan administration, including funds for mass transit, infrastructure maintenance, and grants for subsidized housing. Moreover, government decisions to reduce welfare payments in the 1996 welfare law have made life more difficult for poor urban residents.

• The spreading out of metropolitan areas (urban sprawl) has led to environmental problems. Every day more than fifty acres of green space is plowed under for suburban development (Pedersen, Smith, and Adler, 1999). Not only farm land but also wetlands and forests have been claimed by developers for housing, businesses, shopping malls, roads, and parking lots, resulting in disrupted wildlife habitats and altered streams and rivers. Suburbs have dramatically heightened the use of the automobile, with resulting air pollution (Kay, 1997). Living in the suburbs has increased commuting time to work (Atlantans drive an average of 36.5 daily miles round trip to work). Moreover, the organization of suburbs is such that one must drive to get to work, visit a doctor, shop, bank, go to a park, or whatever. In high-density inner cities, shops, services, and parks are typically within walking distance.

REFERENCES_____

Kay, Jane Holtz. 1997. *Asphalt Nation: How the Automobile Took Over America and How We Can Take It Back.* New York: Crown.

Pedersen, Daniel, Vern E. Smith, and Jerry Adler. 1999. "Sprawling, Sprawling . . . " *Newsweek* (July 19):23–27.

Timmer, Doug A. 2000. "Urban Problems in the United States," in D. Stanley Eitzen and Maxine Baca Zinn, *Social Problems,* 8th ed. Boston: Allyn and Bacon, chapter 6.

Wilson, William Julius. 1996. *When Work Disappears: The World of the New Urban Poor.* New York: Alfred A. Knopf.

24

America's Rush to Suburbia

KENNETH T. JACKSON

Jackson looks at the dark side of the suburbanization trend within the United States. These dysfunctions of our urban landscape, which result in the concomitant decline of the central cities, do not occur in other industrialized countries because of their standing policies that enhance cities and discourage movement to the suburbs. According to the author, the United States would do well to consider the public policy differences between this country and its industrialized peers.

This week in Istanbul, experts from around the globe are attending a United Nations conference on urbanization. The timing is propitious, because in the next few years the world will pass a historic milestone. For the first time, half the earth's population, or more than three billion people, will be living in cities.

At the turn of the century, only 14 percent of us called a city home and just 11 places on the planet had a million inhabitants. Now there are 400 cities with populations of at least one million and 20 megacities of more than 10 million.

But while cities around the world are becoming more dense, those in the United States are moving in the opposite direction. The typical model here is a doughnut—emptiness and desolation at the center and growth on the edges.

Many of the great downtown department stores—including Hudson's in Detroit and Goldsmith's in Memphis—are now closed. Meanwhile, new megamalls, discount centers and factory outlets are springing up every day on the peripheries of America's cities.

Though some cities are still thriving, of the 25 largest cities in 1950, 18 have lost population. For example, from 1950 to 1990, Baltimore lost 22 percent of its population, Philadelphia 23 percent, Chicago 25 percent, Boston 28 percent, Detroit 44 percent and Cleveland 45 percent. (It's true that many cities—Houston, San Diego, Dallas and Phoenix, among them—have grown since 1950, but that is largely because they have annexed their outlying territories. New York City, unique as always, has the same number of people, although its boundaries are unchanged.)

Source: Kenneth T. Jackson. 1996. "America's Rush to Suburbia," *New York Times* (June 9), p. E15.

By contrast, during the same period, the suburbs gained more than 75 million people. In 1990, our nation became the first in history to have more suburbanites than city and rural dwellers *combined.*

Why should Americans care whether Portland, Me., or Portland, Ore., is losing inhabitants? Because our system of governance balkanizes social responsibility in our country, a nation divided by race and income.

Only in America are schools, police and fire protection and other services financed largely by local taxes. When middle- and upper-class families flee from the cities, they take with them needed tax revenues.

In Europe, Australia and Japan, such functions are essentially the responsibility of national or at least regional governments. In any of these places, moving from a city to a suburb does not have much impact on a citizen's taxes or on inequality of services.

Americans tend to regard a move to the suburbs as natural—even inevitable—when people are given choices about where to live. But in fact the pattern arises not because land is abundant and cheap (which it is) and not because we have racial and economic divides (which we do) but largely because we have made a series of public policy decisions that other countries have not made.

First, the tax code allows us to deduct mortgage interest and property taxes for both first and second homes. Most other advanced nations do not allow this.

Second, gasoline is essentially not taxed in this country. The 12-country European Union, which has fewer vehicles on the road than the United States does, takes in more than five times as much in gasoline taxes as America does. Our gasoline is cheap compared to that in other advanced industrialized nations, so living in the suburbs, without public transportation, is an attractive option.

Third, the United States has long had a policy, unique in the developed world, of making the provision of public housing voluntary. For the most part, communities across the country can choose to apply—or not—for public housing. The result of this is that the central cities have become the homes of the poor while the suburbs have become places to escape the poor.

By contrast, the French, British, Germans and Japanese spread public housing around. Indeed, in many countries a demonstrably higher proportion of public housing units go to the periphery than to the central city—and this discourages middle-class urban flight.

Finally, in the United States, government at all levels has affected cities by what it has *not* done. In Europe, land is regarded as a scarce resource that has to be controlled in the public interest rather than exploited for private gain. Thus, governments have acted to preserve open space and deter suburban sprawl.

There are other policies, too, that work against urban areas in the United States, but the larger point is clear: American cities operate under a series of unusual handicaps.

St. Louis offers an extreme example of the consequences of all this. Once the fourth largest city in the nation, the so-called Gateway to the West has become a ghost of its former self. In 1950, it had 857,000 people; by 1990, the population had dwindled to 397,000. Many of its old neighborhoods have become dispiriting collections of eviscerated homes and vacant lots. Aging warehouses and grimy loft factories are now open to the sky; weeds cover once busy railroad sidings.

Will the experience of St. Louis, become typical of other cities in the 21st century?

In recent years, such prominent authors as Paul Hawken, John Naisbitt and Alvin Toffler have predicted that cities are doomed and that new telecommunications have made human interaction unnecessary. In the future, they suggest, our journey to work will be from the breakfast table to the home computer. There, in splendid isolation, we will work, shop and play in cyberspace.

Perhaps the futurists are correct, and the cities of our time, like conquered Carthage, will be razed and sowed with salt. But I doubt it. It is more likely that New York, Chicago, Los Angeles, San Francisco, Boston and a dozen or so other places will remain great cities well into the next millennium, despite government policies that cripple them.

That's because the same catalytic mixing of people that creates urban problems and fuels urban conflict also spurs the initiative, innovation and collaboration that taken together move civilization forward. Quite simply, metropolitan centers are the most complex creations of the human mind, and they will not easily yield their roles as marketplaces of ideas.

Cities are places where individuals of different bents and pursuits rub shoulders, where most human achievements have been created. Whereas village and rural life, as well as life in the modern shopping mall, is characterized by the endless repetition of similar events, cities remain centers of diversity and opportunity. If they express some of the worst tendencies of modern society, they also represent much of the best.

As Charles E. Merriam, a professor at the University of Chicago, told the United States Conference of Mayors in 1934: "The trouble with Lot's wife was that she looked backward and saw Sodom and Gomorrah. If she had looked forward, she would have seen that heaven is also pictured as a city."

25

Going Places: Europe's Cities Are Being Redesigned with People and the Environment in Mind

JAY WALLJASPER

The topics covered in this article could be grouped in both the urban and environmental chapters. Walljasper argues that Europe's cities, unlike those in the United States, are being redesigned with people and the environment in mind. Typically, these new plans involve reducing automobile traffic by banning autos from certain sections, lowering speed limits, improving mass transit, and promoting alternative modes of transportation, especially bicycle travel.

The German city of Heidelberg is world famous as the setting of *The Student Prince*—a sappy operetta whose plot revolves mostly around beer drinking and duel fighting. But if Bert-Olaf Rieck gets his way, this city of 140,000 will also be known for something else: bike riding.

Rieck was recently appointed Heidelberg's bicycle commissioner, a new position arising out of the city's determination to do something about its environmental problems. Fearful of being swamped in traffic, clouded by pollution, and complicit in global warming trends, Heidelberg has instituted new policies aimed at reducing the use of automobiles. That's why Rieck was plucked out of the ranks of a bike activists' group and installed in city hall.

He is now busy working on ways to make bikes the vehicle of choice for at least one-third of all trips around the city—a goal already accomplished by the German city of Münster and surpassed by the Dutch cities of Delft (41 percent of city trips) and Groningen (48 percent). Currently, 22 percent of Heidelberg's non-pedestrian traffic rides on two wheels, a big change from the days when Rieck studied linguistics at the university. "Twenty years ago when I was a student I parked my car right over there," he

Source: Jay Walljasper. 1993. "Going Places: Europe's Cities Are Being Redesigned with People and the Environment in Mind," *Utne Reader,* No. 58 (July/August), pp. 150–151.

said, pointing out his office window at a picturesque city square that is part of the city's pedestrian zone. "Now you can't even park there."

To put the bicycle on a par with the automobile, Rieck plans to double the city's 25 miles of separate bikeways over the next 10 years. He has already added 1,500 new bike parking spots at the main train station and snatched a lane of traffic from cars on Bismarckstrasse, Heidelberg's main thoroughfare, which he triumphantly showed me as we rode bicycles the city bought for its employees to use. For an American bike commuter like me, it was nothing short of euphoric to pedal down a busy avenue in the safety of my own lane.

Heidelberg is one of numerous European cities that offer solid examples of what could be done in North America to revitalize urban life and restore the environment. Although the ecology movement first surfaced in the United States, and for years we were the world's leader in fighting pollution, the nations of Northern Europe are now widely acknowledged to be ahead of us in most aspects of environmental policy. The Scandinavian, Dutch, and German governments have encouraged initiatives ranging from promoting renewable energy to protecting the countryside. Green consciousness has also taken root at the local level, flowering in an array of environmental innovations, especially in the field of transportation, where city governments have the most jurisdiction.

Freiburg, a German city of 200,000 in the Black Forest, showed the way for other municipalities with its early efforts at incorporating environmental awareness into government decision making. In 1972, the city made a radical move by banning cars from certain streets in the city center, establishing one of Europe's first pedestrian zones.

This district is now the pulsing heart of the city, filled with shoppers and tourists strolling from department stores to the open-air market in the Münsterplatz to bustling sidewalk cafés. Freiburg has also established a network of bikeways (now covering 82 miles) and light rail lines (13 miles today, and 9 more miles planned in the next decade), with impressive results. While people climbed into their cars for 60 percent of all vehicle trips around the city in 1975, autos now account for less than half—46 percent—of those trips. In the same period, bike traffic climbed from 18 to 27 percent of local trips, and public transit jumped from 22 to 26 percent.

European successes in weaning drivers away from their autos are generally dismissed as not applicable to North America because Old World cities are more densely populated than our sprawling communities. Freiburg, however, is one of Germany's fastest-growing towns, with development spreading out across a flat valley. Even in its expansive suburban areas you see packs of bicyclists waiting at stoplights and light rail trains gliding past single-family homes.

Freiburg has also pushed environmental initiatives in areas besides transportation. It banned pesticides for urban uses and built a biomechanical refuse plant to salvage organic wastes from the city's garbage. With encouragement from the city council, a local factory that makes cigarette filters switched its fuel supply from coal to natural gas. The city has also established an eco-hotline to answer citizens' questions about environmental matters, and it now subjects all new development projects to in-depth environmental scrutiny.

So what makes Freiburg willing to buck business as usual in favor of environmental innovation? The presence of 30,000 university students helps, but most observers point to the citizens' deep regional pride. People cherish the city's historical charm and the natural beauty of the Black Forest as well as the celebrated local cuisine and fine wines. This gives them a particular stake in protecting their home. This also explains the Green Party's strong showing in Freiburg. Greens have been part of the city council since 1980 and gained 20 percent of the vote in the last municipal election.

Of course, local drivers do a lot of grumbling about the restrictions on automobiles. So far they have shown little political clout in Freiburg, but recent elections in the northern German city of Kassel registered a big backlash from car owners. Members of the Social Democratic Party, who engineered major restrictions on automobile use, suffered significant losses in city council elections.

Like Americans, Germans are notorious for their love affair with the auto. They proudly assert that the cars they manufacture are the finest in the world, and motorists' organizations resist all efforts to impose speed limits on their fabled autobahns. It's estimated that one workplace in seven throughout the nation is in some way connected to the auto industry. That was part of the political picture in Kassel, where a Volkswagen plant employs 20 percent of the local population. But political observers point out that voters' dissatisfaction with local politicians could be blamed on high unemployment and xenophobic reactions to the city's large foreign population as much as on anti-auto policies.

Still, there is a lesson here for advocates of alternative transportation policy about relying too much on sticks rather than carrots in luring people out of their cars. Improving the convenience and safety of walking, biking, and public transit must accompany driving restrictions.

Switzerland, whose cities have also aggressively tackled traffic and pollution problems, experienced an angry backlash several years ago in the form of a new political party dedicated to rolling back transportation innovations. The auto party makes a lot of noise but at election time never wins more than a handful of votes. Swiss municipalities have continued their efforts to promote alternative transportation. Zurich recently eliminated 10,000 parking places in the city, and Geneva recently prohibited businesses from providing free parking for their employees.

All over Northern Europe cities are exploring ways to reclaim their streets and neighborhoods from the auto, providing inspiration and practical examples of what can be done to reorder the relationship between cars and people. Most cities now sport lively pedestrian zones, and bikeways criss-cross even the most crowded metropolises: Berlin, Frankfurt, Munich, Copenhagen, Cologne, Amsterdam. The German cities of Bremen and Lübeck have designated certain streets specially for bicycles—an idea Heidelberg recently adopted. The Norwegian cities of Oslo, Bergen, and Trondheim levy a toll on all cars entering the town center. Seventy-five percent of Denmark's highways have a separate bikeway running alongside them, and 20 percent of all urban trips in that nation are made on bikes.

In Amsterdam last year, voters approved an ambitious plan to eliminate most auto traffic in the three-square-mile heart of the city. The Dutch cities of Maastricht, Enschede,

Leiden, and Groningen are following suit, and 30 other cities and towns throughout Holland are discussing similar measures.

In the past several years, many German cities have lowered speed limits to 30 kilometers per hour (19 mph) on all but the busiest streets—an example of "traffic calming," a new concept that aims to tame the automobile by reducing its speed. One town, Buxtehude in northern Germany, has set 30-kilometer limits on all its streets. Narrowing streets is another widely used method of traffic calming,

"Until recently, American cities with their wide lanes and fast traffic were the model for us," says Joachim Schultis, a city planning professor and deputy mayor of Heidelberg. "But all that has now changed."

These innovations not only fight pollution and congestion but also lend a pleasantly relaxed mood to Europe's cities. Being able to get around by strolling, biking, or taking a train without needing to dodge autos and fight traffic enhances urban life in ways that are hard to imagine until you've experienced them. There's no reason why American and Canadian cities can't follow suit—transforming themselves from conduits for cars into places for people.

26

Metropolis Unbound:
The Sprawling American City and
the Search for Alternatives

ROBERT GEDDES

The geographic growth of American cities has far outpaced their population growth in the late twentieth century. This urban sprawl is characterized by problems of housing, transportation, the environment, and social equity. In this article, the author examines alternative models of urban development used by several American and Canadian cities.

A new form of human settlement has emerged in the twentieth century, radically different from the cities of the past. The city has become a city-region. American city-regions' population growth is now dramatically outpaced by their geographic growth. In the two decades from 1970 to 1990, the New York region had a modest population increase of 8 percent, but it had an explosive growth of 65 percent in its built-up urbanized land. While Chicago grew 4 percent in population, its urbanized land increased 46 percent. Even places that were declining in their population were simultaneously growing in their urban area; Cleveland, for example, had a population decline of 8 percent, while it expanded geographically by 33 percent. This urban growth cycle is similar across America. City-regions are exploding into their surrounding countryside at growth rates that are eight to ten times greater than their population increases.

What is new is not the size of cities, but a change in their form. New York City, for example, used to have a concentric form surrounding Manhattan that resembled the growth rings of a tree. That was how it appeared when New York's Regional Plan Association, a civic organization, published its first plan 60 years ago. The Third Regional Plan published in 1996, however, describes a city-region with a population of 20 million people, extending 150 miles across and covering 13,000 square miles; its form now resembles a flower with petals radiating into five subregions in three states.

Source: Robert Geddes. 1997. *The American Prospect 35* (November/December), pp. 40–46.

Ominously titled *A Region at Risk,* the regional plan warns of the dangers from the vast sprawl for New York's economy, environment, social fabric, and quality of everyday life. "Far more suddenly than people realize," write the authors, Robert Yaro and Tony Hiss, "super-sized metropolitan regions—areas hundreds of miles wide crowded with a dense mixture of aging cities, expanding suburbs, newer edge cities, and older farmlands and wildernesses—are emerging not just as a recognizable place but as humanity's new home base."

The everyday consequences for suburb and city alike are familiar enough: traffic congestion and inefficient transportation, unavailable and unaffordable housing, water and air pollution, social segregation and lack of community. In the decades after World War II, millions of Americans fled the cities to live in the suburbs, but in a sense the city has come after them. Nonetheless, the persistence of old political boundaries prevents the problems they face from being addressed together or even discussed coherently. The problems of transportation, housing, jobs, the environment, and social equity get scattered attention in public policy, but there is hardly any notice of the urban dynamic that lies behind them: the new form that American cities have taken. Nor is there much debate about the alternative paths of development that a few city-regions have taken in North America that could be the basis of a new paradigm for city-regions and neighborhoods in the next century.

THE EVOLVING CITY

The emergence of a new form of human settlement is relatively rare in human history. For thousands of years, human settlements grew slowly and predictably. Generally, they grew outward in concentric rings, each expansion being larger but still recognizably the same as its earlier form. For example, while the European city of Bruges was growing over a period of 500 years, its boundary walls were periodically moved outward, but it kept the same kind of shape. As a pre-industrial city, Bruges faced economic and technological limits on its size, such as everyday walking distances.

The relationships between how things grow and the shapes they take fascinated the biologist D'Arcy Thompson. In his 1917 book, *On Growth and Form,* Thompson analyzed both natural and manmade objects, from marine shells, teeth, fleas, and dinosaurs to soap bubbles and bridges, observing how and when their form accommodated and changed during growth.

If this pattern, as Thompson argued, applies to mechanical constructions like boilers and biological constructions like the marine shell Forminifera, it also applies to social constructions like cities. Before the industrial revolution, the size of towns and cities was constrained by natural limits, such as the capacity of the surrounding countryside to supply foodstuffs and the ability of people to move about by foot or on animals without mechanized vehicles. Railroads changed city form in two ways. Long-distance rail lines connecting to other cities and distant agricultural areas meant that a city's population size was no longer constrained by the food from its surrounding countryside. And short-distance rail lines extending into the country meant that the city's geographic size was no longer limited by walking distances. The city's form evolved into a star pattern, with new settlements—"railroad suburbs"—concentrated around rail stations, spaced a few miles apart. The legacy of America's dependence on rail lines and depots remains with us: The New York region, for example, has a rail network that is aging and somewhat disconnected but still includes 900 railroad stations.

The railroad suburb was a nineteenth-century invention, but it is also an alternative spatial model for the twenty-first century that retains some notable advantages compared to the sprawl of the more recent automobile suburb. The advantages of the star pattern come from its physical and social compactness, its preservation of the surrounding countryside, and its economy and efficiency of transport.

The automobile radically changed city form. The private car provided extraordinary flexibility, adaptability, and choice. Space and time were reconfigured. The city's edges—so clear in the old pre-industrial city and still evident along the finger-like corridors of the industrial city—melted away. Urban centers struggled to accommodate their new inhabitants—moving and parked vehicles. Centers kept their appeal—shopping centers, research centers, sports centers, health centers, to name a few—but each became a separate center. The city became a city-region of disjointed centers. Today, at its best, it is a galaxy; at its worst, it is chaos.

THE LOS ANGELES PARADIGM

Historically, two massive shifts of population have formed American city-regions. The farm-to-city shift after the Civil War is comparable to the massive city-to-suburb shift after World War II. Now more than half the nation's population lives in the suburbs. Although still separate legal jurisdictions, it no longer makes sense to talk of suburbs and cities as if they were separate; they are economically and ecologically joined in a new kind of human settlement, the city-region.

Periodically, a city seems to be the embodiment and image of the new. Historians call it the "shock city" of its time. Los Angeles has been the "shock city" of our time, as Manchester, England, was in the nineteenth century and New York was in this century's first half. Los Angeles is now seen as the first American city to remove itself from the European models of growth and form. Architect and urbanist Richard Weinstein argues that "the structure of the built-environment as it exists in Los Angeles now represents a paradigm of growth that already houses more than half of the [United States] population and is, with variations, the pattern of growth for most new settlements in the developed world."

The Los Angeles paradigm is an extended, open, unbounded matrix laced with linear corridors, from boulevards to commercial strips, and overlaid by freeways. Its keywords are *fragmented, incomplete, ad hoc, uncentered.* Concerning the Los Angeles environment, Weinstein argues that the open extended matrix, with all its in-between spaces, is more supportive of environmental health than denser, more continuous urban structures. There is more green, in-between.

But the Los Angeles urban form has had inequitable social consequences. Ethnic colonies have become isolated, the city fragmented. If the goal is to balance the economy, the environment, and social equity, is the open extended matrix of Los Angeles the inevitable model for American cities?

NORTHERN LIGHTS

On the North American continent, Toronto represents an alternative model of urban growth and form. In contrast to Los Angeles, Toronto generates vitality in its centers. Toronto's downtown is vibrant and pedestrian-friendly, and its neighborhoods retain their strength as places of sociability. By developing mass transit, Toronto succeeded, at least until the mid-1970s, in linking its centers and retarding the land-consuming and smog-producing dependence on the automobile. A key element in this achievement was that Toronto managed its postwar boom with a system of governance called Metro-Toronto that integrated urban and suburban decision-making. Metro-Toronto had jurisdiction over planning not only for five municipalities in the core metropolitan area, but also for the surrounding communities. Among its achievements was a light-rail transportation network financed by the core city.

Toronto has thus become a more equitable city than Los Angeles not only because of Canada's generous social programs, but also because the city has not isolated its less affluent residents. Ethnic minorities, the poor, and the elderly—thanks to public policy—are less segregated in Toronto than in other North American city-regions. Not only did Toronto build the transportation connections; it has also created the continent's largest stock of dispersed mixed-income social housing.

In recent decades, however, the Toronto pattern of development has drifted away from this tradition. In 1972, the Ontario provincial government combined the surrounding communities into four mini-metro governments (Halton, Peel, York, and Durham), each having strong powers over their own region. According to Gardner Church, a political scientist at York University, the province failed to create any comprehensive planning authority or to sustain the earlier commitments to contain growth and coordinate transportation. Sprawl set in and the region stood in danger of becoming, as observers put it at the time, "Vienna surrounded by Phoenix." But recently, in an effort to reverse this backsliding, the province has made Metro-Toronto the unified government of the core metropolitan area and created a new super-regional authority, called Greater-Toronto, for transportation, social services, and economic development. The surrounding areas will share the costs of social services with Toronto. Church believes this new system "offers the potential for a return to comprehensive, progressive planning."

Another model for the future comes from the Pacific Northwest, where a chain of cities—including Portland, Seattle, and Vancouver—form a city-region now often called "Cascadia" (from the Cascade Mountains that parallel the Pacific coastline). Although this new city-region crosses state and international boundaries, the emerging idea of Cascadia provides an economically integrated vision of the settlements along a regional corridor, a "Main Street" called Interstate Highway 5. What is especially notable is that it also includes an ecologically integrated vision of the geology, vegetation, natural species, climate, and movement of water throughout the region.

Cascadia shows that an equilibrium of nature, society, and culture can still be the basis of city building. Think of Cascadia as a candidate for the historians' next "shock city." Its predecessors, Manchester, New York, and Los Angeles, all drew their image from their built landscape. Cascadia draws its power as a new paradigm from its natural landscape.

Portland, Seattle, and Vancouver have each pioneered in planning for environmental protection and the provision of greenspace (parks, riparian corridors, natural habitats) as parts of the urban fabric. Today, however, greenspace is at risk. The greatest challenge comes from rapid population growth and a pattern of human settlement that, like other American city-regions, is consuming land at an even faster rate. Sprawl development has led to inefficient use of land, energy, and other resources and has had profound impacts on air quality, the hydrology of watersheds, and the environmental health of the inhabitants. The question is whether Cascadia will go the way of Los Angeles. Or as Cascadian urbanists Ethan Seltzer, Ann Vernez Moudon, and Alan Artibise put it, "Will the legacy of our times result in the stewardship of the environment, or the destructive consumption of one of the most striking and abundant landscapes on the continent?"

Cascadia has also tried to meet the needs of socially diverse residents by regulating the form of urban development. Unlike most other city-regions, it has tried to define "urban growth boundaries" to promote compact development and "urban villages" with a mix of living, working, and leisure activities. Portland, for example, has set a growth boundary that is the most concrete commitment in North America to reversing trends toward racial and class segregation and the flight from inner cities. But Portland would never have been able to undertake this process if it had not been for action by its state.

LEADERSHIP IN THE STATES

In the American political system, cities have little autonomy. The authority to enact policies and programs that might effectively shape the development of cities lies with their state governments. Two states, Oregon and New Jersey, stand out as leaders.

Since 1973, Oregon has required each city to draw a growth boundary based on its assessment of economic development and community needs in the next 20 years. In turn, the city develops a comprehensive plan, including the steps it will take to create needed infrastructure for water and sewers, roads and transit, and other public facilities within the growth boundary. The growth boundary also influences state expenditures for highways and other roads. By 1986, to meet the state standards, all communities in Oregon had drawn up growth plans to limit their expansion.

Ethan Seltzer, who runs the Institute of Portland Metropolitan Studies at Portland State University, explains that the state expects land inside urban growth boundaries to be developed at urban densities and, in fact, allows developers to go to court for immediate approval if local jurisdictions fail to process permit applications for approved purposes within 120 days. "This means that multifamily development occurs by right and according to plan even in the suburbs!" Seltzer says. But outside the boundaries, he continues, "you cannot develop at urban densities, cannot get urban services, and face strict restrictions on what can be built in farm and forest zones. Even road widening for non-farm uses is closely regulated outside of urban growth boundaries."

Seltzer notes,

> *Creativity comes into play because, especially in recent years, the state is committed to accommodating growth through infill and redevelopment, and not just on vacant land at the edge. Today, the market is responding. In the last six months, 30 percent of our residential growth has been infill development in the region, 15 percent has been in attached housing/townhouses. . . . There is active development of housing in downtown Portland, and we will probably see a new public elementary school in downtown in the next few years.*
>
> *The Oregon program directs cities and investors to steward land committed to urban use much the way a farmer stewards his or her fields. Rather than [allowing] disinvestment, we pursue reinvestment. It comes at a cost. Currently we are struggling with our popularity, and what it means to live not in a cheap region but a desirable, valuable one.*
>
> *I guess what we've proven is that pursuing an end to sprawl is possible and desirable, but it won't by itself solve the problems of poverty or provide needed affordable housing.*

He adds that while urban growth boundaries are not a "silver bullet," they "are great at what they do: stopping sprawl on farmland, directing attention back onto lands already committed to urban use, and in the metropolitan region here, suggesting to local elected officials that their future is a shared one best approached through a partnership with their brother and sister jurisdictions living within the same economy."

The growth and form of cities are critical issues for New Jersey, the only state to be entirely occupied by "metropolitan areas," according to the U.S. Census. In 1992, New Jersey produced its first state plan to "coordinate public and private actions to guide future growth into compact forms of development and redevelopment." Its policies are like Oregon's: "encourage development, redevelopment, and economic growth in locations that are well situated with respect to present or anticipated public services and facilities, and to discourage development where it may impair or destroy natural resources or environmental qualities."

In New Jersey's search for a new model of urban growth and form, the keyword is *compact*. Comparing the traditional trends with the new policies proposed by the state plan, James Hughes and his colleagues at Rutgers University found that compact development would generate more jobs in accessible centers throughout the region, thereby reducing the jobless rates in inner cities. There would also be less destruction of the natural environment because forests, watersheds, and farmlands would be preserved. Local and state governments would save money because there would be less need for new infrastructure. For example, to accommodate growth until the year 2010, the traditional pattern would need 5,500 lane-miles of new local roads. For the same population and economy, the state plan would require only 1,600 new lane-miles. But the greatest benefit would be in the revitalization of neighborhoods.

HERE COMES THE NEIGHBORHOOD

For revitalizing our cities, the "neighborhood" is almost always cited as the basic building block. Today in America there are two different concepts. The first is the idea of a "neighborhood" with a core and boundary. Spatially and socially, this "neighborhood" focuses on its core: local shops, a neighborhood school, perhaps a library and other community facilities for education, health care, and recreation. The neighborhood's population size and density, its network of roads and paths, even its image and character are linked to the neighborhood's core. At its boundary, the neighborhood's edges are marked by landscapes—generally, roads or parkways, or in cities, arterial streets. Neighborhoods, in this concept, are given names and generate loyalty; they are also inward-looking and intentionally static.

The city-building implications of this neighborhood concept are clear: Clusters of neighborhoods can create a district, and clusters of districts create the city. This "cluster" concept of the neighborhood, district, and city is the American vernacular. It is embodied in the postwar comprehensive plans for restructuring such old cities as Philadelphia and for the construction of such new cities as Columbia, Maryland. It is manifest in the power of "community boards" in large cities. And it is given lip-service by developers and their advertising agencies for suburban tracts.

The second concept, a "street-neighborhood," is radically different. It does not have the spatial and social clarity of the "core-and-boundary neighborhood." Instead, it idealizes the natural cohesion that comes from "neighboring" on the street and sidewalk. This sense of neighborhood is the consequence of face-to-face, casual, informal contacts in everyday city life. For the spatial setting of this concept of neighborhood, the gridiron street plan of such cities as Manhattan is especially useful. Paradoxically, the static, predictable, public structural form can support and stimulate the dynamic, small-scale, ad hoc, spontaneous life of everyone—residents and visitors, workers and walkers, insiders and outsiders.

The key to this concept of neighborhood is the street and sidewalk. The street is the armature, the skeleton, the structure of the street-neighborhood. To the streets are attached the social institutions that characterize a neighborhood: the schools, food stores, coffee shops, library and bookstores, movie theaters, local service stores, health clubs, parks and playgrounds, and of course, the workplaces and homes of the neighbors. The street-neighborhood is immensely popular. Throughout the United States, for example, old loft districts are being used for new living-working places; shopping malls are trying to simulate the life of a downtown street and sidewalk; and cities are recognizing that the key to the neighborhood is the street and its quality of life.

CITY PROSPECTS

How can these concepts of neighborhoods serve an emerging new society profoundly affected by changes in communication and information technologies? They offer both positive and negative possibilities.

The core-and-boundary neighborhood can create a human-scale community and sense of place within a large city-region. Because it is a development unit that itself has edges, it can help establish an urban growth boundary. But the core-and-boundary neighborhood can turn pathological if the territorial boundary becomes hard-edged and gated, excluding outsiders from a segregated community.

The street-neighborhood has the advantage that it does not intentionally create physical boundaries that exclude people. At its best, it is open, welcoming, and place-making. Diverse street-sidewalk places would be welcome insertions into conventional core-and-boundary neighborhoods, or even more, into the fabric of suburban sprawl. But the street-neighborhood also has pathological possibilities: The streets can be the territorial setting for intimidation and crime and, at their worst, these threats can destroy our cities.

Increasingly, "Main Street" is once again valued as a lively center of a surrounding neighborhood. In Toronto, for example, the ethnic diversity of the city-region is expressed by its many neighborhoods—Greektown, Chinatown, Portuguese Village–each with its own "Main Street." What had been St. Claire Avenue is now Corso Italia. Similarly, in northern Manhattan, Harlem's neighborhoods are anchored by their crosstown streets. The most famous is 125th Street, but others such as 116th and 135th Streets are each a string of lively places, central arteries for economic and cultural activity.

If, as Peter Drucker predicts, our future organization of work will be more akin to that in pre-industrial cities, with an intimate mixture rather than separation of living and working places, then the neighborhood street will once again be the vibrant setting for everyday life. More than ever, we will value places to meet, to see and be seen, to drink coffee together, and maybe, to bowl together.

But this will not happen automatically; the form of a city is a consequence of public policies. Four kinds of policies are needed: regional compacts to build and maintain infrastructure for transportation, water, and waste systems; community growth boundaries to contain the urban built-up land uses; regional compacts to preserve greenspaces and natural ecological systems; and public initiatives to support the centers of cities and neighborhoods.

Streets and sidewalks, buildings and plazas, gardens and parks profoundly affect our everyday lives and ought to be the subject of public debate. "By its form, as by the manner of its birth," wrote the French anthropologist Claude Levi-Strauss, "the city has elements at once of biological procreation, organic evolution and aesthetic creation. It is both a natural object and a thing to be cultivated; something lived and something dreamed. It is the human invention par excellence." We need the courage to create our cities again.

SECTION 11

Environment

THE UNITED STATES CONTEXT

The United States has 4.5 percent of the world's population, yet it uses about 25 percent of the earth's resources and contributes more than 20 percent to global emissions of carbon dioxide, the major culprit in global warming (Ehrlich, 1997:104). The country consumes 25 percent of the world's fossil fuel, 20 percent of its metals, and 33 percent of its paper, and produces 72 percent of the world's hazardous waste (Crews and Stauffer, 1997).

> While developing countries severely tax their environments, clearly the population of rich countries leave a vastly disproportionate mark on the planet. *The birth of a baby in the United States imposes more than a hundred times the stress on the world's resources as a birth in, say, Bangladesh.* Babies from Bangladesh do not grow up to own automobiles and air conditioners or to eat grain-fed beef. Their life-styles do not require huge quantities of minerals and energy, nor do their activities seriously undermine the life-support capability of the entire planet. (Ehrlich and Ehrlich, 1988:917; italics added)

The United States also produces more garbage than any other nation, on average 4.4 pounds per person per day. A typical McDonald's restaurant serving 2,000 customers a day produces 238 pounds of waste per day (Rathje, 1999). In 1997 the amount of garbage generated by Americans amounted to 217 million tons, up from 88 million tons in 1960 and 152 million tons in 1980 (Gavzer, 1999).

A critical health danger is related to the production and disposal of toxic wastes (lead, asbestos, detergents, solvents, acids, and ammonia), fertilizers, herbicides, and pesticides that pollute the air, land, and water. A major source of air pollution is automobiles, which emit five gases implicated in global warming: carbon monoxide, carbon dioxide, nitrous oxide, chlorofluorocarbons, and ozone. The United States has 561 cars per 1,000 people; the other industrialized nations average 366 cars per 1,000 people, whereas there are only 68 cars per 1,000 Latin Americans, 14 per 1,000 Africans, and 2 per 1,000 Chinese (Livernash and Rodenburg, 1998:17).

REFERENCES

Crews, Kimberly A., and Cheryl Lynn Stauffer. 1997. *World Population and the Environment.* Washington, DC: Population Reference Bureau.

Ehrlich, Paul R., and Anne H. Ehrlich. 1988. "Population, Plenty, and Poverty," *National Geographic, 174* (December): 914–945.

Ehrlich, Paul R., Gretchen C. Daily, Scott C. Daily, Norman Myers, and James Salzman. 1997. "No Middle Way on the Environment," *The Atlantic Monthly 280* (December): 98–104.

Gavzer, Bernard. 1999. "Take Out the Trash, and Put It . . . Where?" *Parade Magazine* (June 13): 4–6.

Livernash, Robert, and Eric Rodenburg. 1998. "Population Change, Resources, and the Environment," *Population Bulletin 53* (March).

Rathje, William. 1999. "Talking Trash," *Washington Post National Weekly Edition* (February 15): 22.

27

The Green Revolution in the Making

CURTIS MOORE

Germany, in contrast to the United States, has instituted policies based on the principle that increased environmental regulation of industry will result in economic success. The reduction of all forms of pollution gives Germany a competitive edge over the United States and Japan because in doing so Germans must be more efficient in producing goods. Resulting innovations range from manufacturing wallboard for homes out of the residues of air pollution to developing new systems to generate electricity from wind and sun that can be marketed globally.

All in all, it's been a pretty tough 14 years for Americans seeking to make a buck by protecting the environment, and this factory in the heart of Germany says it all. As wide ribbons of heavy, brown kraft paper unspool from massive rolls onto a production line, a coverall-clad worker stands with his beefy left hand gripping a switch. A constant stream of cream-colored gypsum paste squirts between the kraft sheets, forming an endless plaster sandwich that disappears into a flat, shimmering oven where it is baked to rock hardness. With his back arched and his head cocked, the worker peers down the production line as mile after mile of what Americans call "Sheetrock" or "wallboard" thunders through the factory, bound for building sites in Germany and across Europe to form the walls and ceilings of offices and bedrooms, closets and boardrooms.

Just another factory making one of the thousands of products so common that they are scarcely worth noting, a casual observer might say—but not so. This factory represents the leading edge of a new technological revolution, one that could transform the industrial world from a cauldron of pollution to a relatively safe haven. For this wallboard is made from—are you ready?—air pollution.

This process of making wallboard, mortar, and other construction materials—and from them, homes and offices—out of the residues of air pollution is emblematic of the innovations that have sprung up as Germany, propelled by a fierce environmental ethic, has leapt to the forefront of the global environmental movement.

Source: Curtis Moore. 1995. "The Green Revolution in the Making," *Sierra 80* (January/February), pp. 50–52, 126–130.

The German passion for environmental protection was fueled initially in the late 1970s and early '80s by reports of *Waldsterben,* or "forest death"—the widespread damage to the country's forests caused by air pollution. After that, the meltdown at Chernobyl and mounting fears of stratospheric-ozone depletion and global warming established a firm ecological consciousness, leading the *Los Angeles Times* to comment that in Germany, "environmental correctness has come to rival tidiness and punctuality as a national obsession." As ethically committed as Germany's citizens and government are to protecting the earth, they also perceive the process of eliminating pollution as an opportunity to further strengthen their nation's economy.

Already running a close race with the United States as the world's leading exporter of merchandise, Germany is convinced that its environmental regulations, easily the world's most stringent, will stimulate the development of a wide range of new "green" technologies that can be marketed globally just as demand for them is beginning to increase sharply. The Germans also believe that new efforts to curb pollution by boosting efficiency will further reduce operating expenses in their already efficient economy, providing them with a competitive edge over Japan and (especially) the United States.

The homes-from-pollution process illustrates how environmental concerns have stimulated German innovation, causing many of the country's firms not only to launch their own research programs, but to raid the workshops of less-alert competitors—including the United States, where many of these new technologies were developed. Like any number of other emerging technologies, ranging from super-efficient electrical generators to add-on pollution-control systems, the homes-from-pollution process is a product of Yankee ingenuity. It was originally installed in 1973 at the Cholla I power plant in Arizona during the first wave of air-pollution regulation in the United States, but the process was exported to Germany in 1980, where it has thrived and been perfected. This is how it works:

When coal is burned to generate electricity, prodigious amounts of pollutants pour into the air, including sulfur dioxide, which causes acid rain. Some nations, though not many, require modest controls over these emissions. If the regulations are stringent, scrubbers are usually installed to remove the sulfur dioxide by spraying the exhaust with a watery mist containing limestone. The pollution/limestone reaction produces a sludge that is usually dumped on the ground or into pits or waterways.

But in Germany, where all power plants are equipped with pollution controls, the sludge can't be dumped because the law prohibits it. Such waste must be put to some use, leaving German power plants with two options: develop a means other than scrubbers to eliminate the air pollution, or find a way to use the scrubber sludge. German industry has done both, yielding two simultaneous streams of innovation, one aimed at developing pollution-control systems superior to scrubbers, the other at devising better ways to use scrubber waste. Both streams not only help make the German economy itself more efficient, but create products that can be sold on the world market, boosting employment and income at home.

When the homes-from-pollution system was exported to Germany in 1980, it was initially marketed by Knauf-Research Cotrell (KRC), a subsidiary of its U.S. developer and Knauf Gypsum. Rapidly improved there in response to the German air-pollution and waste requirements, the technology was acquired in October 1986 by the Salzgitter Group, which now sells the system globally.

One place where the technology has been installed is New Brunswick, Canada, where the 450-megawatt, coal-fired Belledune power station went into operation in 1993. The production of market-grade gypsum was "a fundamental requirement" contained in the specifications for the Belledune plant, in the words of an executive of New Brunswick Power, because it not only solved waste-disposal problems, but was less expensive than competing systems. Thus, a North American innovation traveled to Europe and back again in the space of 20 years (though the profits are being made by Germans) and is selling globally because it is, quite simply, better than the alternatives.

Sadly, the U.S. market for the homes-from-pollution process was destroyed in the 1970s when the federal government allowed utilities to build "tall stacks" for dispersing sulfur dioxide over wide areas—thus creating a new acid-rain problem—rather than requiring them to eliminate it. Even if strict controls on power plants had remained in effect, however, lax waste-disposal regulations might have had the same ultimate impact. In Germany, though, the process has proved so effective and profitable that in 1990 Knauf Gypsum opened a British plant at Sittingborne-on-Thames, where German air-pollution residues are made into building materials for homes and factories. Flowing in the opposite direction, of course, is profit that can be plowed back into the German economy— perhaps to acquire still more products of U.S. origin.

There are other examples of remarkable innovation stimulated by Germany's tough attitudes toward pollution:

• The Ford auto plant in Cologne complied with new requirements by modernizing its paint-spray line, cutting pollution by 70 percent and the cost of painting a car by about $60—a savings that makes German-built cars marginally more salable.

• The "4P" plastic-film manufacturing and printing plant in Forchheim, where plastic bags for frozen french fries and other foods are printed and stamped by the millions, was forced to cut pollution by 70 percent. The company installed a recycling system that reclaims up to 90 percent of the Plant's solvents, saving so much money that the 4P pollution controls will not only pay for themselves, but actually start saving the company money by reducing the cost of solvents. A sister plant with a similar system already recaptures solvents—once again lowering its overhead while increasing profit.

Little wonder that Edda Müller, former chief aide to Germany's minister for the environment, declares emphatically that "what we are doing here is economic policy, not environmental policy."

She is not alone in this view of the future, nor is Germany. For example, Takefumi Fukumizu, U.S. representative of Japan's powerful Ministry of International Trade and Industry, says that industrialists in his country see "an inescapable economic necessity to improve energy efficiency and environmental technologies, which they believe would reduce costs and create a profitable world market."

With virtually no coal, oil, or natural gas, and limited mineral resources, Japan has historically been forced to do more with less than its principal industrial competitors, the United States and Germany. As a result, it makes steel, automobiles, and a wide range of other goods with greater efficiency and less pollution than any other nation. That national thrift and the technologies it has spawned are now global commodities as other nations increasingly search for cleaner, more efficient manufacturing methods and energy use. "The potential profit in such a market," explains Fukumizu, "is limitless."

In the United States, however, governments and businesses alike remain so focused on short-term profits and quarterly earnings that they overlook the true source of long-term wealth: innovation. Necessity breeds invention, and during the 1970s, when protecting the environment and saving energy were seen as essential elements of national policy, the United States brought hundreds of new products and processes to the verge of commercial reality.

These ranged from systems to generate electricity from wind and sunlight with zero pollution to little-known devices such as fuel cells that can power everything from homes to locomotives with zero or near-zero pollution and noise, while requiring minimal space. Yet these and thousands of other born-in-the-U.S.A. environmental products were abandoned during the 1980s as the Reagan and Bush administrations, the Congress, and many state officials turned their backs on environmental protection, orphaning technologies that now stand to generate billions, perhaps trillions, of dollars for their new proponents.

Solar photovoltaics, for example, were originally developed to generate electricity for space satellites, then modified for ground-based uses, making the United States the world's leading producer. But when Ronald Reagan took office, he slashed federal funding for the program from more than $150 million to zero. Then he rejected the "energy independence" policies of presidents Nixon, Ford, and Carter, substituting a "cheap oil" strategy expressly designed to increase U.S. reliance on Persian Gulf oil by driving prices down through secret negotiations with Saudi Arabia. As oil prices plummeted, they destroyed the U.S. market for solar and other forms of renewable energy, allowing the Japanese, Germans, and others to buy companies, patents, and production licenses for pennies on the dollar. Now Japan is the world's leading producer of solar cells. The United States is second, but the nation's largest factory is owned by the German conglomerate Siemens. If its production were assigned to Germany instead of the United States, America's photovoltaic sector would drop to a level on par with those of developing nations like Brazil.

A similar fate befell fuel cells, compact and virtually silent devices that chemically convert fuel to electricity. When run on hydrogen, fuel cells produce zero pollution or, if a hydrogen "carrier" such as natural gas is used, almost zero. First developed for the space program, they still meet all of the electrical needs of NASA's space shuttles. But in the 1980s, U.S. companies such as General Electric and Englehard turned their backs on fuel-cell technology. As a result, the world's first fuel-cell assembly line was Japanese, and the first zero-polluting, fuel-cell-powered bus is Canadian. Both employ technologies that were developed with hundreds of millions of U.S. tax dollars. The governments of both Canada and Japan helped their nation's companies acquire and develop the fuel-cell technology.

The list goes on and on, and includes technologies ranging from high-efficiency light bulbs to new ways of burning coal, all developed in large part with U.S. capital, but now wholly or partially in the hands of others. In the United States, the cheap-oil strategy remains in place, energy taxes have been rejected by Congress, and environmental laws continue to fall further and further behind those of Germany, Japan, Sweden, the Netherlands, and other industrialized nations. Once the world's environmental leader, the United States is now a laggard, its political landscape hostile to those seeking to pioneer in what many regard as a new industrial revolution greening the global economy.

Germany, meanwhile, has been restructuring the technological basis of its economy to make it sustainable over the long run, leading to a profusion of new environmental products and processes spurred by the world's most aggressive protection programs. Consider, for example, the following:

- It is retrofitting all power plants. While politicians in North America were arguing about whether acid rain was real, Germany listened to its scientists and adopted rules requiring every power plant within its borders to slash the air pollutants that cause acid rain by 90 percent. By 1989 the German retrofit was complete. Today, seven years before the U.S. control program will take full effect in 2002, Germans are selling Americans and the rest of the world anti-pollution technology and know-how.

- It is aggressively phasing out chemicals that destroy the ozone layer and cause global warming. In 1989 Germany mandated a ban by 1995—five years before the rest of the world—on chlorofluorocarbon (CFC) gases, the primary culprits in the destruction of the ozone layer that protects Earth from solar radiation. It had also committed to reducing emissions of carbon dioxide, the principal cause of global warming, by 25 percent by the year 2010. These are the swiftest and toughest phase-downs in the world, and they required German industries to respond quickly, creating new products and processes that can be marketed globally as other nations begin to follow suit.

- It is revolutionizing the trash business. Aiming not only to reduce the volume of trash swelling landfills and clogging incinerators, Germany has also fostered a new industry by adopting a "take back" program that requires everything from cameras to yogurt cartons—and the scrubber sludge from which Knauf Gypsum makes wall-board—to be collected by manufacturers and recycled. The program was so fabulously successful that the volume of trash quickly outstripped the nation's recycling capacity, thus creating even further pressure for industry to minimize packaging and other waste. Although the program was originally meant to include cars as well, German manufacturers staved off formal government action by agreeing to mount voluntary take-back programs, thus starting a global movement among car makers to develop vehicles that can be recycled. Some are already rolling off the assembly line with bar-coded parts and instructions for dismantling an auto in 20 minutes.

Like most of Germany's environmental laws, the take-back rule imposes explicit, numeric requirements: as of this year, 90 percent of all discarded glass and metals must be recycled, as well as 80 percent of all paper, board, plastics, and laminates. Incineration, even if used to generate power, has been ruled out as a solid-waste-disposal method because the burning of materials pollutes the air, especially with highly toxic dioxins and furans.

Because the take-back law sweeps virtually every form of waste into its ambit, its results were almost immediate: 400 German companies randomly surveyed less than 18 months after the law took effect on December 1, 1991, said they had completely abandoned use of polyvinyl packaging, plastic foams, and 117 other types of packaging. All but one of 146 companies had stopped using "blister" packs, which are both tough to recycle and yield dioxins when burned. One of every four companies was using packaging made at least in part from recycled materials. Companies were running full-page newspaper advertisements touting the recyclability of their products. And with good reason, as almost two-thirds of Germany's consumers shop for environmentally friendly products. Indeed, public insistence on recycling has become so widespread in Germany that the amount of recycled plastic rocketed from 41,000 tons in 1992 to ten times that amount a year later. Now, the nation has become a favorite testing ground for products to be marketed as environmentally safe. When in 1991, for example, Procter & Gamble introduced Vidal Sassoon "Airspray" hair spray in the United States, it did so only after testing in Germany. Similarly, two years earlier, P&G launched its "Enviro-pak" containers for laundry detergents in the United States only after testing in Germany.

Companies such as P&G have no choice but to develop such products if they wish to do business in Germany. One reason for this is the government's Blue Angel environmental labeling program. Introduced in 1977, Blue Angel is a symbol owned by Germany's environment ministry, which describes it as "a market-oriented instrument of government" that informs and motivates environmentally conscious thinking and acting among manufacturers and consumers. The ministry licenses the label's use for about 3,500 products selected on a case-by-case basis by the independent, nine-member Environmental Label Jury. The label depicts a blue figure with outstretched arms encircled by the laurel wreath of the United Nations. Inscribed in the border for each product is a brief explanation of the product's qualities, such as "low-polluting," "low-noise," or "100-percent recycled." Although there are imitators in other countries—the Green Cross of Canada, for example—Germany's Blue Angel remains far and away the most famous and successful environmental-labeling program.

In the United States, efforts to establish such a government-sponsored labeling system have foundered on industry opposition. A private effort, Green Seal, is struggling to establish itself, but is hampered by high testing costs and a lack of publicity. In Germany, however, the Blue Angel offers its bearers the prospect of winning an edge over competing brands and products in the environmentally conscious German marketplace. The prospect of its award—and attendant profits—has made it possible for a wide variety of environmentally friendly products ranging from low-pollution paints to mercury-free batteries to establish themselves. Public recognition of and enthusiasm for the Blue Angel program has boosted the market share of many products. For instance, before water-soluble lacquers were awarded a Blue Angel in 1981, these products commanded a meager one-percent market share. Today, 40 percent of Germany's do-it-yourself wood finishers and 20 percent of its professionals buy the less-toxic coatings. Similarly, biodegradable chainsaw lubricants are in high demand by the foresters who manage virtually every acre of Germany's woodlands. First introduced in 1987, the formula eliminates up to 7,000 tons a year of highly toxic oil otherwise absorbed by forest floors and nearby streams. After receiving a Blue Angel, these oils achieved a dominating position in the market.

Having deployed these weapons in their battle against pollution of air, water, and soil, some German officials believe they have all but exhausted the reductions that can be achieved through conventional cleanup means such as wastewater-treatment plants and scrubbers. Nevertheless, pressured by voters to cut pollution further, the government is imposing a wide range of increasingly tough requirements designed to reduce pollution by further increasing efficiency both in factories and on the highways.

Regulations now being implemented, for example, will force drivers out of gas-guzzling cars and onto energy-efficient public transit. Inner cities are being systematically closed to auto traffic, while highway, bridge, and other tolls are being raised, and long-term "green passes" for public transportation are sold in all of Germany's major cities. A Berlin green pass costs about $40 a month, and is valid for an unlimited number of rides. A comparable pass in Washington, D.C., costs roughly twice as much. Germany also intends to increase bicycle ridership by providing specially marked lanes on sidewalks and at intersections.

Systematically shifting people and goods in this fashion not only reduces pollution, but boosts the overall efficiency of Germany's economy by cutting transportation costs. Commuting by train, for example, slashes both fuel consumption and air pollution by up to 75 percent compared with cars, and 90 percent compared with planes. Traffic congestion and the pollution it generates, as cars creep through crowded roadways or idle at stoplights, is also cut, because trains occupy only a quarter of the road space required by buses and 1/13th that needed by cars. Because trains run on electricity generated by Germany's domestic coal, oil imports required to fuel diesel buses or gasoline cars are likewise reduced.

The nation's self-imposed target of reducing carbon dioxide emissions from the former West Germany by 25 percent and from the former East Germany by 30 percent—both by the year 2010—requires the economy to become even more efficient. One way the country intends to achieve this is to put energy that is now being wasted to some useful purpose.

In most power plants and factories, only about one-third of the energy in coal, oil, or gas is actually used. The rest escapes as waste heat. The German government has prepared regulations that will require large- and medium-size industries and utilities to market this waste energy. It can be used to heat homes and factories (or, by running CFC-free "absorption chillers," to cool them), operate paper mills and chemical plants, and even generate a few more kilowatts with super-efficient technology. Officials estimate that use of this waste heat will boost efficiency to roughly 90 percent and that air pollution—already at the world's lowest levels—will be chopped by at least half.

Because of the immense cost of bringing the former East Germany into compliance with the environmental requirements of the former West Germany, the waste-heat law has been delayed while officials turn to more pressing needs. Work is already under way, for example, on shutting down 80 percent of the former East Germany's power plants while retrofitting the remaining facilities that generate 10,000 megawatts—that's slightly more than Thailand's entire electricity consumption—with state-of-the-art pollution controls.

The cumulative effect of all these programs is to place Germany in a commanding position as nations beset with environmental problems search for ways to reduce pollution quickly and inexpensively. Thailand, for example, decided to install scrubbers on its coal-fired power plants after a single episode of air pollution in Mae Mo District sent more than 4,000 of its citizens to doctors and hospitals. Smog-bound Mexico City has been forced to implement emissions controls on cars and factories. Taiwan is even going so far as to require catalytic converters for motorcycles. Such mandates will almost inevitably benefit Germany because, as Harvard Business School economist Michael Porter explains, "Germany has had perhaps the world's tightest regulations in stationary air-pollution control, and German companies appear to hold a wide lead in patenting— and exporting—air pollution and other environmental technologies."

In the United States, however, where environmental standards were relaxed by a succession of Reagan/Bush appointees, often in the name of competitiveness, "as much as 70 percent of the air pollution control equipment sold . . . is produced by foreign companies," according to Porter, whose 855-page study of industrial economies, *The Competitive Advantage of Nations,* examines the impact of environmental regulations on competitiveness.

Germany's actions continue to contrast sharply with those of the United States, even under President Clinton, whom most environmentalists supported as the green answer to George Bush. Germany's emissions limits on power plants and incinerators are 4 to 300 times more stringent than those of the United States. German companies that generate electricity from wind, solar, or other renewable forms of power are reimbursed at twice to three times U.S. levels. German recycling is mandatory, while American programs are usually voluntary where they exist at all.

Still, support for Germany's environmental initiatives is by no means unanimous. Wolfgang Hilger, for example, the chairman of Hoechst, Germany's largest chemical company, complained bitterly in 1991 that the government had lost all sense of proportion. He claimed that regulations had jeopardized 250 jobs at his company, and threatened it with a $100-million loss. But Hilger represents a minority view. Most German citizens and businesses remain convinced both that environmental protection is essential and that the technological innovation stimulated by stringent environmental requirements will, over the long term, strengthen their national productivity and competitiveness.

Tragically, U.S. political leaders continue to embrace the outmoded and false view that the environment can be protected only at the expense of the economy, when the truth is precisely the opposite. Meanwhile, products of American genius continue to depart for Japan, Germany, and other nations, only to be sold back to U.S. industry sometime in the future. So far, the homes-from-pollution process hasn't traveled full circle back to its place of invention in the United States. But don't be surprised if sometime soon you see a piece of wallboard being nailed into a new office or a remodeled home only to find it boldly emblazoned: "Made in Germany."

28

Late to the Station

DAVID MOBERG

Despite recent government initiatives, the United States remains behind Japan and Europe in the construction of high-speed rail systems. In addition to the obvious environmental benefits of high-speed rail, the consequences of not having such a developed system will hurt the United States in a wide range of areas including jobs, economic efficiency, public convenience, safety, and even foreign trade. U.S. businesses in particular will be damaged because their economic rivals in other countries are able to produce goods using only half the amount of energy used in the United States.

By the turn of the millennium, Japan expects to begin construction on a second-generation high-speed train system. Depending on the results of tests now underway, the Japanese government will choose one of two technological options. It may decide to upgrade the steel-wheel-on-steel-rail technology used in Japan's nearly 30-year-old 130-mile-per-hour bullet train. Or it may opt for a new "maglev" technology—a concept that eliminates old-fashioned wheels and track in favor of powerful superconducting magnets that suspend the train above a guideway and propel it at 300 miles per hour.

Also around the year 2000, the major cities of Europe will be increasingly linked by 200 mile-per-hour steel-wheel trains of principally French and German manufacture. Other important routes will be improved to accommodate trains at 125 miles per hour or more if the German government gives its approval later this year; construction may also start in 1994 on a $5 billion maglev line that would link Hamburg and Berlin using Germany's well-tested Transrapid technology. A trip that now takes three hours by modern train would zip by in only 55 minutes on the Transrapid.

By contrast, in the United States there may be a few corridors in densely populated regions that have been improved enough to run European-designed trains at 125 miles per hour by the year 2000. If all goes well, there will also be a U.S. maglev prototype ready to begin testing. In the unlikely event that any high-speed steel-wheel trains are

Source: David Moberg. 1993. "Late to the Station," *In These Times* (June 14), pp. 14–17.

deployed by then, the technology will almost certainly be European or, at best, the product of a joint venture with U.S. companies.

Yet even this anemic U.S. performance will be possible only because the Clinton administration is seeking a hefty increase in high-speed train funding. The administration proposes spending $1.3 billion over five years on high-speed trains, including $300 million on technology development. That includes $228 million over five years for maglev research. The administration also plans to continue separate funding of improvements on the Amtrak line from Boston to Washington that will permit running higher speed trains. In addition, President Clinton is seeking a change in tax law to enable states to issue tax-free revenue bonds to finance rail projects.

George Bush had proposed no funds for any passenger trains—including Amtrak—and froze even some of the more modest high-speed rail spending approved by Congress in 1991. Clinton's high-speed train proposal reflects the best of his campaign promises—economic stimulus through public investment that will strengthen the economy for the long run. Yet even Clinton's projected spending will leave the United States lagging far behind other industrial countries. Meanwhile, America's rail gap will continue to hurt the country on many fronts—jobs, trade, economic efficiency, public convenience, safety, energy efficiency, the environment and even foreign policy.

Trains have been a missing link in the transportation infrastructure of the United States, the victim of private mismanagement and unsupportive, even hostile, public policy. Even so, rail freight has made a small comeback, especially with "piggyback" trains hauling truck trailers. Amtrak has also made vast improvements, though it still isn't a match for even the most backwater European trains. Because we've slipped so far, however, there is far less of a built-in constituency for trains—except for a dwindling club of train buffs—than there is for cars, trucks and planes. Yet even in such auto shrines as Southern California, modestly modernized rail has proven popular.

Contemporary high-speed trains make sense. They can carry travelers over distances of several hundred miles as quickly as planes, based on overall travel time, thus offering an alternative to gridlocked highways and airports. They require roughly one-third the energy per passenger mile of autos and about one-fourth to one-sixth the fuel of airplanes.

Japan's and Europe's more efficient transportation systems help these U.S. economic rivals produce goods with about half of the energy that this country does, giving their businesses a competitive edge. Electrified trains do not rely on oil and could free the United States from its dangerous and costly reliance on the Mideast, which skews U.S. foreign and military policy. The energy advantage of trains yields an environmental reward, despite the pollution and radiation waste disposal problems of power plants for electrified trains. And if photovoltaics and wind generators were used, trains might prove an environmental bonanza.

Trains use far less space than highways or even airports and operate more quietly than airplanes (although they still pose noise problems at high speeds). They are the safest form of transportation: after billions of passenger miles on high-speed trains in France and Japan, there have been only two fatalities—and those occurred when the French TGV (*train a grande vitesse*) was nearing a station at a low speed. Trains also encourage denser urban settlement, which is more efficient and less environmentally destructive than auto-induced sprawl.

The existing U.S. transportation system is less and less effective even at moving people at reasonable speeds. Highway gridlock wastes more than 3 billion hours each year for commuters, truck drivers and travelers. By 2005, we'll be wasting 12 billion hours. Figuring that a person's time is worth, say, $10 an hour, the cost is staggering.

Delays at airports are also costly. Larry Johnson, director of the Center for Transportation Research at Argonne National Laboratory near Chicago, calculates that passengers lose more than 12 million hours each year in delays at O'Hare airport alone. In 1986, according to the Federal Aviation Administration (FAA), airline delays cost $5 billion, including $2 billion in extra fuel and labor costs for the ailing airline industry.

Building new highways and airports is often unpopular, and such construction creates as many new problems as it solves by contributing to urban sprawl and further lengthening commuting time. It's also costly. Relieving airport congestion will cost $117 billion over the next decade, according to the FAA. Maintaining the interstate highway system could run $3 trillion over the next several decades.

High-speed railroads could relieve many of these problems, but the biggest obstacle is financing. Building a new rail system requires a long-term strategic outlook that government must provide—either as a major investor and guarantor or as the outright owner and operator.

At first glance constructing a new train system seems very expensive. Yet comparison of the costs of different transportation modes is complicated. Although railroads were heavily subsidized in the 19th century, government policies have favored highways and airports at the expense of rail for more than 50 years. Highway and airport trust funds receive fuel and airport taxes, but for many years railroad taxes went not for rail improvements but for general federal programs. There are also direct subsidies to highways (about 40 percent of total costs) and air travel (more than [the FAA's] final report recommending that the United States go ahead with further development and narrowing of options). All of the U.S. maglev concepts employ superconducting magnets; three of the four use electromagnetic repulsion. At a recent international maglev conference at Argonne, U.S. Army researcher James Lever argued that the four U.S. proposals promised higher performance than the Transrapid or the French TGV at comparable cost.

There are still technical issues to be resolved, especially with the new U.S. concepts. No prototypes have been built or tested yet. But the issue of cost still emerges immediately in most discussions.

At this point maglev seems likely to be more expensive than high-speed steel-wheel rail. Typical ballpark figures suggest an average of $10 million to $15 million a mile for high-speed trains, $20 million to $30 million a mile for maglev. Maglev proponents claim they could build a system for under $20 million a mile. Costs could be reduced dramatically if maglev could use interstate highway right-of-ways. Most maglev designs assume that tracks would be elevated, but money could be saved if the guideways could operate at ground level for long stretches in rural areas. Most urban expressways cost in this same $20 million to $30 million range (or even more), but average overall highway costs are lower.

John Harding, research director for the Federal Railway Administration, says that at these prices maglev could pay its full operating and construction costs in the San Diego-Los Angeles-San Francisco corridor and in the Northeast, from Washington to Boston. In several other densely populated areas, maglev could pay full operating costs out of fares but probably not all construction costs, Harding says.

Steel-wheel advocates argue their technology is now ready to go and has proven that it can reach speeds on test runs of over 300 miles per hour. Maglev advocates argue that their systems start at 300 miles per hour and represent the inevitable triumph of electronic over mechanical systems. They doubt steel-wheel technology is viable at the highest experimental test speeds. Yet maglev's higher speeds may offer only insignificant time savings for short- and medium-range travelers. For example, on a 50-mile trip, improving speeds from 50 miles per hour to 150 miles per hour cuts a one hour ride to 20 minutes. But jumping from 150 miles per hour to 300 miles per hour only reduces that already short 20-minute trip to 10 minutes.

Although maglev has often been presented as more energy efficient than rail, research presented at the Argonne conference suggested maglev may be more energy intensive—but not enough to make a big difference at current energy prices. Both are far more efficient than planes, but steel-wheel technology may run into problems of maintenance and reliability at the upper range of its speed.

Maglev appeals to strategists who see it as an opportunity for U.S. corporations—possibly including converted defense suppliers—to leapfrog to a new generation of transportation technology and overcome the nation's neglect of rail over the past 50 years. There is only one U.S.-owned company with a limited capacity now to make passenger locomotives (Morrison Knudsen) and two weakened freight locomotive manufacturers (General Electric and General Motors). Two foreign-owned firms have locomotive factories in the U.S.

With steel-wheel technology, American producers may be locked into an inferior position, relying on technological leadership from overseas. Hard bargaining could move some production jobs here or encourage joint ventures, however. Clinton's program provides some help for non-electric high-speed locomotive development as well as maglev in the hope that U.S. firms can carve out a new niche. It will be a tricky balancing act for government to mesh industrial strategy and transportation objectives without letting either policy distort the other.

Much of the rail infrastructure work is now being left to private investors, who are notoriously skittish about such long-range commitments. Consequently, many rail advocates think the federal government should assume primary responsibility for the track infrastructure. This would be accomplished not through tax revenue, but by issuing bonds to raise private funds. There could be competition for operation of the trains, with Amtrak as one likely contender. But the same competitive model that governs airlines or trucking firms is likely to work even less well on railroads. That's especially true for maglev, since the choice of a guideway design will essentially determine the train design as well.

The national transportation strategy must balance immediate incremental improvements in conventional rail with efforts to develop new technology, both steel wheel and maglev. The nation can't wait for maglev breakthroughs, for example, nor can it rely solely on gradual modernization.

Some skeptics doubt whether government has the will or ability to pull off such a massive mission—comparable to the interstate highway program started under Eisenhower or the space program under Kennedy. A new high-speed ground transportation system will be costly. Yet there are less obvious costs of delay—inefficiency and damage to human health and the environment. Without strong government leadership, the nation will pay a hidden price it can't afford.

29

Creating Markets for Recycling

FRED FRIEDMAN

There are few economic incentives in the United States to motivate peo-ple to recycle. A number of European countries have recycling systems in which producers take responsibility for recycling reusable materials and for designing products that can be easily recycled. The author argues that the key to a successful recycling system is making it a prof-itable venture. Factors preventing the development of a recycling mar-ket in the United States are discussed.

When a school child, a parent, or a business-person comes into the Environmental Pro-tection Agency's New England Research Library where I work to talk about how they can "help" the environment, they usually talk about recycling. Recycling is the best known pro-environment action that you can take without major investments in time, equipment or social organizing. Anyone can do it. Anyone can collect recyclables or buy products made with recycled materials.

Because recycling is so easy, some environmentalists distrust it, branding it a "feel-good activity" with questionable environmental worth. Since it's so accessible and since businesses push their products emphasizing recycled content, isn't it really just hype?

WHY DO WE RECYCLE?

As of 1997, Americans were recycling about 27% of their municipal solid waste, burn-ing and burying the rest. Since 1988, recycling has just about doubled. Why? The answers produced by public opinion polls are usually "because it is something that we can easily do to conserve resources and/or help the environment" and "it's the best way to deal with waste."

The same polls reveal many public misconceptions about recycling. In 1994, fewer than half of the consumers and business executives polled believed that recycling was expensive and most (74% of consumers, 68% of executives) believed that recycling paid for itself. Wrong on both counts.

Source: Fred Friedman. 1999. *Dollars and Sense 224* (July/August), pp. 29–33.

Common sense says recycled goods should be cheaper than those made from "virgin" materials because recycled material need nor be mined or milled, nor does it require the energy and pollution containment needed to manufacture new materials. This is not always the case, sometimes because companies charge the same for both products no matter what their costs, but also because it can still be costly to process recycling.

Recycling has made good sense and good business for one unsung recycling industry that takes old or broken wooden pallets and turns them into new pallets for the transport industry, or into furniture. Recycled and virgin-made pallets perform equally well, and manufacturers charge about the same for both. Though not all pallet recyclers have struck it rich, businesses such as Pallet Resources of North Carolina, Quality Pallet of Seymour, Wisconsin, and AAA Pallet & Lumber Co. of Phoenix, Arizona, are thriving.

But economic incentives to recycle are not so strong everywhere. We still need markets (such as the one the transportation industry provides for pallets) and we need to create recycled materials for manufacturers more efficiently. Recycling is not free. Every time waste is touched, costs are incurred.

Curbside collection is the best way to sustain the public's participation in recycling programs—though a committed community has proven it can sustain drop-off recycling too. But costs are high until many people participate and as they gain experience in properly sorting materials, and where there is competition among haulers. The more centralized the operation of the entire recycling process—from hauling waste from the curb, through processing and remanufacture—and the fewer middlemen involved, the more cost effective recycling becomes.

Dumping and incineration, meanwhile, are cheaper than the public imagines. This depresses the incentive of cities to recycle. The United States is not on the verge of running out of landfill space. The Great American West (the interior, not the Coast) has ample landfill capacity waiting with attractive "tipping fees." In fact, these fees are far more attractive than they should be. Recycling is a more attractive form of waste management when "full-cost accounting," including environmental costs, is employed. The cost of dumping or incineration, which degrade land, water, and air quality, and may cause "downstream" health hazards, cannot be assessed in the amount of the tipping fee or the incinerator's bill. A full accounting must include these environmental costs, starting from the production of the raw materials involved, and continuing through each stage of the manufacturing process to disposal of whatever unusable waste remains at the end. But we don't know how widely full-cost accounting for waste is used.

Three recent developments, however, promise to make recycling more economically viable. The first is the "pay as you throw" system of municipal garbage disposal. Here, municipalities charge households for trash pick-up based on how much they put out on the curb, usually calculated per container, much as utilities charge homes for the amount of electricity they use. When residents pay for trash collection and disposal directly, instead of indirectly through property taxes, they cut back on their waste and recycle more. This has been seen in most communities where it was tried, from Tacoma, Washington, to Gainesville, Florida, and from San Jose, California, to Falmouth, Maine.

The second development is called "producer responsibility." Here governments require that producers recycle reusable materials and dispose of unusable wastes or ask them to voluntarily arrange for recycling and disposal. This is particularly important for dangerous materials where no recycling infrastructure exists as yet. Cellular telephones, industrial batteries, and certain auto parts all fall in this category, as do hard-to-dispose-of products that contain hazardous materials like computers, fluorescent lights, and medical apparatus, or those which are merely a social nuisance such as packaging.

Europe has taken this approach for a while—beginning with Germany's "Green Dot" system, and continuing with similar programs in France, Belgium, and the Netherlands. It has just started to catch on in the United States, notably with the manufacturers of rechargeable batteries and some home computers. The Portable Rechargeable Battery Association (including the manufacturers Energizer, Panasonic, Saft, Sanyo Energy, and Varta) will take back used rechargables, nickel-cadmium cells, and some other batteries. Compaq and Apple both offer battery take-back programs through their authorized dealers. Dell Computer USA offers some customers an asset recovery service which is a take-back, refurbish and resale program even if the equipment wasn't made by Dell. Hewlett-Packard offers take-back on a case-by-case basis; as of 1994, the company processed 900,000 pounds of equipment per month; they also take back laser toner cartridges. IBM has a similar program in eight European countries, and plans to expand it to the United States.

The third sustainable development is "green design." For recycling, this means designing products to separate cleanly and quickly into reusable materials. Unless the parts of more products can be easily separated and recycled, recycling's rapid growth will come to a halt. Green design is already employed in car production, making cars the world's most recycled product; about 70% of a vehicle's parts, mostly metals, are recycled. Plastics, glass, rubber, and carpet from cars are usually not recycled. Where green design is in place, cars are easily disassembled with most parts resold as replacements or reused as feedstock for new car parts or raw material for other recyclers.

In the United States, the Big Three auto makers have been at work on this agenda for five years while European firms such as Mercedes Benz, BMW, and Peugeot have more fully implemented green design. The Europeans aim to avoid nonrecyclable or hazardous materials, and to avoid parts whose distinct materials cannot be separated. Their cars are easier to disassemble, and they use plastics that are easily identifiable by resin type. Whether green design ever catches on in other industries will depend in part on whether a market develops for the component materials.

Whether recycling in general can succeed right now rests on whether it can be made into a profitable enterprise. Recycling firms recycle for profits. Except for companies that receive their recycled raw materials for low or no cost, however, there is no guarantee that recycling will be profitable. When recycled high grade paper can be sold for $100 per ton as in 1995, it will be profitable to recycle. When the same material is sold for $20 per ton as in 1998, it may not be profitable, unless sold in sufficient quantities, to certain export markets, or under long-term contracts which do not reflect the spot market price.

Markets for recycled materials do not just spring up on their own. It has taken the efforts of the EPA, many state environmental departments, and some private trade associations, among others, to help create what markets do exist. Some states provide tax breaks to recycling industries. The EPA's Waste-Wi$e program gives technical help to businesses interested in using recycled products or reducing their waste. Its Jobs Through Recycling program offers grants of up to $200,000 to help states develop their recycling industries. And the National Office Paper Recycling Program of the U.S. Conference of Mayors helps businesses and local governments collect and market recycling.

Even so, the current recyclables market is not nearly what it could be, except perhaps in paper. Few large consumers are buying recycled content products whenever they can. All too few procurement departments at government offices, businesses, universities, and hospitals are buying recycled products for their offices or core operations. By 1998, 47 states had followed the federal government's lead and told their procurement officers to buy certain recycled products when possible even if they have to pay a premium. Since State and local government purchasing accounts for 15% of the U.S.'s gross national product (the feds account for about 6%), these governments could have a big impact on recycling.

Just look at paper. Federal procurement programs, which started tentatively in 1983, and expanded aggressively after 1990, largely created the market for recycled office papers. But you cannot sustain recycling without knowing and using the sources of recycled products. The "Official Recycled Products Guide" is the most comprehensive compendium of recycled-content products available. Yet only one of the six New England states had a current edition of this vital "buy recycled" directory available when I recently surveyed them. Not a single hospital that has called the Research Library for recycling information in the past three months had it either.

Meanwhile, regulatory differences from one state to another keep standards and markets for recycling decentralized. Only about 12 states, for example, authorize the use of recycled asphalt for use in road construction. Some states permit the use of fly ash, glass, and tire rubber in road construction or civil engineering projects. Others do not.

At the same time as the government mandates recycling in some areas, it sometimes undercuts that effort by subsidizing the manufacture of virgin materials that compete in the same markets as unsubsidized products with recycled content. The timber industry got about $400 million in subsidies in 1991, but recycled wood or composting firms were ignored. The same holds in steel—the virgin steel industry gets subsidies, recycled steel does not. Some state and local governments are historically tied into tax-break, tax-rebate, or tax-advantage systems for manufacturing industries which mine, mill, or manufacture chiefly from virgin raw materials. Only recently have a few states (Massachusetts, New York, Washington, and California) given similar subsidies to recycled-content-based industries.

Another factor, almost never mentioned, which may stand in the way of recycling, is that the remanufacturers of recycled-content products are also manufacturers of virgin materials. Paper producers put out both virgin, and virgin-plus-recycled content products. Steel producers put out virgin, recycled and virgin-plus-recycled steel alloy. Aluminum manufacturers control the remanufacturing of virgin aluminum alloy, as well as virgin-plus-recycled aluminum. The two largest producers of recycled-content aluminum are Alcan and Kaiser, the two largest manufacturers of all aluminum. The same is true of major manufacturers of PET and HDPE plastics, replacement auto parts, glass, and tire rubber.

TABLE 29.1 Timber Subsidies by U.S. Government

SUBSIDY	AVERAGE OVER 1 YEAR ($MILLIONS)	TOTAL OVER 5 YEARS ($MILLIONS)
Timber Tax Breaks	635	3,175
Below-Cost Timber Sales	111	555
Forest Roads Construction	31	157
Forest Service Salvage Fund	34	171
Total	811	4,058

Source: Grassroots Recycling Network. "Welfare for Waste: How Federal Taxpayer Subsidies Waste Resources and Discourage Recycling." April, 1999.

By controlling the prices of both virgin and recycled plastic, major manufacturers and processors ensure that consumers see little of the potential savings from the lower cost of recycled materials. Sometimes recycled-content products are as expensive as, or even more expensive than, their virgin-content equivalents. This is not universally the case, but it is the case frequently enough to have an important economic impact— depressing the benefits, which could accrue to all of us, of using recycled materials.

To revisit the question posed at the outset, "Why do we recycle?" An alternative view comes from Denmark, where a summary of polling and other literature suggests complex motives that begin with public altruism. Recycling offers an all-too-rare opportunity for each member of society to participate with their neighbors in socially beneficial behavior. According to the Danish scholar John Thorgeresen, morality, not the market, is the true context for recycling. Yes, calculations of public benefit, economic savings, and resource conservation are motivators. But the key to understanding the motivation for recycling lies in a moral choice between the environmental and the economic, where the environmental wins. He concluded that market-based solutions were not the principal concern of people in the several countries (including the United States) that he studied.

Recycling cuts pollution from manufacturing. Recycled materials can be transformed into new products with far less energy than can virgin materials. Recycling avoids the costs of disposal in landfills or incinerators. If well designed, a recycling system contributes to cost-competitive waste management. It creates jobs, makes industry more competitive, and saves resources both renewable and nonrenewable. Recycling, however, is not a panacea, and it cannot be all things to all people at all times. Recycling can be profitable in the financial sense, but it should not always be expected to make money. Recycling can lead to creative invention and adaptation of materials into new products, but to expect this to be true for all recyclables, all of the time, is to set the bar too high. We do not expect other forms of waste management to be cost-free, nor to pay for themselves. We do not expect wastes sitting in landfills to be used inventively and creatively. Why expect the same of recycling?

PART FIVE

Individual Deviance

Crime and Crime Control

THE UNITED STATES CONTEXT

International comparisons of crime data, while inexact, do provide rough approximations of how crime is patterned geographically. The following is from Eitzen and Baca Zinn: What is accepted is that among the industrialized nations there is not too much difference in burglaries, bicycle thefts, and other property crimes. (2) What is striking, however, is that among these nations, the United States has much higher rates of violent crimes (robberies, assaults, murders, and rapes) (2000:478–479). "For at least a century and probably longer we have been the most murderous 'developed' society on earth" (Harwood, 1997:27). Criminologists are in general agreement that the extraordinarily high rate of violent crime in the United States is the result of the confluence of at least four major forces. First, countries where there is a wide gap between rich and poor have the highest levels of violent crime. The United States has the greatest inequality gap among the industrialized nations.

Second, the greater the proportion of the population living in poverty, the higher is the rate of violent crime. The United States differs from the other industrialized nations "in having an underclass that is not merely poor, but has few chances of escaping poverty" (Rubenstein, 1995:20). Criminologist Elliott Currie says, "[We] know that the links between disadvantage and violence are strongest for the poorest and the most neglected of the poor . . . [The] people locked into the most permanent forms of economic marginality in the most impoverished and disrupted communities [have] the highest concentrations of serious violent crime" (Currie, 1998:127).

Third, violent crime is worse in those societies with weak "safety nets" for the poor. As Currie puts it: "[The United States] though generally quite wealthy, is also far more unequal and far less committed to including the vulnerable into a common level of social life than any other developed nation" (Currie, 1998:120).

Fourth, the greater the availability of guns in a society, the higher the level of violent crime. Without question, the United States has more guns per capita than any other industrialized nation—an estimated 240 million guns and adding about 4 million more annually in a population of 270 million (Symonds and Woellert, 1999). The 1995 rate of gun ownership per capita in Great Britain was 0.006 compared to 0.853 in the United States.

The U.S. solution to crime has been to ignore these sources of criminal behavior—the inequality gap, the relatively high proportion living in poverty, the weak "safety nets" for the poor, and the wide range of gun ownership—and focus rather on imprisoning criminals. In 1998 the various levels of government had 1.8 million people in prison or jail. This amounted to an incarceration rate of 668 inmates per 100,000 people, up from 458 in 1990 (Gilliard, 1999). Only Russia's incarceration rate is higher. Another way to capture the enormity of this statistic: one out of every 150 U.S. residents in 1998 was in prison or jail, up from one out of every 217 in 1990. Even more revealing is that one out of every thirty-four adults (5.9 million) is under police supervision for crime, either in prison or jail or on probation or parole. Finally, 40 percent of all African American men in the United States between the ages of eighteen and twenty-five are either in prison, in jail, on parole, or on probation (Estrich, 1999).

The United States imprisons seven times as many people (proportionately) as does the average European country (*The Economist,* 1996). The size and growth of the U.S. prison population is largely the result of tough legislation in the 1980s, which increased the sentences for many crimes, especially drug offenses (Witkin, 1998). "Between 1980 and now, the proportion of those sentenced to prison for non-violent property crimes has remained about the same (two-fifths). The number of those sentenced for drugs has soared (from one-tenth to over one-third)" (*The Economist,* 1996:24).

REFERENCES_____

Currie, Elliott, 1998. *Crime and Punishment in America.* New York: Metropolitan Books.

The Economist. 1996. "Crime in America: Violent and Irrational—and That's Just the Policy" (June 8):23–25.

Eitzen, D. Stanley, and Maxine Baca Zinn. 2000. *Social Problems,* 8th ed. Boston: Allyn and Bacon.

Estrich, Susan. 1999. "Willie Horton, R. I. P." *Denver Post* (August 26):11B.

Gilliard, Darrell. 1999. "Prison and Jail Inmates at Midyear 1998," *Bureau of Justice Statistics Bulletin,* NCT 173414 (March).

Harwood, Richard. 1997. "America's Unchecked Epidemic," *Washington Post National Weekly Edition* (December 8):27.

Rubenstein, Ed. 1995. "The Economics of Crime," *Vital Speeches of the Day* (October 15):19–21.

Symonds, William C., and Lorraine Woellert. 1999. "Under Fire," *Business Week* (August 16):62–68.

Witkin, Gordon. 1998. "The Crime Bust," *U.S. News & World Report* (May 25):28–33, 36–37.

30

Cultural Divide over Crime and Punishment

LINNET MYERS

*This article examines America's tendency to focus on the punishment
rather than the prevention of violent crimes. U.S citizens commonly
respond to rising violent crime rates by demanding more prisons and
harsher punishments. Europeans, by contrast, enjoy lower crime rates
by focusing their public policies on the roots of crime such as poverty,
drugs, and guns. The types of penalties issued to offenders also differ
considerably, with Europeans favoring community service and other
alternatives to prison.*

Huntsville, Texas—Month after month, Thomas Miller-El wrote from Death Row to
someone he'd never met, thousands of miles away.

Miller-El, 44, was convicted of the robbery and murder of a hotel clerk in 1985. The
following year, a Texas court decided he should pay for the crime with his life. He has
been waiting ever since for his date with the world's busiest death chamber.

His pen pal was a citizen of Denmark, a 56-year-old woman with her own grown sons,
wife of a cement company owner. Like many other Europeans, the woman, an activist with
Amnesty International, believed that Miller-El's scheduled execution was a moral outrage.

To her, the death sentence also was a tragic example of America's tendency to focus
on punishment rather than prevention when dealing with its most vexing problem—
violent crime.

The differing views across the Atlantic on how to deal with Miller-El's fate reflect
a broader debate on crime and criminals that is under way in Washington and the capi-
tals of Europe.

From Boston to San Diego and from Miami to Seattle, Americans see crime as the
nation's No. 1 problem, a disease infecting America's soul and making its streets, schools
and towns unsafe.

The prescribed cures are more prisons and harsher punishments.

Source: Linnet Myers. 1995. "Cultural Divide over Crime and Punishment," *Chicago Tribune* (October 13),
pp. 1, 8.

Texas last week marked its 100th execution since it resumed capital punishment in 1982, adding to a rising toll since the U.S. reinstated the death penalty in 1976. The current hot trend is "three strikes and you're out" laws that put criminals behind bars for life after three felony convictions. And every politician worth his PAC has a get-tough-on-crime plank in his campaign.

But experts from abroad think the American approach is worse than wrong; it doesn't work. They point to the dramatically low crime rates in Europe and other parts of the world as evidence that they know a better way.

Instead of spending so much money on building new prisons, they argue, Americans should focus on the roots of crime, using radically different approaches toward drugs, guns, television violence, wealth and poverty—even the way they raise their children.

"It looks very simple. If someone commits murder, you stick him in prison for life," says Irvin Waller, Director of the International Center for the Prevention of Crime in Montreal. "The problem is, what you do to that one person doesn't stop what is causing other people to be violent."

"It's exactly like building cancer wards to stop cancer that is caused by smoking."

If crime rates in various nations are a measure of who is right, America's critics may have a point.

Although property-crime rates in the U.S. and Western Europe are often similar, the U.S. is "the Mt. Everest of Western industrialized societies" when it comes to violent crime, said Wesley Skogan, a Northwestern University professor of political science.

The figures are startling. According to the Council of Europe, England and France each had a homicide rate of 1.1 per 100,000 in 1990; the Swiss rate was 1.4 and Germany's was 1.2. The U.S. rate was 9.4, according to the FBI.

Even after recent crime drops, New York City, with a population of about 7 million, had 1,572 homicides last year. But London, a city of almost the same size, had 169.

Chicago, with about 2.8 million people, reported 930 homicides. Paris, with about 2.2 million, had 88.

In most cases, the striking differences cannot be attributed to foreign laws and penalties that are tougher than those in America.

The U.S. had 519 prisoners per 100,000 population in 1993, according to the Sentencing Project, a nonprofit research group. In comparison, the Netherlands had only 49 prisoners per 100,000; France had 84 and England, 93.

"Most Americans think countries with low crime rates are tougher on crime, but that's not true. That's where Americans are fooled," said Jerry Neapolitan of Tennessee Technological University, a member of the Homicide Research Working Group, which studies murder worldwide.

But many of America's critics fail to appreciate how this country differs from Europe and other parts of the world. The U.S. has a unique culture, political system and population that make fighting crime especially tough. There is no guarantee that a solution that works in Europe would work in America.

And many American advocates of stronger laws and penalties say their programs are starting to pay off.

ATTITUDES TOWARDS PUNISHMENT

For the crime of burglary involving the theft of a television, attitudes toward the type of punishment differ greatly among nations.

▶ **International survey**

• In a 1990 survey, percent of people who favored imprisonment:

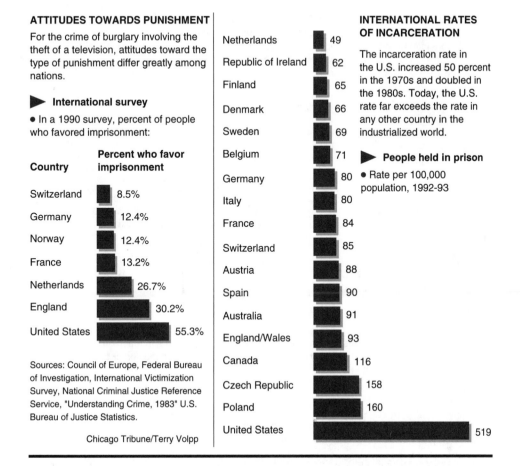

Country	Percent who favor imprisonment
Switzerland	8.5%
Germany	12.4%
Norway	12.4%
France	13.2%
Netherlands	26.7%
England	30.2%
United States	55.3%

Sources: Council of Europe, Federal Bureau of Investigation, International Victimization Survey, National Criminal Justice Reference Service, "Understanding Crime, 1983" U.S. Bureau of Justice Statistics.

Chicago Tribune/Terry Volpp

Netherlands	49
Republic of Ireland	62
Finland	65
Denmark	66
Sweden	69
Belgium	71
Germany	80
Italy	80
France	84
Switzerland	85
Austria	88
Spain	90
Australia	91
England/Wales	93
Canada	116
Czech Republic	158
Poland	160
United States	519

INTERNATIONAL RATES OF INCARCERATION

The incarceration rate in the U.S. increased 50 percent in the 1970s and doubled in the 1980s. Today, the U.S. rate far exceeds the rate in any other country in the industrialized world.

▶ **People held in prison**

• Rate per 100,000 population, 1992-93

FIGURE 30.1

As executions increase and new prisons go up around the country, violence has started to drop especially in some big cities.

Dallas police boast of crime decreases for six consecutive years. Houston has shown drops in homicides each year since 1992; last year that city had 383 killings compared with 633 in 1991.

Some experts say the figures prove that tough punishment has been the key all along.

"It's worked," said Raymond Teske Jr., a professor of criminal justice at Sam Houston State University in Huntsville. "We've gotten them off the streets."

Many Americans are heartened by the recent crime decreases and argue that—in this society at least—prisons make sense.

John DiIulio, a criminologist at Princeton University, presents these frightening figures: Ex-convicts on parole in Florida committed 4,656 violent crimes between 1987 and 1991, including 346 murders and 185 sexual assaults.

The United States has the highest homicide rate of any Western industrialized country and a growing prison system to match. The nation's state and federal prisons had to find room for 83,294 more inmates last year—the second largest increase in history. Including local jails, almost 1.5 million people were incarcerated in the U.S. in 1994, 690,158 were on parole and 2,962.166 were on probation.

HOMICIDE RATES

• Homicides and attempts recorded by police in selected Western industrialized nations.
Rates per 100,000 population, 1990:

England/Wales	France	Germany	Norway	Sweden	Switzerland	Scotland	Italy	Hungary	United States
1.1	1.1	1.2	1.2	1.3	1.4	1.7	2.6	3.0	9.4

PEOPLE IN JAIL OR PRISON

Of the almost 1.5 million persons held in the U.S. in 1994, two-thirds were in federal and state prisons. Local jails, which primarily hold people awaiting trial or serving sentences of a year or less, held the other third.

► **Number of adults in jail or prison**

• Number by year, 1980–1994

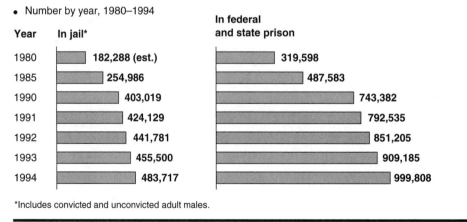

Year	In jail*	In federal and state prison
1980	182,288 (est.)	319,598
1985	254,986	487,583
1990	403,019	743,382
1991	424,129	792,535
1992	441,781	851,205
1993	455,500	909,185
1994	483,717	999,808

*Includes convicted and unconvicted adult males.

FIGURE 30.2   Crime and Incarceration

"Make no mistake: Imprisoning violent and repeat offenders most definitely prevents crime," he said.

But the American arguments obscure a key issue: How much of the get-tough policies can America afford? And will they ever bring violent crime rates in the U.S. down to the level of other countries?

INMATES AND THEIR CRIMES

More than a quarter of federal and state inmates were in prison for drug offenses (234,600 prisoners) in 1993. In federal prisons, inmates sentenced for drug law violations were the single largest group—60 percent in 1993, up from 25 percent in 1980.

▶ **Federal prison inmates**

● In percent by category of crime, 1993

▶ **State prison inmates**

● In percent by category of crime, 1993

▶ **Combined federal and state**

● Inmates in state and federal prisons. In percent by category of crime, 1993

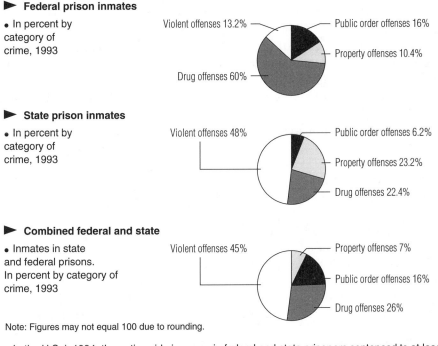

Federal prison inmates:
Violent offenses 13.2%
Public order offenses 16%
Property offenses 10.4%
Drug offenses 60%

State prison inmates:
Violent offenses 48%
Public order offenses 6.2%
Property offenses 23.2%
Drug offenses 22.4%

Combined federal and state:
Violent offenses 45%
Property offenses 7%
Public order offenses 16%
Drug offenses 26%

Note: Figures may not equal 100 due to rounding.

● In the U.S. in1994, the nationwide increase in federal and state prisoners sentenced to at least a year's incarceration translated to a need to confine an additional 1,602 inmates each week.

FIGURE 30.2   Continued

Texas has executed more inmates than any other state since the Supreme Court brought back the death penalty in 1976. Some 400 inmates sit on Huntsville's Death Row, crowded into tiers of 5-by-9 foot cells, waiting for their turn to die. A frantic construction program, set to end next year, is adding 75,000 new prison beds in Texas. The cost: $1.5 billion.

Some Americans and Europeans view prisons as a growth industry. Towns in Texas started bidding for prisons after the oil boom collapsed and jobs were sorely needed, said David Nunnelee, spokesman for the Texas Department of Criminal Justice.

Texas now has the highest prison population rate in the U.S., which has the highest such rate in the Western world.

The same thing is happening elsewhere in America. The U.S. has more than tripled its number of prisoners since 1980, almost reaching an astounding 1.5 million people behind bars, according to the Justice Department.

The cost is estimated at $26 billion a year.

All of that money isn't necessarily buying a safer America. Even with the decreases in crime, Texas still has one of the highest crime rates of any state in the country and far exceeds any in Europe.

Some experts argue that demographics may be mainly responsible for the decrease in reported crime. The homicide rate for youths 18 and under more than doubled between 1985 and 1992, though no increase was noted for adults 24 and over, according to Alfred Blumstein, a criminologist at Carnegie Mellon University.

There is now a drop in youths 18 and under, which could explain much of the decline in crime, Blumstein said. But the number of boys about to reach that age group is larger, he warned—an ominous sign that violent crime may rise again.

Even DiIulio and other American prison advocates, like Teske, agree that tough punishment isn't enough.

"The increase in prison space is a stopgap matter," said Teske. "We had to address the hard-core repeat criminals. . . . Now we've got to take a hard look at what's causing this."

That is where things get a lot more complex. Americans and Europeans have far different attitudes about crime, and that affects their attitudes toward punishment and prevention.

The differences don't show up in opinions about serious crime, such as homicide. Western European sentences for homicide are similar to America's, except for the death penalty, said criminologist Jim Lynch of American University.

The big difference lies in property and especially drug crimes, where the U.S. is becoming more harsh in its punishment, Lynch said.

In 1983, 8.3 percent of state prison admissions were for drug offenses; by 1992, that had grown to 30.4 percent.

A UN study showed that Americans are less forgiving, even of property crimes. When asked what should happen to a burglar who had a prior conviction and then stole a television set, 55.3 percent of Americans said he should get prison time.

Just over 39 [*sic*] percent of the English said so; only 12.4 percent of Germans and 13.2 percent of the French did.

That may be because many Europeans view the criminal as "one of us," said Jan Van Dijk, crime prevention chief at the Dutch Justice Ministry. Americans, with wide ethnic and racial divisions, often show a "them-versus-us" mentality, he said.

With less violence—and fear—Europeans more readily accept alternatives to prison, particularly for young criminals.

In the Netherlands, juveniles who commit crimes such as theft are often sentenced to return to the scene of their crime, and often put to work. If you stole from a store, "you have to mop the floor of that same shop," said Van Dijk.

Another Dutch program, called "Beware, Watch Out," puts more serious young criminals under the wing of Officer Rob Raat, who said he came up with the idea after watching youths who "lived in a circle—to the police, the judge, the jail and the police again."

Today Raat has his disciplined ex-criminals patrolling an Amsterdam shopping center, where they have helped lower the rate of shoplifting by 50 percent. Watching Raat work is like seeing an affectionate, strict father overseeing a big family.

Many Americans would have difficulty imagining such programs working for the street-tough youths of U.S. cities.

Speaking from Death Row, convicted killer Miller-El said that his European supporters gave him a glimpse of "a totally different type of environment—more neighborly, friendly, caring."

Each month for four years, he and the Danish woman wrote each other. Then the letters stopped. Finally one of her sons wrote, telling him she had died.

"It was like losing someone in the family. . . . It was a really difficult experience for me to get over her death," said Miller-EL. "We had a wonderful correspondence."

Writing from a nation with a murder rate that is a tiny fraction of America's, the Danish woman saw Miller-El simply as a man with thoughts and feelings.

In a country where brutal murders are too common to keep track of, Americans see him as a cold-blooded killer.

Europe's anti-death-penalty activists know the statistics that document the carnage in America, but "that's not the same as living with it," said Rick Halperin, head of the Dallas office of Amnesty International. "I don't think they can grasp how deep the pain is."

That pain is one reason that Americans support the death penalty by margins of 75 to 80 percent, according to most polls.

Polls show that many Europeans still support the death penalty as well, but it rarely is a big issue there.

When talk of restoring it comes up, "it always happens around a particular crime— some children murdered, maybe an act of terrorism," said Richard Dieter, director of the Death Penalty Information Center in Washington, D.C., an anti-capital-punishment advocacy group. "Then it sort of goes away."

Despite the great social differences between the U.S. and Europe, European police and criminologists say the U.S. could learn from its allies across the sea.

The Europeans argue that they have built relatively violence-free societies without locking up their citizens in record numbers or hanging, electrocuting, or injecting them with poison.

And they are willing to bet that America won't conquer crime with prisons and punishment alone.

31

The Secret of Japan's Safe Streets

THE ECONOMIST

This article describes how intensive but friendly neighborhood policing, a forgiving attitude toward petty misbehavior, and a ruthlessness to presumed criminals are helping to preserve the order of Japanese cities and to reduce serious crime.

It is Friday night in a bar district of Tokyo, and the Japanese miracle is under way. A few paces from the porno shops and pin-ball parlours stands a brightly lit *koban,* a police box. Inside, three policemen sit behind a long, low table spread with detailed maps, old-fashioned telephones, and a box of red-tipped seals for stamping documents. Little local police stations like this one, sometimes manned by only one person, are to be found in 15,000 places across Japan. They represent one of the secrets behind Japan's enviably low crime rate.

Every few minutes somebody comes in to ask for help. A man dressed exclusively in leather is looking for a certain night club; this is pointed out for him on one of the maps. Another caller wants to report a lost bag; this involves official stamps. Then a grizzled man with a crew-cut enters, bows deeply to the policemen, and hands over ¥200 ($1.95). He is repaying a loan: if you are caught short without money for a bus journey home in Tokyo, the police can be relied upon to help out.

This remarkable cosiness between police and civilians comes with a correspondingly low crime rate. In 1990 Japan suffered 12 thefts per 1,000 people, compared with America's 53 and Germany's 44. The contrast between Japan's present and its past is even more remarkable, although the headline figures obscure the nature of the change. Between 1970 and 1990 the total number of recorded crimes jumped 15%, reflecting the growth in petty theft that naturally accompanied the spread of property. But the striking figure is that, over the same period, violent crime dropped by two-thirds.

What can other countries learn from this? Deriving lessons from Japan involves distinguishing between two kinds of reason for the country's social peace. The first is the particular nature of its society: homogeneous, disciplined, imbued with a fear of ostracism

Source: "The Secret of Japan's Safe Streets." 1994. *The Economist 331* (April 16), pp. 38–40.

that encourages conformity. The second kind of reason, which may hold transportable lessons, lies in the special strength of its police.

It is tempting to ascribe Japan's low crime rate entirely to social causes. Japan has almost no underclass. Illiteracy is practically unheard of. Tramps remain a rare sight. Immigrants, whose children in some rich countries form a crime-prone underclass, are rare too.

Four decades of remarkable economic growth have rewarded disciplined work both handsomely and evenly. GNP per head has doubled since 1970. Income inequalities have remained remarkably low: at the age of 50, high-school graduates working in big firms get paid 85% as much as their university-educated contemporaries. Even in its worst post-war recession, the government's (admittedly optimistic) statistics say that unemployment remains below 3%. In short, the fat rewards of accepting society's rules have made it foolish to rebel.

Drug-taking is minimal: in 1991 a mere 60 people were arrested for offences relating to cocaine, and 110 for ones relating to heroin. Japanese people, explains Akira Kawada of the National Police Academy, disapprove of drugs. Last year a publishing magnate was arrested for importing cocaine; to show their distaste, some Japanese vowed to stop buying his books.

Yet the social causes of Japan's respect for the law, though powerful, can only suggest why Japan is more peaceful than other rich countries. They cannot explain why Japan is more peaceful today than in the past. Indeed, Japan's serious crime has dwindled even though some of the social conditions that tend to restrain crime have eroded.

HARDER TIMES

Immigrants, for example, may be scarce, but they are more numerous than they were. Cocaine and heroin were even rarer ten years ago than today. Conservative, multigeneration households are giving way to nuclear families and people living alone. Closeknit, village-like communities are being replaced by modern anonymity.

Nobody is more aware of this last point than the Japanese police. In 1992 the National Police Agency complained of "the borderless rampancy of crimes," meaning that society, and therefore crime, has grown more mobile.

In 1970 one Japanese in five had a car; in 1990 one in two. Driving, rather than walking, cuts people off from their neighbours: they lose opportunities to greet each other in the street. Cars also encourage shoppers to go less to friendly local stores, and more to distant discounters where customers avoid each other's eyes. And cars enable families to abandon cramped town centres, where everybody knows the neighbours, in favour of spacious suburbs, where anonymity reigns.

All this weakens the old social ties that both deterred crime and made investigating it easier. In the motorised age, a criminal can escape faster from the scene of his crime. He may drive to the scene too, so the old assumption that he is somebody who lives nearby is no longer safe. Even if he does turn out to be a local, his neighbours may never have spoken to him. Personal relations are "thinning," in the police agency's phrase.

In May 1990 a small girl was found dead in Ashikaga, a quiet town in Tochigi pre-
fecture, on the border between the Japan Alps and Tokyo's Kanto plain. Over the next
18 months, the police distributed an average of ten leaflets to each of Ashikaga's 53,000
homes, asking for useful information. But Ashikaga had suffered the transition to mobility: since the early 1970s cars had reduced the number of pedestrians in its shopping
streets on the average July Sunday by two-thirds. Leaflets and door-to-door questioning
produced few results. When a suspect was eventually arrested (he confessed to murder-
ing two other children previously), it transpired that none of his neighbours had known
his name, his job, or anything else about him.

THE NEIGHBOURLY POLICEMAN

Japan's policing triumph—the reduction of serious crime despite more awkward social
circumstances—has been achieved through skillful adaptation. The most important
instance of this is to be found in the maps and friendly grins in that Tokyo police box.
The stream of callers asking for help testifies to a triumphant campaign to ensure that a
traditional system has not been left behind by social modernisation, but has been adapted
and extended as the central feature of policing in Japan.

The importance of neighbourhood policing was recognised decades ago. In 1967 the
patrol police, who, as a subsection of the traffic police, had been considered the dregs of
the force, were dignified with the status of a division.

These days, some 6,000 police boxes are manned day and night in Japan's towns;
in the countryside, the boxes, which double as policemen's homes, number 9,000. By
deploying manpower widely rather than concentrating it in big police stations, Japan's
police aim to be more accessible than their western counterparts. They spend much time
dispensing friendly services like telling people the way, taking charge of lost property,
or sheltering stray pets. A wife in a live-in police box is expected to help, handling reports
of lost goods if her husband is out when someone calls.

To maintain good community relations, the police take part in local events with
deadly earnestness. Two years ago in Kanazawa, a small provincial town, the police used
to commandeer the top floor of a civic centre for band practices, drowning out this cor-
respondent's Japanese lessons. The National Police Agency claims that police bands give
about 5,000 performances each year, and that these are heard (whether with pleasure the
statistics do not relate) by some 20 million people.

This cosiness traditionally encouraged the public to co-operate with the police, and
to volunteer information about suspicious characters. To reinforce this, police-box officers try to call on each family, shop and company in their area twice a year.

But, as the Ashikaga murder showed, social change has undermined the efficacy of
traditional police methods. The need to adapt has been clear since the late 1970s, when
Masayuki Murayama, a legal academic at China University, accompanied patrolmen on
their rounds in Tokyo. He found that women were increasingly going out to work, so it
was becoming harder to find householders to survey. Such residents as could be found
were becoming less welcoming; only janitors and landlords seemed eager to help. Mr

Murayama even found that policemen sometimes forged visit reports in order to escape this unrewarding duty.

Mr Murayama's patrolmen were scarcely more enthusiastic about handling routine callers at the police box. However essential this work might have been to preserving the police force's reputation, patrolmen considered it mundane. In the past, callers had occasionally volunteered information that led to arrests; by the 1970s this was rare, so handling calls gave policemen few opportunities to win points that might lead to promotion.

Instead, more and more arrests resulted from spot checks on suspicious-looking characters in the street—a few questions, an inspection of belongings. Mr Murayama found that patrolmen reserved their enthusiasm for this, since arrests won promotion points. This research was later backed up by official surveys, which found that police boxes were often left unmanned while their occupants were on patrol, much to the public's frustration.

Rather than resign itself to the decline of the police box, however, Japan's police force has fought back. In the mid-1980s, the police began to change the system of evaluating officers, to encourage helpfulness to the public rather than just notching up arrest scores. The visiting system has been adapted to make it more effective: visits concentrate on the people who need them most (the old, for instance) and the areas where they can be most useful (places where mobility is high and it is harder to keep tabs on people). To improve the quality of simple services, the police force has also started rehiring retired policemen, who concentrate exclusively on less taxing jobs like dealing with lost pedestrians and objects found in the street.

The retired policemen are also meant to reduce the number of occasions when police boxes are deserted. But this problem also has a high-tech solution. The police have installed about 100 "automatic" boxes: when a caller enters an empty box, a policeman from a nearby station appears on a video screen to answer questions. If the caller wants a local map, this is immediately faxed to him.

The range of help dispensed from the police box has been broadened so as to keep the public interested. In 1991 the police recorded 188,000 requests for personal advice, a modest expansion on 1990. Just under a third related to crime prevention; advice on family problems accounted for more than a quarter of the questions, and civil affairs (such as personal finance) accounted for nearly a fifth.

Social mobility has increased the number of old people living alone and uncared for by their children, and so vulnerable to crime. Community policemen have seen in this an opportunity: at the end of 1991 they claimed to be paying regular visits to some 140,000 people over 65 living alone, about one in seven such households. As well as dispensing advice on crime prevention, the police make it their business to report on the state of the elderly to their relations, so bolstering their reputation for helpfulness.

All this seems to be working. The public's continued willingness to co-operate with the police is revealed in the lost-and-found statistics. In 1991 the number of articles handed in to the police (4.1 million) astonishingly exceeded the number of reported losses (2.9 million). Fully ¥18.5 billion ($137 million) in lost cash was found and handed over to the police by dutiful citizens.

Could other countries emulate this system? Some have tried: in 1991 alone, 13 countries sent missions to Japan to study community policing. Frustratingly for foreigners, the friendly style of Japan's patrolmen does in part depend on the friendliness of the people they work with. In 1991 only three policemen died while carrying out their duties; of these, two were killed by an erupting volcano. Not being brutalised, Japanese policemen tend not to be brutal.

Yet this does not mean that Japan's policing friendliness is impossible to copy. For one thing, society can be encouraged to be gentle: gun control is one obvious measure whose absence in America is reckoned crazy in Japan. And the relaxed style of Japan's police owes much to two replicable policies: generous staffing, and leniency.

Japan's policemen claim that they are understaffed, noting that, in 1990, the country had one policeman per 556 Japanese, proportionately fewer than in America (one per 379) or France (268). But Setsuo Miyazawa, a legal academic at Kobe University, points out that Japan's police force is big relative to the number of crimes it must cope with. In 1990 Japan's thefts per policeman were just two-thirds of France's and less than a tenth of America's. Japan's policemen have less work, so their relaxed style should not come as a surprise.

The small number of crimes per policeman is the result of a 73% expansion in police staff between 1960 and 1990. Expansion made promotion easier to come by, which further helped morale; this was reinforced by several redefinitions of ranks. The latest came in 1991, when middle ranks (inspector and assistant inspector) expanded from 19% to 36% of the force, while the numbers of lowly patrolmen shrunk.

Good morale is reflected in the competition to join the police force. In 1991, even before the current recession made private-sector jobs hard to get, 8.6 candidates applied for each available job. More than a third of the 7,500 successful applicants had been to college or university.

Then there is the leniency. In 1990, 31% of offenders caught and questioned by the police were dismissed after signing an apology for some minor offence. The prevailing attitude of forgiveness achieves three objects. Police are spared the job of collecting evidence to support the prosecution of minor cases. The public is reinforced in its view that policemen are decent. And the stigma of judicial action is reserved for serious crimes.

THE UNNEIGHBOURLY POLICEMAN

None of this means that Japan's policemen are soft. Far from it: a big reason for the low rate of serious crime is that it is so hard to get away with. In 1989 Japan cleared 96% of its murder cases—for which the penalty may be death—and 76% of its robberies, a far higher proportion than elsewhere. The reasons for this are replicable too, though some may not be desirable.

The scattered deployment entailed by the police-box system enables patrolmen to get to the scene of a crime quickly. Those at the bar-district box could walk to the boundary of their allotted area in two minutes. In 1989 it took the police an average of five minutes and 49 seconds to reach the scene after receiving an emergency telephone call.

Japan's police force is experimenting with new methods. It is developing a central computer database of photographs and notes on suspects that can be easily consulted by prefectural police agencies. New roadside machines check number-plates of passing cars against those of wanted vehicles. More gadgets check fragments of fingerprints left by suspects against vast numbers of fingerprints held in a computer. Technological advance helps to derive clues from infinitesimal quantities of material left behind by criminals.

Next come the less desirable causes for Japan's high clearance rate, which come down to the fact that suspects have few civil rights. In theory, Japanese have the right to silence and legal help when they are arrested. In practice, suspects can be held for 23 days without being charged, and often without access to a lawyer.

Japan's police therefore have plenty of opportunities to force confessions. These are neither recorded verbatim nor tape-recorded. Instead, detectives write up the results of their interrogations into coherent statements, and tell the suspects to sign them.

In 1990 fully 91.5% of defendants tried at district and summary courts had signed such confessions, according to Mr Murayama. Japan's constitution declares that forced confessions, or confessions made after unduly long periods of detention, shall not be admitted in court; and that confession alone is insufficient basis for conviction. In practice, confessions carry a lot of weight, in part because those who are accused of crimes are given little chance to collect evidence for their defence.

In 1990 36% of defendants tried at district and summary courts had no witnesses at all to give evidence on their behalf. Among the rest, the average number of witnesses was just 1.5. Press reports of arrests and trials often assume that the accused is guilty. It is only slightly amazing, therefore, that in 1990 the conviction rate in district and summary courts was 99.8%.

Leniency and friendliness are thus matched with illiberal ferocity towards those presumed guilty; inducements to respect the law and the police are backed by harsh treatment for those who fail to do so. Other rich countries, with longer traditions of civil liberties, may balk at the second half of Japan's formula. But the first—the friendly policeman in a little local box—plus the blending of police work with some of the roles usually played by social workers—provides a valuable lesson for outsiders.

32

Deaths Reflect Gun Use in U.S.

MICHAEL BOOTH

The gun-related death and homicide rate of children in the United States is many times higher than that of other industrialized countries. Whereas the United States has few restrictions on guns, other industrialized nations either restrict gun ownership or ban guns entirely. In the wake of shootings like those at Columbine High School, other countries have instituted strict gun regulations that have received extensive popular support.

Painful as it was to hear, while bombs were being defused and memorials were being planned in the Columbine High School community, there was an unmistakable chorus last week of "only in America."

The debate rages in the nation on how to sell, register, store, conceal and regulate guns. But there is agreement, among statistical experts in the United States and observers overseas, that guns make America a nation apart.

The gun-related death rate of U.S. children under the age of 15 is nearly 12 times higher than the combined totals of 25 other wealthy, industrialized nations, according to a major study by the Centers for Disease Control and Prevention in Atlanta.

The homicide rate by all causes for U.S. children is five times that in all those nations combined.

The United Nations compared firearms death rates around the world from 1994 and 1995 and found similar disparity. Of the 1,107 children around the world killed by firearms that year, 86 percent died in the United States.

The numbers for adult deaths from firearms are just as striking. Total firearm deaths in the United States in one year reached 35,957.

Japan had 93.

Of course, the United States has a much larger population than most industrialized nations, but that doesn't go far in explaining the difference. Broken down per capita, the U.S. rate of firearm deaths is more than triple the next closest nation, Canada.

Source: Michael Booth. 1999. *The Denver Post* (April 25), pp. IA, 19A.

In the year the CDC conducted its exhaustive study, three of four Asian countries surveyed reported no firearm deaths among children.

"I don't think American children are inherently worse, or parents are less good parents. There can't be something unusual about Americans that they are more determined to commit violence," said Rebecca Peters, an Australian lawyer who consults around the world on violence issues.

"Our violence is just more lethal," said Franklin Zimring, a law professor at the University of California at Berkeley who compiles youth crime statistics. "So it must be the availability of the means. It's hard to explain how obviously it looks that way to people in other countries."

Guns were only part of the Columbine assault by teenagers Eric Harris and Dylan Klebold; they also exploded a series of homemade bombs assembled from household items that maimed victims with shrapnel. But they did carry an arsenal of rapid-fire handguns and shotguns. Their heavy weaponry was a factor they had in common with recent school killings in Jonesboro, Ark., Paducah, Ky., and Springfield, Ore.

Colorado State University violence expert Ernie Chavez noted that "in one year alone, Los Angeles County had more murders than Canada. I'd be hard pressed to think of any country not in the midst of a revolution that has more violence and weaponry than us."

Estimates on the number of existing firearms in the United States, including handguns, rifles and shotguns, range between 230 million and 250 million.

Other nations have either had longtime restrictions on gun ownership, ranging from careful licensing and registration to outright bans on handguns, or severely tightened their laws in the wake of tragedies similar to Columbine's.

The United States and its local governments have made incremental changes in basic gun-ownership rights, but even those have been sharply opposed by many gun owners. There are now severe restrictions in the United States on the sale or purchase of fully automatic weapons, and a national waiting period and background check were instituted in recent years.

Like most states, Colorado has no requirement to register or obtain a license for guns.

Guns laws did not change significantly in the United States in the wake of the terrible string of school shootings in the 1997–98 academic year.

U.S. and international child advocates say it would horrify them if gun laws did not change in the wake of the Columbine shootings.

International colleagues of Chicago pediatrician and violence expert Dr. Katherine Christoffel "can't understand how or why America tolerates the level of gun violence that we do," she said. "People in the rest of the world don't live like this."

The strongest U.S. advocate for the rights of gun ownership, the National Rifle Association, declined this week to debate political and international differences.

"I don't think now is an appropriate time to debate public policy, as the tragedy (in Colorado) continues to unfold," said Bill Powers, an NRA spokesman in Washington.

"Anything beyond continued heartfelt sympathy and prayers for the community is just not fitting. Anything beyond those sorts of feelings of respect are just out of line right now," Powers said.

In Great Britain, the 1996 massacre of 16 elementary school children and their teacher in Dunblane, Scotland, prompted an immediate call for a total ban on handguns. The clamor quickly resulted in a British ban on handguns above .22 caliber, and the turning in of 80 percent of the 200,000 handguns around the country.

After a gunman with automatic rifles killed 35 people in Port Arthur, Tasmania, in 1996, Australia banned all automatic and semiautomatic weapons, including pump-action shotguns. The government bought back 700,000 weapons out of an estimated 4 million in the nation, melted them down and instituted strict licensing laws for the remainder, under which owners must justify in detail their need for a weapon.

Outright bans are politically unthinkable in the United States, even among strong advocates of handgun control.

"But there are two things consistent around the world, outside the U.S.," said Mark Pertschuk, Washington, D.C., legislative director for the Coalition to Stop Gun Violence. "No. 1, they have licensing and registration of firearms. No. 2, they have radically lower levels of death. It's not even a gray area," he said.

"It's not that licensing and registration is a one-step fix-it for all of our gun problems. But that's what characterizes an effective, modern system of firearm regulation."

Even after 15 deaths at one school in Colorado, the spectrum of voices speaking out for change in firearms laws remains extremely narrow. Some of the most schooled researchers in the field studiously avoid political comment.

Jim Mercy is one of the directors of a 10-year study on violence as a disease at the CDC. Researchers have concluded that access to firearms is one of the factors pushing America's violent death rates into the epidemiological warning zone.

But on the chances or the need for stricter U.S. gun control, Mercy says, "I think that's an issue I need to stay away from."

	TOTAL FIREARMS DEATHS	FIERARM HOMICIDES	FIREARM SUICIDES	FATAL FIREARMS ACCIDENTS
(1995) United States	35,563	15,835	18,503	1,225
(1994) Australia	536	96	420	20
(1994) Canada	1,189	176	975	38
(1995) Germany	1,197	168	1,004	25
(1995) Japan	93	34	49	10
(1992) Sweden	200	27	169	4
(1994) Spain	396	76	219	101
(1994) United Kingdom	277	72	193	12
(1995) Vietnam	131	85	16	30

FIGURE 32.1   Deaths Due to Firearms
Researchers who have studied gun violence as if it were a disease have noted striking differences between the United States and other countries.
Source: Coalition to Stop Gun Violence. The *Denver Post*/Jonathan Moreno.

SECTION 13

Drugs

THE UNITED STATES CONTEXT

The United States has defined some drugs as legal and others as illegal. The contradiction in this policy is in that the legality of a drug is not correlated with its health consequences. The most dangerous drugs—nicotine and alcohol—are legal. Nicotine, the active ingredient in tobacco, which is a stimulant for blood pressure and heart rate, is responsible for a relatively high probability of heart disease and strokes. The tars and gases inhaled in tobacco smoke also increase the chances of lung cancer, throat cancer, emphysema, and bronchitis. According to the Centers for Disease Control, tobacco addiction kills more Americans than alcohol, cocaine, crack, heroin, homicide, suicide, fires, car accidents, and AIDS combined (cited in Ellerbe, 1995). Alcohol claims about 100,000 Americans a year, twenty-five times as many as all illegal drugs combined. Yet tobacco and alcohol remain legal drugs, while the government defines others as illegal and wages a costly war against their use.

The prohibition against heroin, cocaine, marijuana, and various others, and the official policies to combat their use (the Drug War), are intended to deter crime but they have the opposite effect. The following information is from Eitzen and Baca Zinn (2000:526–528). By making drugs illegal and dangerous to produce, transport, and sell, the price increases many times more than if the drugs were legal. Thus, many users turn to crime (shoplifting, burglary, prostitution, selling drugs) to sustain their costly habit. Crime is also encouraged as organized crime imports, processes, and distributes the illicit drugs through its networks. This in turn promotes crime as violence between rival gangs develops over disputed territorial boundaries. Moreover, the huge amounts of money involved sometimes corrupt police and other government agents. At another level, making drug use illegal creates crime by creating criminals. If there were no laws regulating such behavior, then there would be no criminals. Prior to 1914, in the United States heroin users were not criminals, nor were marijuana users before 1937. The drug laws, then, have created large numbers of criminals. By labeling and treating these people as criminals, the justice system creates further crime by stigmatizing them, which makes their reintegration into society after prison very difficult (about one-third of the prison population are drug offenders). The result, typically, is for the drug users to join together in a deviant drug subculture.

Another irony is that the drug war is intended to reduce the use of illicit drugs by the populace, yet it does not. As shown in the articles found in this section, the Netherlands follows a public health approach (in contrast to the U.S. criminal approach) to drug use. Their more lenient approach, interestingly, results in *lower* drug use than found in the United States. For example, the percentage of Americans who have ever used marijuana was more than twice as high as the percentage in the Netherlands; for cocaine, the percentage of Americans was five times as great as for the Dutch and three times greater for heroin (Common Sense for Drug Policy, 1999). At least one reason for this seeming anomaly is that "many users of illegal drugs—particularly kids—do so not just because they like the feeling but because it sets them apart from 'straight' society, allows them (without any effort or thought) to join a culture of dissent" (Shenk, 1999:52).

The United States has taken a strong moralistic stand against certain drugs. In doing so we create the moral from the immoral, the good from the bad, and, thus, reinforce strong moral boundaries.

> The real power of prohibition is that it creates the forbidden world of danger and hedonism that the straights want to distinguish themselves from. A black market spawns violence, thievery, and illnesses—all can be blamed on the demon drugs. . . . For anyone who is secretly ashamed, or confused, about the explosion in legal drug-taking, here is reassurance: the people in handcuffs are the bad ones" (Shenk, 1999:52).

REFERENCES

Common Sense for Drug Policy. 1999. "Dutch Drug Policy *Even* More Effective Than Previously Thought!" *The Nation* (September 13).

Eitzen, D. Stanley, and Maxine Baca Zinn. 2000. *Social Problems,* 8th ed. Boston: Allyn and Bacon.

Ellerbe, Linda. 1995. "A Wrong I Taught My Children," *Rocky Mountain News* (February 4):43A.

Shenk, Joshua Wolf. 1999. "America's Altered States," *Harper's Magazine* 298 (May):38–52.

33

The View from Platform Zero:
How Holland Handles Its Drug Problem

DANIEL M. PERRINE

This article combines the author's direct observations of "Platform Zero," an area set aside for drug use just outside of Rotterdam's central train station, with a more general analysis of Holland's drug policies. While areas such as "Platform Zero" are controversial, even by the tolerant Dutch, there is a pragmatic acceptance by the government and most citizens that these areas minimize the harm that drug users do to themselves and society.

It is a beautiful summer afternoon, and I find myself regretfully remembering the lush scents of loam and freshly cut flowers in the Dutch greenhouses I visited yesterday. I am sitting on a pile of filthy blankets between two young junkies: Jimmy, who is British, and Anton, who has taken advantage of the European Community's open border policy to escape his native Prague and make it here to Holland, where he can find clean needles, relatively pure dope and greater safety to shoot up. Even the stiff breeze that snaps the Netherlands tricolor over Rotterdam's central station is unable to dissipate the nauseous sweet-sour stench. It is the smell of the homeless, and I find myself remembering the subways of Chicago and New York. It comes from the blankets I am sitting on, and it comes from Jimmy, Anton and Dirk, the Dutch teen-ager sitting across from me with the dirty yellow hair and the dying blue eyes.

Dirk is "cooking" cocaine base. In a bottle cap, he dissolves an off-white powder in a little ammonia he bought at the grocery store. Then he makes the freebase by heating the mixture in a bottle cap over the flame of a Bic lighter. After the liquid has boiled off, he scrapes up the oily tan residue with a knife blade and smokes it in a tiny metal pipe with a wire screen. Rotterdam is the world's largest port, its massive docks stretching for miles along the banks of the canalized Nieuwe Maas, which is the principal outlet for the waters of the Rhine and for Germany's industrial heartland. Here the cocaine comes

Source: Daniel M. Perrine. 1994. "The View from Platform Zero: How Holland Handles Its Drug Problem," *America* 171 (October 15), pp. 9–12.

right off the boat, purer and cheaper, they say, than any other city's streets can provide. But it is cocaine hydrochloride, the kind that is snorted in lines or injected. In the United States, the land that brought us TV dinners and instant coffee, you can buy your crack ready made. Crack is free-based cocaine made by heating the hydrochloride form with baking soda. It is not only more convenient, it provides a cheering Rice Krispies crackle when you light up. The base Dirk is smoking burns silently; but pharmacologically it has the same effect as crack, giving an intense but short-lived rush.

This is Platform Zero, *Perron Nul,* an ironic designation for the "open scene" just outside Rotterdam's central train station. It is an area about 200 feet by 200 feet between a small police station and the main parking lot, zoned in by a graffiti-scarred plexiglass wall. Within the perimeter is a drinking fountain, a cold-water faucet for makeshift washups, a foul-smelling open-air urinal and two blue steel cabins.

To the rear of the area is a large walk-in bus where volunteers from the Pauluskerk, a Dutch Reformed parish just around the corner from my hotel, operate a methadone dispensary and a needle exchange. Open scenes are designated areas where drugs can be used, and permitting such areas is controversial, even in tolerant Holland. Proponents say they keep users from shooting up in apartment doorways or city streets; opponents find the whole thing too revolting to be endured. This is the most notorious open scene in the country, partly because it is the most open of them all and partly because it owes its existence not to the civic authorities but to the Rev. Hans Visser, pastor of the Pauluskerk, who runs a more controlled—and much cleaner—open scene in his own parish hall.

Even within Platform Zero, the junkies are supposed to shoot up only inside one of the blue cabins. But for some reason the cabins were locked today—no one seems to know why. The policeman who escorted me into the area shrugged his shoulders and introduced me to Jimmy. I will be safe, he assures me, if I stay with Jimmy; and Jimmy should escort me back to the police station in a half an hour. With this, the policeman shakes hands all round and returns to the station.

After some conversation with Jimmy, I realize why I will be safe with him. He is a longtime, low-echelon dealer of heroin and crack, and the others respect him as their source. And he has no need to rob me, since his business provides him with more than enough cash for his needs. This is one reason many of the police think Platform Zero is a good idea: They know exactly who the dealers are. While possession of small amounts of hard drugs is not prosecuted in the Netherlands, selling them is. If Jimmy's activities get out of hand, the police can move in; and by close observation of the small-time distributors, they can trace the path of the drugs back to the big smuggling operations on the docks.

Jimmy is caught between a rock and a hard place. If he stops selling, he will have to support himself by stealing or worse; if he tries to expand his business, it can be snuffed out by the police or by the big-time dealers, who like Jimmy just as he is— imprisoned already by the twin addictions of his dealing and his using. He tells me that he once tried saving his profits so he could start on his own. When he had amassed almost 4,000 guilders (about $2,300), he was beaten and robbed. He thinks it was the work of the big-time dealers.

Jimmy is trying to use now, and it is making me writhe inwardly. He is trying to find a vein for the "cocktail" that Anton has thoughtfully mixed for him after mixing and shooting his own. A cocktail is a combination of cocaine and heroin, what American users call a speedball. Watching Anton mix and shoot his didn't bother me. Anton has a maze of prominent blue veins on his arms—they remind me of the maps of Holland's delta estuaries—and he finds one and injects with clinical ease. Jimmy, unfortunately for his chosen career, has only one visible vein in the crotch of each arm, and both are covered with red welts of scar tissue. He makes a half-hearted stab into one of these calloused swellings, but it is no use. So he starts digging for a vein the way a Texas wild-catter back in the 1920's would randomly drill a well anywhere, just on the chance of finding some oil. He sticks the needle into a barren patch of grimy arm, pulls it half out, angles it about 45 degrees, sticks it all the way in again and repeats this process over and over, up and down the arm, until there are rivulets of blood running down each arm and he looks like Jesus being scourged in a Spanish cathedral.

Seeming not to feel any pain—perhaps one good effect of the heroin—Jimmy continues to talk to me. Most of his conversation sounds like what you might hear in a cafe frequented by second-rate existentialists. It is all about death and the haunting awareness of death that he and all his young friends here endure. I am not sure whether this is really what he thinks or whether he is trying to con me. Maybe he doesn't know either. In any case, I find the needle jabbing too distracting, and I involuntarily wince. He notices and comments reassuringly, "I used to use my neck, but I quit doing that." I notice now the large scars on his neck. Finally, Dirk moves over and puts his hands around Jimmy's left arm at the shoulder, squeezing them into a tourniquet. A vague pattern of veins emerges on Jimmy's upper arm, and after a few minutes digging he has finally found a vein. He sucks blood back into the hypodermic to be sure, then presses the plunger home.

I expect him to show some signs of pleasure, or satisfaction or . . . but there is nothing. I am the only one experiencing any relief; everyone else seems even more bored than ever. For the first time, I begin to understand what many of the people who work with addicts here in Holland have told me: If all the heroin and cocaine in the world were overnight transformed into sugar, these people would still be using the next day. An exaggeration, of course. But it makes the point that the drug is only one small part of the picture. They are lost in an endless web of using, finding, dealing, stealing, using. . . . And the peculiar dead-end subculture of their fellow users and dealers, each of whom regularly betrays, robs and sometimes kills the other, is the only society they know.

This is nothing new. It was observed a quarter of a century ago by the anthropologist-economist team of Preble and Casey in their study of New York City junkies: "The brief moments of euphoria after each administration of a small amount of heroin constitute a small fraction of their daily lives. . . . The quest for heroin is the quest for a meaningful life, not an escape from life. And the meaning does not lie, primarily, in the effects of the drug on their minds and bodies. . . ."

I become lost in my own thoughts, images of numerous vivid encounters like this one over the two weeks I have been studying drug policy in the Netherlands—conversations with drug-using prostitutes, with the Union of Junkies, with the Union of Cannabis Retailers, with Hans Visser, with the police. . . . I find myself wondering, do drugs marginalize a subpopulation? Or is it the other way around? Are illegal drugs, precisely because they are illegal, used by already marginalized groups as a quasi-sacramental symbol of the bond formed by their own alienation from mainline society?

There is an almost Hegelian progression to the development of prohibitionist legislation. A drug like smoked opium or marijuana that has been constructively integrated into a given culture, like that of immigrant Chinese or Mexicans, is perceived by xenophobic elements in U.S. culture as symbolic of the threat that the alien culture is imagined to pose. Prohibitionist legislation is enacted and harshly enforced with the result that other marginalized groups in the culture take up the drug. However, the sacrament effects what it symbolizes: The groups become increasingly alienated because of their use of the drug and welcome it in the increasingly concentrated and more toxic formulations in which the market will naturally supply any banned product.

Even the demographics of the various forms of a legal drug display the same dynamic. The scorn of mainline society for grain alcohol or fortified wines like Thunderbird is an expression of its scorn for the population that uses it. And the scorn is generously reciprocated. Unfortunately for the mainline culture, it will always bear within itself a group—adolescents—that naturally feels itself alienated, not yet accepted, driven by an irresistible evolutionary force to challenge the dogmas of the quiet past. This is exactly the group, its own future, which the mainline culture sets out to protect from contamination by the feared alien culture. And thus the whirligig of time brings in its revenges. The largest group using marijuana, LSD, ecstasy, in American society consists of middle- and upper-class adolescents. A surprising number of them also use grain alcohol and "Mad Dog" wine.

In the United States, the War on Drugs often sounds like a call for a crusade or an exterminatory witch-hunt. In the Netherlands, the focus is pragmatically centered on minimizing the harm that the addict population does to itself and the rest of society. The record speaks for itself: American adolescents use marijuana at about twice the rate of their counterparts in Holland, where marijuana and hashish have been freely available for more than 17 years (available, by the way, in quiet, rather boring "coffee shops" patronized almost exclusively by small numbers of superannuated hippies and gawking tourists). The only drug that causes traffic fatalities and violence in Holland is the same one that causes these problems here—alcohol.

Over the same 17-year period in Holland, during which possession and use of hard drugs have been treated as a medical, not a criminal issue, the percentage of Dutch youth under 22 years of age who use heroin or cocaine has dropped from 15 percent to less than 3 percent. However disagreeable, the visible presence of junkies in places like Platform Zero plays its part. Dutch adolescents have no difficulty seeing what I have just seen—that this is hardly a glamorous and exciting life-style and that it does not even provide much pleasure. Reality, even disagreeable reality, is remarkably educational; and the attempt to legislate reality out of existence is remarkably counterproductive.

I realize my mind is rambling. Jimmy has had his fix, and my time at Platform Zero is up. He walks me to the entrance, shakes my hand and asks me to send him a copy of my book. I smile politely, but I do not ask the obvious question about his address. I suppose I could send it care of the Rotterdam police; they will always know where he is.

From the train station it is a short walk to the immaculate Holiday Inn on the Schouwburgplein. When I get to my room, I notice a faint sweet odor. . . . I shudder, strip off my clothes, shower and send everything I had been wearing out to be laundered.

34

The Netherlands:
Let's Be Realistic

HERBERT P. BARNARD

The Dutch use a holistic approach to deal with drug use that contains elements of cure, prevention, and punishment. These government programs and policies have been successful in minimizing the risks associated with drugs for both users and nonusers.

Drug use is a fact of life and needs to be discouraged in as practical a manner as possible.

"The Dutch policy on drugs is a disastrous mistake. The Netherlands regrets its liberal policy and is about to turn back the clock." "Drug use has increased by 250 percent in two years, armed robberies by 70 percent, shoot-outs by 40 percent, and car thefts by 60 percent." "In the Netherlands, 1,600 addicts receive daily injections of heroin on government orders." "In Amsterdam recently, a father who was addicted to cannabis massacred his whole family." "There's plenty of heroin for sale in every Dutch coffee shop."

Do you believe all this? I am quoting just a few statements by foreign politicians and other "experts" who disagree with the Netherlands' drug policy. There is evidently an audience willing to believe all this, which gives such critics a reason to continue spreading these stories. Aside from questioning the honesty of this approach, one should ask what purpose is served by repeating such nonsense. It is certainly not in the interest of drug users, their immediate neighbors, the government, or health-care and social service institutions.

The drug problem is too serious an issue to be used as a political football by ambitious politicians. Nor should it be the subject of speculations about reality, making the facts of the matter irrelevant. As a representative of the Netherlands government, I take this opportunity to present the facts.

Source: Herbert P. Barnard. 1998 *The World & I 13* (October), pp. 66–69.

To understand the Dutch drug policy, you need to know a little about the Netherlands and the Dutch people. After all, a country's drug policy has to fit in with the nation's characteristics and culture.

The Netherlands is one of the most densely populated countries in the world, with around 15.5 million people in an area one-quarter the size of New York State. Commerce and transport have traditionally been important sectors of industry in our country. Rotterdam is the busiest port in the world, handling almost 5 million containers a year. In fact, the Netherlands is generally seen as the gateway to Europe.

The Dutch have a strong belief in individual freedom. Government is expected to avoid becoming involved in matters of morality and religion. At the same time, we feel a strong sense of responsibility for the well-being of the community. The Netherlands has a very extensive system of social security, while health care and education are accessible to everyone.

What is the Dutch drug policy? The main objective is to minimize the risks associated with drug use, both for users themselves and those around them. This objective was formulated in the mid-1970s and can be characterized as harm reduction *avant la lettre.*

Many elements of the harm-reduction approach are very similar to Dutch drug policy. Our policy does not moralize but is based on the idea that drug use is a fact of life and needs to be discouraged in as practical a manner as possible. This calls for a pragmatic and flexible approach that recognizes the risks for both drug users and those around them.

Our policy focuses on reducing demand as well as supply. A combination of these two instruments requires close cooperation with public health and law enforcement authorities on all policy levels, Furthermore, we invest a lot of money in cure and prevention. Since the 1970s and early '80s, respectively, low-threshold methadone provision and needle exchange programs have been important elements in our harm-reduction approach.

Our policy is based on two important principles. The first is the distinction between types of drugs, based on their harmfulness (hemp products on the one hand and drugs with unacceptable risks on the other). The second legal principle is a differentiation according to the nature of the punishable acts, such as the distinction between the possession of small quantities of drugs for one's own use and possession with intent to deal. This makes it possible to pursue a finely tuned policy based on the application of criminal law.

The possession of up to 30 grams of cannabis is a petty offense punishable with a fine. The sale of small amounts of cannabis, through what are known as "coffee shops," subject to strict conditions, is not prosecuted. The idea behind the policy on coffee shops is that of "separating the markets." The reasoning is that if retailers of cannabis are not prosecuted under certain conditions, the experimenting user will not be forced to move in criminal circles, where higher profits are made by urging users to take more dangerous drugs (such as heroin).

People often think that drugs are available legally in the Netherlands and that we do not focus on combating the supply side of the drug market. Nothing could be less true. Aside from the retail trade in cannabis, a high priority is given to tackling all other forms of drug dealing. The police and customs authorities seize large consignments of drugs almost every week, working closely with other countries in the fight against organized crime.

Some people think that harm reduction and legalization are synonymous. I disagree and would like to emphasize that harm reduction is not legalization in disguise. Harm reduction is first and foremost concerned with reducing the risks and hazards of drug taking. Harm reduction is meant to reduce the risks for not only the drug user but the immediate environment (i.e., the public) and society as well. This implies that intensive cooperation at all times between those providing care for addicts, the criminal justice authorities, and the government is an essential element in the harm reduction approach.

What are the results of our policy? The Dutch government recently issued a document discussing its drug policy, evaluating the policy of the last 20 years, and mapping out approaches for the future. This paper can be compared with the yearly *National Drug Control Strategies of the White House Office of National Drug Control Policy.* I will summarize the main outcomes.

Regarding the evaluation of Dutch policy on hard drugs, the document makes the following points:

Our policy of harm reduction has been quite successful. Thanks to a high standard of care and prevention, including extensive low-level and nonconditional methadone prescription, social and medical assistance for drug users, and a large-scale free needle-exchange program, we have reached a situation that is matched by few other countries.

The number of addicts in the Netherlands is relatively low compared with that in many countries. This implies that harm-reduction measures do not increase the use of drugs.

The population of addicts is rather stable and rapidly aging. This suggests that few new users are joining in. Heroin is not fashionable among youngsters. The average age of Amsterdam methadone-provision clients increases by almost one year every year, and the *number* of young heroin users using services like methadone provision has shrunk over the years to a handful. The average age of Amsterdam methadone-provision clients was 36.2 years in 1995. The average age of newly registered drug clients in the Netherlands was 32 years in 1995.

The mortality rate among drug users is low, due to the low-threshold methadone programs that provide protection against overdose.

The damage to health caused by the use of hard drugs has been kept within limits. The number of addicts infected with HIV is exceptionally low. In the Netherlands, the percentage of intravenous drug users (IDUs) among the total cumulative number of AIDS cases is low. In addition, the incidence of HIV infections among IDUs has decreased since 1986. An evaluation study concluded that a combination of harm-reduction measures (i.e., methadone provision, needle exchange, training, and counseling) has resulted in safer sexual and drug-taking behaviors. Safe sex practices among addicted prostitutes have increased as well.

Another result of our policy is that a comparatively large proportion of drug users in our country has been integrated into society to a reasonable extent.

The number of regular hemp smokers has gradually increased in recent years. Lifetime prevalence and last-month prevalence have increased substantially since 1984. An annual survey among older pupils in Amsterdam showed, however, that the prevalence of cannabis use has stabilized since 1993–94. This might indicate that we have reached the peak of the upward trend of the past years.

Can the increase in cannabis use, especially among students, be attributed to the existence of coffee shops in the Netherlands? An analysis of surveys shows an upward trend in many other European countries. Since the late 1980s, cannabis use among youngsters (as well as the general population) has increased in France, the United Kingdom, Germany, and the United States.

Compared with the U.S. prevalence, the figures for the Netherlands are considerably lower. According to the results of the 1995 *Monitoring the Future Surveys,* published by the University of Michigan, cannabis use has increased tremendously among American youngsters. To my knowledge, this increase cannot be attributed to any significant change of policy.

The fact that the rate of cannabis use in the Netherlands is comparable with that in other countries (and even lower than in the United States) shows that government policy probably has less influence on use than we think. Other factors, such as trends in youth culture, social differences, and other social influences, probably play a far more important role. In our view, this does not mean that it makes no difference whether one pursues a liberal or a restrictive drug policy. The difference is that a tolerant policy prevents the marginalization of the user. A situation often encountered in other nations, where the user—in most cases a minor—runs the risk of getting into trouble with the police, is seen as highly undesirable in my country.

SOME CONCLUSIONS

1. Comparisons with other countries show no indications that our policy has led to an increase in the number of cannabis users. Therefore, there is no reason to change our policy on cannabis.

2. Our policy on cannabis has not led to an increase in the number of hard-drug users. In the Netherlands, the stepping-stone hypothesis cannot be confirmed.

3. The wide range of provisions for care and prevention has held down the number of hard-drug users, and has ensured that the health of these users can be described as reasonable. Harm reduction actually works, if you invest in it.

4. By definition, the Dutch drug policy requires an integral cooperation with public health, law enforcement, and public order officials.

The Dutch drug policy, therefore, is not a disastrous experiment but a serious effort to tackle a serious issue. Our policy has produced results that are demonstrably better than those in many of the countries criticizing us. While we realize that an ongoing dialogue with all those involved with the drug problem is a precondition for any progress, we are not going to change our policy on the basis of unjustified criticism.

35

Does Europe Do It Better?
Lessons from Holland, Britain
and Switzerland

ROBERT J. MacCOUN AND PETER REUTER

*This article debunks some common myths associated with so-called lib-
eral drug policies in Europe. The authors discuss innovative programs
in Europe that use decriminalization, legalization, and drug-maintenance
to address problems associated with drug use.*

Listen to a debate among drug policy advocates and you're likely to hear impassioned
claims about the brilliant success (or dismal failure) of more "liberal" approaches in certain European countries. Frequently, however, such claims are based on false assumptions. For example, we are told that marijuana has been legalized in the Netherlands. Or
that addicts receive heroin by prescription in Great Britain.

Pruned of erroneous or excessive claims, the experience in Europe points to both the
feasibility of successful reform of US drug laws and the drawbacks of radical change.
What follows are descriptions of some innovative approaches being tried over there, with
judgements of their applicability over here. They fall into three broad categories: eliminating user sanctions (decriminalization), allowing commercial sales (legalization) and
medical provision of heroin to addicts (maintenance).

DECRIMINALIZING MARIJUANA: THE CASE OF
THE DUTCH COFFEE SHOPS

Dutch cannabis policy and its effects are routinely mischaracterized by both sides in the
US drug debate. Much of the confusion hinges on a failure to distinguish between two
very different eras in Dutch policy. In compliance with international treaty obligations,
Dutch law states unequivocally that cannabis is illegal. Yet in 1976 the Dutch adopted a
formal written policy of nonenforcement for violations involving possession or sale of
up to thirty grams (five grams since 1995) of cannabis—a sizable quantity, since one

Source: Robert J. MacCoun and Peter Reuter, 1999. *The Nation* (September 20), pp. 28–30.

gram is sufficient for two joints. Police and prosecutors were forbidden to act against users, and officials adopted a set of rules that effectively allowed the technically illicit sale of small amounts in licensed coffee shops and nightclubs. The Dutch implemented this system to avoid excessive punishment of casual users and to weaken the link between the soft and hard drug markets; the coffee shops would allow marijuana users to avoid street dealers, who may also traffic in other drugs. Despite some recent tightenings in response to domestic and international pressure (particularly from the hard-line French), the Dutch have shown little intention of abandoning their course.

In the initial decriminalization phase, which lasted from the mid-seventies to the mid-eighties, marijuana was not very accessible, sold in a few out-of-the-way places. Surveys show no increase in the number of Dutch marijuana smokers from 1976 to about 1984. Likewise, in the United States during the seventies, twelve US states removed criminal penalties for possession of small amounts of marijuana, and studies indicate that this change had at most a very limited effect on the number of users. More recent evidence from South Australia suggests the same.

From the mid-eighties Dutch policy evolved from the simple decriminalization of cannabis to the active commercialization of it. Between 1980 and 1988, the number of coffee shops selling cannabis in Amsterdam increased tenfold; the shops spread to more prominent and accessible locations in the central city and began to promote the drug more openly. Today, somewhere between 1,200 and 1,500 coffee shops (about one per 12,000 inhabitants) sell cannabis products in the Netherlands; much of their business involves tourists. Coffee shops account for perhaps a third of all cannabis purchases among minors and supply most of the adult market.

As commercial access and promotion increased in the eighties, the Netherlands saw rapid growth in the number of cannabis users, an increase not mirrored in other nations. Whereas in 1984 15 percent of 18- to 20-year-olds reported having used marijuana at some point in their life, the figure had more than doubled to 33 percent in 1992, essentially identical to the US figure. That increase might have been coincidental, but it is certainly consistent with other evidence (from alcohol, tobacco and legal gambling markets) that commercial promotion of such activities increases consumption. Since 1992 the Dutch figure has continued to rise, but that growth is paralleled in the United States and most other rich Western nations despite very different drug policies—apparently the result of shifts in global youth culture.

The rise in marijuana use has not led to a worsening of the Dutch heroin problem. Although the Netherlands had an epidemic of heroin use in the early seventies, there has been little growth in the addict population since 1976; indeed, the heroin problem is now largely one of managing the health problems of aging (but still criminally active) addicts. Cocaine use is not particularly high by European standards, and a smaller fraction of marijuana users go on to use cocaine or heroin in the Netherlands than in the United States. Even cannabis commercialization does not seem to increase other drug problems.

TREATING HEROIN ADDICTS IN BRITAIN

The British experience in allowing doctors to prescribe heroin for maintenance has been criticized for more than two decades in the United States. In a 1926 British report, the blue-ribbon Rolleston Committee concluded that "morphine and heroin addiction must be regarded as a manifestation of disease and not as a mere form of vicious indulgence," and hence that "the indefinitely prolonged administration of morphine and heroin" might be necessary for such patients. This perspective—already quite distinct from US views in the twenties—led Britain to adopt, or at least formalize, a system in which physicians could prescribe heroin to addicted patients for maintenance purposes. With a small population of several hundred patients, most of whom became addicted while under medical treatment, the system muddled along for four decades with few problems. Then, in the early sixties, a handful of physicians began to prescribe irresponsibly and a few heroin users began taking the drug purely for recreational purposes, recruiting others like themselves. What followed was a sharp relative increase in heroin addiction in the mid-sixties, though the problem remained small in absolute numbers (about 1,500 known addicts in 1967).

In response to the increase, the Dangerous Drugs Act of 1967 greatly curtailed access to heroin maintenance, limiting long-term prescriptions to a small number of specially licensed drug-treatment specialists. At the same time, oral methadone became available as an alternative maintenance drug. By 1975, just 12 percent of maintained opiate addicts were receiving heroin; today, fewer than 1 percent of maintenance clients receive heroin. Specialists are still allowed to maintain their addicted patients on heroin if they wish; most choose not to do so—in part because the government reimbursement for heroin maintenance is low, but also because of a widespread reluctance to take on a role that is difficult to reconcile with traditional norms of medical practice. Thus, one can hardly claim that heroin maintenance was a failure in Britain. When it was the primary mode of treatment, the heroin problem was small. The problem grew larger even as there was a sharp decline in heroin maintenance, for many reasons unrelated to the policy.

"HEROIN-ASSISTED TREATMENT": THE SWISS EXPERIENCE

What the British dropped, the Swiss took up. Although less widely known, the Swiss experience is in fact more informative. By the mid-eighties it was clear that Switzerland had a major heroin problem, compounded by a very high rate of HIV infection. A generally tough policy, with arrest rates approaching those in the United States, was seen as a failure. The first response was from Zurich, which opened a "zone of tolerance" for addicts at the so-called "Needle Park" (the Platzspitz) in 1987. This area, in which police permitted the open buying and selling of small quantities of drugs, attracted many users and sellers, and was regarded by the citizens of Zurich as unsightly and embarrassing. The Platzspitz was closed in 1992.

Then in January 1994 Swiss authorities opened the first heroin maintenance clinics, part of a three-year national trial of heroin maintenance as a supplement to the large methadone maintenance program that had been operating for more than a decade. The motivation for these trials was complex. They were an obvious next step in combating AIDS, but they also represented an effort to reduce the unsightliness of the drug scene and to forestall a strong legalization movement. The program worked as follows: Each addict could choose the amount he or she wanted and inject it in the clinic under the care of a nurse up to three times a day, seven days a week. The drug could not be taken out of the clinic. Sixteen small clinics were scattered around the country, including one in a prison. Patients had to be over 18, have injected heroin for two years and have failed at least two treatment episodes. In fact, most of them had more than ten years of heroin addiction and many treatment failures. They were among the most troubled heroin addicts with the most chaotic lives.

By the end of the trials, more than 800 patients had received heroin on a regular basis without any leakage into the illicit market. No overdoses were reported among participants while they stayed in the program. A large majority of participants had maintained the regime of daily attendance at the clinic; 69 percent were in treatment eighteen months after admission. This was a high rate relative to those found in methadone programs. About half of the "dropouts" switched to other forms of treatment, some choosing methadone and others abstinence-based therapies. The crime rate among all patients dropped over the course of treatment, use of nonprescribed heroin dipped sharply and unemployment fell from 44 to 20 percent. Cocaine use remained high. The prospect of free, easily obtainable heroin would seem to be wondrously attractive to addicts who spend much of their days hustling for a fix, but initially the trial program had trouble recruiting patients. Some addicts saw it as a recourse for losers who were unable to make their own way on the street. For some participants the discovery that a ready supply of heroin did not make life wonderful led to a new interest in sobriety.

Critics, such as an independent review panel of the World Health Organization (also based in Switzerland), reasonably asked whether the claimed success was a result of the heroin or the many additional services provided to trial participants. And the evaluation relied primarily on the patients' own reports, with few objective measures. Nevertheless, despite the methodological weaknesses, the results of the Swiss trials provide evidence of the feasibility and effectiveness of this approach. In late 1997 the Swiss government approved a large-scale expansion of the program, potentially accommodating 15 percent of the nation's estimated 30,000 heroin addicts.

Americans are loath to learn from other nations. This is but another symptom of "American exceptionalism." Yet European drug-policy experiences have a lot to offer. The Dutch experience with decriminalization provides support for those who want to lift US criminal penalties for marijuana possession. It is hard to identify differences between the United States and the Netherlands that would make marijuana decriminalization more dangerous here than there. Because the Dutch went further with decriminalization than the few states in this country that tried it—lifting even civil penalties—the burden is on US drug hawks to show what this nation could possibly gain from continuing a policy that results in 700,000 marijuana arrests annually. Marijuana is not harmless, but surely it is less damaging than arrest and a possible jail sentence; claims that reduced penalties would "send the wrong message" ring hollow if in fact levels of pot use are unlikely to escalate and use of cocaine and heroin are unaffected.

The Swiss heroin trials are perhaps even more important. American heroin addicts, even though most are over 35, continue to be the source of much crime and disease. A lot would be gained if heroin maintenance would lead, say, the 10 percent who cause the most harm to more stable and socially integrated lives. Swiss addicts may be different from those in the United States, and the trials there are not enough of a basis for implementing heroin maintenance here. But the Swiss experience does provide grounds for thinking about similar tests in the United States.

Much is dysfunctional about other social policies in this country, compared with Europe—the schools are unequal, the rate of violent crime is high and many people are deprived of adequate access to health services. But we are quick to draw broad conclusions from apparent failures of social programs in Europe (for example, that the cost of an elaborate social safety net is prohibitive), while we are all too ready to attribute their successes to some characteristic of their population or traditions that we could not achieve or would not want—a homogeneous population, more conformity, more intrusive government and the like. It's time we rose above such provincialism.

The benefits of Europe's drug policy innovations are by no means decisively demonstrated, not for Europe and surely not for the United States. But the results thus far show the plausibility of a wide range of variations—both inside and at the edges of a prohibition framework—that merit more serious consideration in this country.

Credits